The Rising Star

Built under the directions of

LORD COCHRANE,

For the War of Independence in Spanish South America, upon the principle of Navigating either by Sails or by Steam, the impelling Apparatus being placed in Hold, and caused to operate through Apertures in the bottom of the Vessel.

COCHRANE

THE LIFE
AND EXPLOITS
OF A
FIGHTING CAPTAIN

ROBERT HARVEY

CARROLL & GRAF PUBLISHERS, INC.
New York

Carroll & Graf Publishers, Inc.
19 West 21st Street
New York
NY 10010-6805

First published in the UK by Constable,
an imprint of Constable & Robinson Ltd 2000

First Carroll & Graf edition 2000

ISBN 0–7867–0769–0

Printed and bound in the EU
10 9 8 7 6 5 4 3 2

For my mother

'Some ten or eleven years ago a respectable American publisher suggested that [I] should write a book about the Royal Navy of Nelson's time; [I] was happy to agree, since both the period and the subject were congenial, and [I] quickly produced the first of the [Aubrey-Maturin] series, a novel based upon Lord Cochrane's early days in command of the *Speedy*, which provided [me] with one of the most spectacular single-ship actions of the war as well as a mass of authentic detail. . .'

Patrick O'Brian, 1984

CONTENTS

PART THREE
SAILOR OF FORTUNE

PART FOUR
HONOUR IN HIS OWN COUNTRY

ACKNOWLEDGMENTS

When I was commissioned to write *Liberators*, the story of the freeing of South America from the Spaniards, I became fascinated by one of them – Thomas Cochrane. As the section on him in *Liberators* was confined to his life in South America, I was unable to write about his Napoleonic war exploits and subsequent career in Greece in any detail. While his South American exploits are amazing enough, his achievements in the western Mediterranean, the Atlantic and off the coast of France, as well as later in the eastern Mediterranean are even more remarkable. He was a man who terrorized the eastern coast of Spain, inflicted fear upon the western shores of France, defeated the Spanish fleet off the Pacific coast of South America, tricked the Portuguese in northern Brazil into surrender, and then performed a major role in the Greek war of independence. By any measure, these were amazing feats. Yet there had been no new biography of Cochrane in twenty years.

Cochrane was much more than perhaps Britain's greatest sea-captain. He was a Radical MP who unashamedly espoused the cause of the oppressed of the time. He won one of the most spectacular battles of the Napoleonic wars, in defiance of his own commander-in-chief. He was immersed in an intricate stock-exchange scandal straight out of the pages of Wilkie Collins – perhaps the greatest criminal *cause célèbre* of its day – and he was one of the most far-sighted and greatest innovators of naval strategy of his times, as well as a prodigious inventor.

I owe a great debt to many people in preparing this book. They include the present Earl of Dundonald, Douglas Cochrane, David and Suzanne (Cochrane) Howell, all of whom have given me invaluable insights into their families' distinguished forebear. The two best academic biographies remain Donald Thomas's *Cochrane* and Ian Grimble's *The Sea Wolf*, both were published in the 1970s. The former is finely written and researched while Grimble first had access to the Cochrane family archives and his book contains detail unavailable elsewhere, as well as being well-written. Anyone who wants to pursue Cochrane's career in greater detail would be well advised to read these two books. Christopher Lloyd's *Cochrane*, although dating back to 1947, is a fine short summary of his life by a distinguished naval historian.

On the judicial front, it remains fascinating how the polemics have continued down the generations. Cochrane's own autobiography, a large part of which is devoted to defending himself from the charges for which he was sent to jail, was answered by the grandson of Lord Ellenborough, the trial judge, which in turn was supported by Henry Cecil's *The Guilt of Lord Cochrane*, whose arguments were convincingly rebutted in a pamphlet by Douglas Cochrane, a direct descendant. The war of words goes on, and I have offered my own tentative verdict in these pages.

I owe, as always, a great debt to Raleigh Trevelyan, whose writing and advice have inspired my own; to Gillon Aitken, whose encouragement and wisdom are without parallel; to my enthusiastic and painstaking editors Nick Robinson and Roger Hudson; to Jan Chamier and Anna Williamson; to Christine, Richard and Emma and all our friends in Meifod; to my sister Antonella and her family for their warm and cheerful support; to my uncle, Peter, Lord Harvey of Tasburgh, whose love of sailing helped to inspire this book; to my wonderful assistant, Jenny Thomas, who put up with so many unreasonable demands without a word of complaint, and her equally patient historian husband, Geoffrey; to my dear mother for all her help – which included first suggesting that I write this book, and to my darling Jane and Oliver, the best companions a writer ever had.

LIST OF ILLUSTRATIONS & MAPS

Thomas Cochrane (from picture by Stroeeling)
(© *National Maritime Museum*)

Earl of St Vincent (by Sir William Beechey)
(*courtesy of the Hulton Getty Picture Collection*)

The *Speedy* and the *Gamo*
(*courtesy of the Hulton Getty Picture Collection*)

Recruiting poster for the *Pallas*
(© *National Maritime Museum*)

Broadsheet announcement of Lord Cochrane's sentence
(published 21 June 1814)
(*courtesy of the Octopus Publishing Group Ltd.*)

Cochrane in the stocks (cartoon, 1814)
(*courtesy of the Octopus Publishing Group Ltd.*)

Maria Graham
(*courtesy of the Hulton Getty Picture Collection*)

Kitty, wife of the 10th Earl of Dundonald, with eldest son,
Thomas
(*courtesy of the Earl of Dundonald & Octopus Publishing Group Ltd*)

The Battle of Aix Roads, 12 April 1809
(*courtesy of the Octopus Publishing Group Ltd.*)

Thomas Cochrane, 10th Earl of Dundonald
(*courtesy of the National Portrait Gallery, London*)

The Rising Star (inside covers)
(*courtesy of the Earl of Dundonald & Octopus Publishing Group Ltd*)

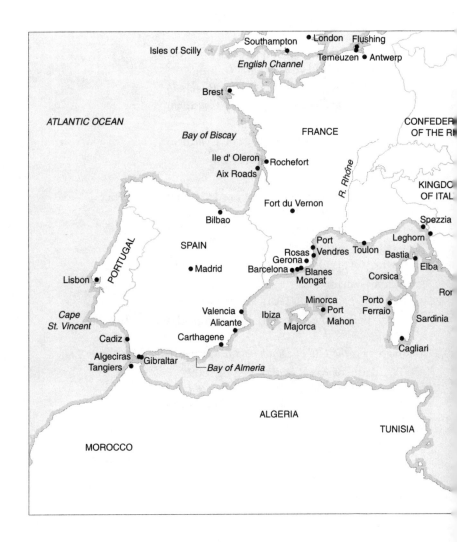

Isles of Scilly

Southampton •London Flushing
English Channel Terneuzen •Antwerp

Brest •

ATLANTIC OCEAN

Bay of Biscay FRANCE CONFEDER
OF THE RI

Ile d' Oleron •Rochefort
Aix Roads

R. Rhône KINGDC
OF ITAL

Fort du Vernon Spezzia

Bilbao

SPAIN Leghorn

Port
Rosas •Vendres Toulon Bastia
•Madrid Gerona• Elba
Barcelona••Blanes Corsica
Mongat Ror

Lisbon •

PORTUGAL

Cape
St. Vincent Minorca Porto
Valencia • •Port Ferraio
Alicante • Ibiza Mahon Sardinia
Cadiz • Carthagene • Majorca
Algeciras Cagliari
Tangiers • •Gibraltar
Bay of Almeria

ALGERIA TUNISIA

MOROCCO

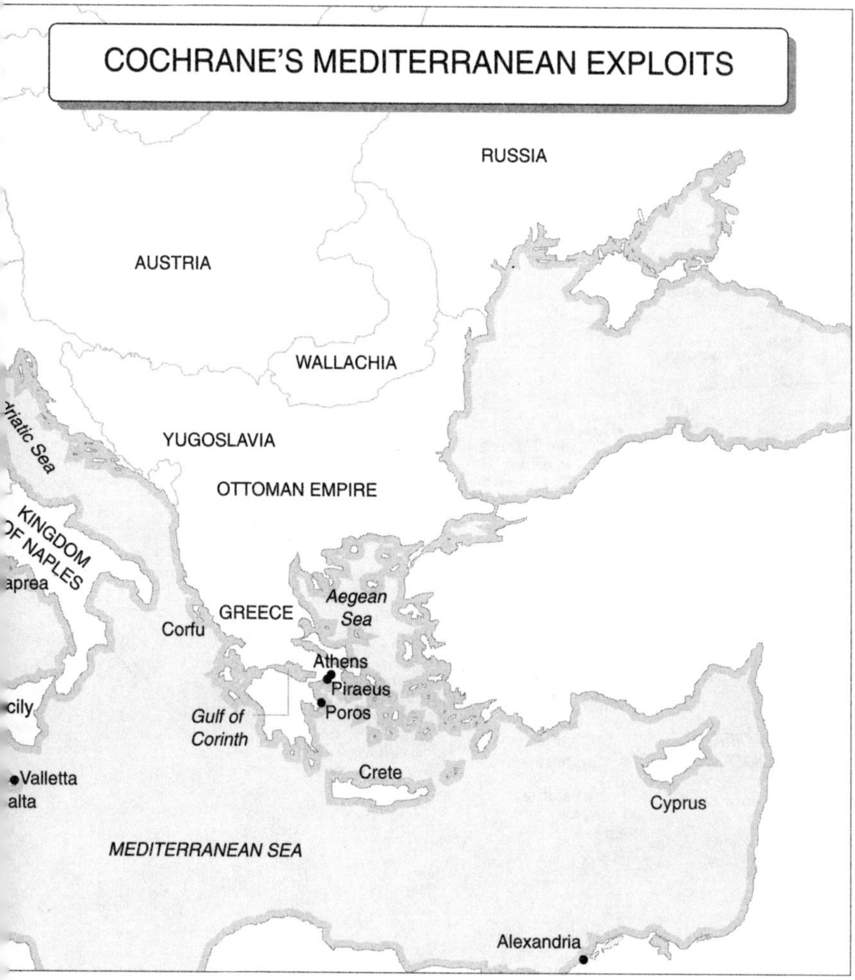

COCHRANE'S MEDITERRANEAN EXPLOITS

RUSSIA

AUSTRIA

WALLACHIA

Adriatic Sea

YUGOSLAVIA

OTTOMAN EMPIRE

KINGDOM OF NAPLES

aprea

Aegean Sea

GREECE

Corfu

Athens

Piraeus

Gulf of Corinth

Poros

cily

Crete

Valletta

alta

Cyprus

MEDITERRANEAN SEA

Alexandria

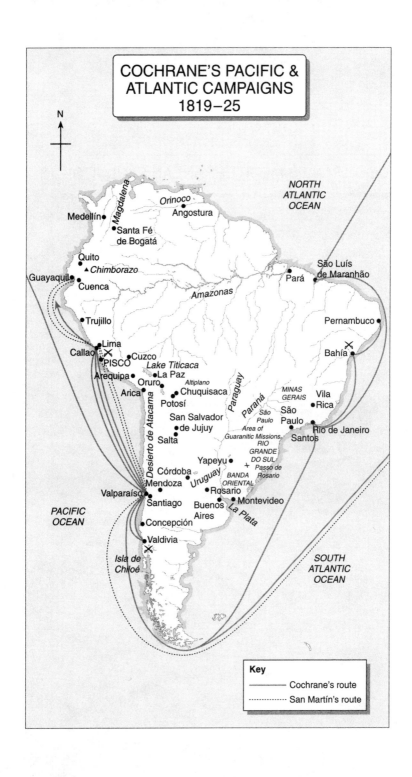

COCHRANE'S PACIFIC &
ATLANTIC CAMPAIGNS
1819–25

N

NORTH
ATLANTIC
OCEAN

Medellín
Santa Fé
de Bogatá
Orinoco
Angostura

Magdalena

Quito
Chimborazo
Guayaquil
Cuenca

Amazonas

São Luís
de Maranhão
Pará

Trujillo

Pernambuco

Lima
Callao
PISCO
Cuzco
Lake Titicaca
La Paz
Arequipa
Oruro
Altiplano
Arica
Chuquisaca

Bahía

Paraguay
Paraná

*MINAS
GERAIS*
Vila
Rica

Potosí
São
Paulo
São
Paulo

Desierto de Atacama

San Salvador
de Jujuy
Area of
Guaranitic Missions
*RIO
GRANDE
DO SUL*
Santos
Rio de Janeiro

Salta
Yapeyu

Uruguay

Passo de
Rosario
*BANDA
ORIENTAL*

Córdoba
Mendoza
Rosario

Valparaíso
Santiago
Buenos
Aires
Montevideo
La Plata

PACIFIC
OCEAN

Concepción
Valdivia

*Isla de
Chiloé*

SOUTH
ATLANTIC
OCEAN

Key
———— Cochrane's route
------------ San Martín's route

PROLOGUE

On 20 June 1814, while the world went about its business on a cheerful summer's day in central London, a man was taken from the court-house of King's Bench, Westminster, and escorted to the nearby prison to begin a twelve-month sentence. He had also been fined £1000 and sentenced to the indignity of an hour in the pillory opposite the Royal Exchange – along with his co-defendants the last man ever so sentenced. Although humbled, he was no ordinary criminal, but had the bearing of a major public figure, and was clearly from a privileged background, with a deeply distinctive appearance. In the words of a contemporary, writing a little later:

> He was a tall young man, cordial and unaffected in his manner. He stooped a little, and had somewhat of a sailor's gait in walking; his face was rather oval; fair naturally, but now tanned and sun-freckled. His hair was sandy, his whiskers rather small, and of a deeper colour, and the expression of his countenance was calm and self-possessed.

On this occasion his countenance was lacerated with humiliation. He was shown to the spartan two rooms – comfortable by the standards of common prisons – on the upper floor of the building, for which he had to pay rent and accommodation. He was told he would be given the privilege of being allowed to exercise within a half-mile radius from the prison, but in his bitterness he declined. His jailers left him to the turbulence of his thoughts. He wept bitterly.

In his new surroundings, his mind raced back to the freedom of wind and ocean over twenty years of one of the most extraordinary careers in British naval history. He had been prepared a little for confinement by the small cabins and close quarters of life at sea – but that was different because on deck, he enjoyed the liberty of racing about on the world's oceans.

This was no ordinary prisoner, and his crime no small misdemeanour. Thomas Cochrane was perhaps the greatest fighting captain that this sea-faring huddle of islands off Europe's coast has ever produced, a hand-to-hand fighter, a figure of almost mythical dash, courage, intrepidity and romanticism. He was now utterly disgraced.

He had taken on not only the huge, visible Napoleonic foe, but had dared to oppose one far more elusive: Britain's often corrupt naval establishment. In addition to being Britain's greatest living sea-hero, he had become an enemy of the state. His reputation has been indelibly tarnished ever since to the point, almost, of being erased from the nation's historical consciousness, a non-person. He had been ruthlessly despatched on a trumped-up charge in a trial staged after one of the most colourful criminal mysteries of the nineteenth century.

Examining the details of the case his innocence seems clear – as certain as, for example, that of Alfred Dreyfus in France more than a century later (although the latter was a far less prominent personality, he suffered much more). What is much less obvious is the motive behind Cochrane's persecution. His supporters believed at the time that this was an act of exemplary revenge by the defenders of the status quo against one of their most formidable opponents, the removal by a governing cabal of a man who uncovered scandals and corruption that had caused untold suffering and death among thousands of ordinary sailors. But it could have been more complicated still – the cover-up of a scandal surrounding the most dubious clique ever to hold sway within the royal court.

Either way, the persecution of Cochrane was to have an enduring effect. For in spite of a series of admirable scholarly biographies, he is now largely unknown to a wider public. But he is not altogether forgotten: in an astonishing tribute to his reputation and personality, this apparently flawed idol became the model for three of the greatest writers of British naval fiction after him. All three are far too eminent and skilful as authors to relate his exploits verbatim – indeed those exploits would be too incredible to relate as fiction.

The first, Captain Frederick Marryat, who founded the genre of Napoleonic naval fiction, actually served under Cochrane, and was unrepentant about his debt to him as the basis for Captain Savage; the second, C. S. Forester, in his Hornblower series, repeatedly evokes the incidents and venues of Cochrane's own career; and the third, the contemporary Patrick O'Brian, with his unique style and skilful development of character and plot, clearly owed a huge debt to Cochrane's extraordinary life. Indeed the full irony of Cochrane's career, with its perverse changes of fortune, is well reflected by the personality of Captain Jack Aubrey, O'Brian's hero – a golden-haired, plain-speaking seaman, fond of prize money, accurate gunnery and 'go straight at 'em' tactics, who loses several fortunes, finds disfavour with the Admiralty and, although pilloried as a result of a Stock Exchange scandal, ends up an Admiral himself. The savage old men who sought to destroy Cochrane's reputation may instead have condemned him to an altogether more interesting fate: as the seaman who has given birth to one of the most exciting branches of English literature – the Napoleonic War sea-adventure.

PART ONE

The Napoleonic Wars

The lieutenant of the watch . . . looked with attention at the approaching figure. It was that of a skinny young man only just leaving boyhood behind, something above middle height, with feet whose adolescent proportions to his size were accentuated by the thinness of his legs and his big half-boots. The newcomer was dressed in a badly fitting uniform which was soaked right through by the spray; a skinny neck stuck out of the high stock, and above the neck was a white bony face . . .

'How old are you?'

'Seventeen, sir,' stuttered Hornblower.

'Seventeen!' The disgust in the speaker's voice was only too evident. 'You must start at twelve if you wish to become a seaman. Seventeen! Do you know the difference between a head and a halyard?'

C. S. Forester, *Mr Midshipman Hornblower* (1950)

CHAPTER 1

Mr Midshipman Cochrane

Left in the unaccustomed peace and solitude of his prison lodgings, as Thomas Cochrane's racing thoughts became reconciled to his predicament, a particular memory came flooding back: of his arrival as a tall and gangling seventeen-year-old aboard a navy ship – the *Hind*, a small armed schooner based at Plymouth, nearly twenty-one years before to the day, on 27 June 1793. The youth was six foot two, with a mop of distinctive red hair, dreamy yet penetrating blue eyes, a prominent hook nose and a broad, strong mouth with a slightly quizzical, humorous expression. As he climbed aboard ship, it was evident that he was both shy and polite. He must have seemed anything but promising material to the first lieutenant of the little ship, Jack Larmour.

Above all, Cochrane was – or appeared to be – a child of privilege. Descended from a long line of one of the most distinguished military families in Scotland, he was the eldest son of the ninth Earl of Dundonald, a title that dated back to as far as 1648, whose forebears had married into one of Scotland's most ancient and distinguished families, the Bruces. The Cochranes were warriors by profession: one had been killed in 1758 in the attack on Louisberg during the Seven Years War. Another had died at Yorktown, where he had served as an aide in the last disastrous campaign of General Cornwallis which sealed the outcome of the American War of Independence.

Now young Thomas Cochrane had been appointed to his first ship by its captain – none other than his uncle, the Hon. Alexander Cochrane, who had pulled strings for him, providing him with a fictitious naval record as a volunteer at the age of seven who had served in no fewer than four ships before he came aboard the *Hind*. This deception was necessary so that he could start his career as a midshipman rather than having to work his way up from the lower deck. Larmour, a tough, self-made master seaman who had done just that, looked upon his new charge with contempt and decided to teach him his first lesson. When Thomas's huge chest of personal possessions was brought on board, Larmour ordered it opened, scattered its contents, and sawed it nearly in half, before ordering the boy to take it below.

It was the first harsh introduction to his new life. But the youngster was far from being the stranger to humiliation and even hardship that his illustrious pedigree suggested. Thomas's childhood had been highly unusual, and had helped to forge his strong independence of spirit. His father Archibald, the ninth Earl, who had inherited the title when Thomas was aged three, was master of Culross Abbey House, built in 1608 next to the ruins of a thirteenth-century Cistercian monastery. The house was sited on an evocative inlet of the Firth of Forth 12 miles across the waters from Edinburgh. Although endowed with great prestige and a large amount of land which contained coal mines, the family was far less wealthy than previously, and Cochrane's brilliant, eccentric and vigorously inventive father set about restoring its fortunes – with disastrous results.

The boy's lack of team spirit or subservience was established by not being sent to the smart but brutal public schools of the time, such as Eton or Harrow. Instead he was educated by a succession of private tutors, which left him considerable time to devote to the pleasures of exploring an extensive estate in beautiful surroundings. Cochrane amusingly recalled two of his teachers, one:

> of whom my most vivid recollection is of a stinging box on the ear, in reply to a query as to the difference between an interjection and a conjunction; this solution of the difficulty effectually repressing further philological inquiry on my part.
> We were, after a time, temporarily provided with a French

tutor, a Monsieur Durand, who, being a Papist, was regarded with no complacent eye by our not very tolerant Presbyterian neighbours. I recollect this gentleman getting into a scrape, which, but for my father's countenance, might have ended in a Kirk Session.

As a matter of course, Monsieur Durand did not attend church. On one side of the churchyard was the Culross Abbey cherry-garden, full of fine fruit, of which he was very fond, as were also the magpies, which swarmed in the district. One Sunday, whilst the people were at church, the magpies, aware no doubt of their advantage, made a vigorous onslaught on the cherries – provoking the Frenchman, who was on the watch, to open fire on the intruders from a fowling-piece.

The effect of this reached farther than the magpies. To fire a gun on the Sabbath was an abomination which could only have emanated from a disciple of the Scarlet Lady, and neither before nor after did I witness such a hubbub in the parish. Whatever pains and penalties were to be found in Scottish church law were eagerly demanded for Monsieur Durand's benefit, and it was only by my father's influence that he was permitted to escape the threatened martyrdom. Annoyed at the ill-feeling thus created, he relinquished his engagement before we had acquired the rudiments of the French language.

Cochrane had three younger brothers and appeared to be devoted to his beautiful mother Anna who died when he was nine, at perhaps the most sensitive age in a child's life, contributing to the lifelong emotional vulnerability that lay beneath his extraordinary physical courage.

Archibald Cochrane was a scientific innovator at a time when new discoveries and patents were all the rage, and he set about turning his gift to restoring the ailing family fortunes. One day a sudden explosion of light at midnight from the little inlet alarmed those awake on both sides of the Firth of Forth. As the young Thomas later described it:

Having noticed the inflammable nature of a vapour arising

during the distillation of tar, the Earl, by way of experiment, fitted a gun barrel to the eduction pipe leading from the condenser. On applying fire to the muzzle, a vivid light blazed forth across the waters of the Forth, becoming, as was afterwards ascertained, distinctly visible on the opposite shore.

It was a discovery of great importance: coal gas, which was soon to be used for street-lighting across the developed world. The young Thomas was proudly taken to see the great inventor, James Watt, who appreciated its possibilities. Yet it was one of Watt's disciples who was to patent the invention in 1804, depriving Archibald of the commercial benefits of his discovery.

In fact, the Earl had stumbled across coal gas entirely by accident. He had invested £22,500 of his own money and that of other investors to set up four furnaces to extract tar from the abundant coal on his estate for another purpose altogether. With characteristic foresight he had realised that coal tar could be used to coat the hulls of ships which were periodically invaded by worms, something which until then could be prevented only by the hugely expensive process of hobnailing them with iron nails (or by 1780, the equally expensive process of 'coppering'). Archibald Cochrane had indeed hit on the solution.

But there was a snag: the monopoly of ship's repair in the naval dockyards was enjoyed by the Admiralty; and the latter was completely uninterested in the new invention. The reason was straightforward – as a shipbuilder in Limehouse explained it: 'We live by repairing ships as well as by building them, and the worm is our best friend. Rather than use your preparation, I would cover ships' bottoms with honey to attract worms.'

The young Cochrane had seen his first experience of the vested interests and corruption that was eating away, like those worms, at the underbelly of the Royal Navy. Not until 1822 was coal tar adopted – and it was the celebrated Sir Humphry Davy who gained the credit.

Now in financial trouble, the Earl engaged in one experiment after another: for manufacturing salt (discovering in the process how to produce soda artificially, which was to be used widely by others for making soap and glass), sal ammoniac, alumina for silk and calico printing, and white lead. This latter-day alchemist also tried to create a kind of bread extracted from potatoes. In 1795, he published his pioneering *Treatise Showing the Intimate Connection between Agriculture and Chemistry*. Nearly two decades later, Davy once again trumped him, publishing his *Elements of Agricultural Chemistry* along much the same lines, and secured the credit for revolutionizing farming methods.

Life at Culross, once so idyllic, was now tinged with foreboding. With the death of his beloved first wife, four children on his hands, and his creditors closing in, in 1788 the Earl remarried, a good-looking and wealthy widow, Isabella Raymond, who saved the estate from bankruptcy. He despatched his two eldest sons to a fashionable military academy at Kensington Square in London, with a view to army careers.

The prickly and sensitive child was deeply upset by the move from Culross and returned six months later, saying he detested army life, and wished instead to go to sea – his mother having been the daughter of a frigate captain and his favourite pastime having been to sail about in a makeshift boat in the little inlet. His irascible father, who had endured a brief spell of naval life and hated it, had no time for such rebellion and sent Thomas down to join the 104th Foot under the patronage of an uncle, Andrew Cochrane-Johnstone, who, much later, was to have a fateful influence on Cochrane's life.

The boy was dressed, on his father's insistence, in a bright yellow waistcoat and trousers – the Whig colours – while his hair was shaven and a mixture of candle-grease and flour applied to what remained of it. A horde of jeering street urchins followed the unhappy youth down London's streets. His reception at the barracks was no better. After a few weeks he returned home to face the wrath of his father. This account is Thomas's, and was probably nearly as highly coloured as his waistcoat; the truth was that the already quirky and unsociable boy had no interest in the dreary regimentation and institutionalized high jinks of army life and saw in his romantic vision of a life at sea an outlet for his individualism.

He stayed at Culross another three years. After the excitement and independence of his youth, life under the eye of his step-mother began to pall and when Thomas was seventeen, the Earl at last acceded to Thomas's requests to be allowed to go to sea (something in which he was supported by his uncle, Alexander). Culross Abbey House was once again in imminent danger of being sold, and Dundonald was eager to get him off his hands.

These experiences were undoubtedly defining: highly intelligent, with a surprisingly thin skin towards slights and humiliations for someone later to prove so brave in combat (not an uncommon combination), a restless and independent individual with a love of personal freedom and open spaces, he had acquired two major traits: an obsession with making money in his own right, and an almost pathological rebelliousness towards authority, now represented by his father.

Fortunately, this was not on display when he was first ridiculed as an apparently spoilt young aristocrat by the earthy Larmour on that fateful June day in Plymouth harbour. The huge natural crescent was an awesome bustle of ships, small boats, sailors and vendors. He meekly went below. Six months earlier King Louis XVI of France had been executed in the latest excess of the French Revolution, and war had been declared between Britain and France – a war that was to last for nearly three decades. The boy midshipman belonged to a service which boasted 45,000 men and cost some £4m a year. There were some 150 ships in commission in the mightiest navy in the world.

Thomas's life was hard going at first, although the navy was hardly the sink of institutionalized brutality that is popularly conceived. The schooner was a small, fast ship. It had two masts, each rigged with fore and aft sails. Its twenty-eight nine-pound guns were assembled on a single deck. The quarters for the midshipmen were damp and dark, below the gun-deck, though more spacious than for the seamen, and were only dimly illuminated by candles and the few cracks of light that showed from the decks above. The lonely Thomas, on his first few nights aboard, would have found the quarters stiflingly close, hunched in a 'cot' – a hammock of canvas stretched across a frame – with only a shelf for his possessions, a far cry from the windy spaciousness of Culross. In port the seamen's cots actually touched each other. At sea there was much more room, as men took turns to take the watch.

He would, surprisingly, have been a comparatively senior member of the ship's company. More than four-fifths of ordinary seamen, and half of able seamen, were aged under twenty-five. Only about a fifth were married. Boys of between six and eighteen were to be found aboard ship, many of them engaged simply in playing as well as learning the ropes. There were also plenty of animals aboard, including the inevitable rats, but also such livestock as cattle, sheep, pigs and goats, for food. The dirt can be imagined, but British ships were rigorously kept clean. About half of the crew would have been 'impressed' – that is, involuntary – but only merchant seamen could be so recruited.

The damp below the decks could be pervasive, depending on the condition of the timbers. In summer, especially in the tropics, the heat and stench could be overpowering, although in winter the cramped conditions meant that men rarely suffered from the cold; on this, his first sea journey on a northern station, the heat was probably not too bad for Cochrane.

As Mr Midshipman Cochrane became accustomed to being awoken at 6 a.m. to hurry about his new duties, he would quickly have understood the no-nonsense approach to naval discipline, although its harshness varied enormously from ship to ship. Such discipline and inflexible routines were essential to keeping order among so many men at such close quarters. Alexander Cochrane had a reputation as a strict captain; this would at least have had the advantage for the young Thomas of ensuring that bullying and abuses below deck were strictly controlled.

In less-well-ordered ships, young midshipmen were at the mercy of 'oldsters' – men passed over for preferment who would probably have to spend the rest of their lives in their jobs. Even youngsters could be venomous. As one seaman observed:

We had a midshipman on board of a wickedly mischievous

disposition, whose sole delight was to insult the feelings of seamen and furnish pretexts to get them punished . . . He was a youth of not more than twelve or thirteen years of age; I have often seen him get on to the carriage of a gun, call a man to him, and kick him about the thighs and body, and with his feet would beat him about the head; and these, though prime seamen, at the same time dared not murmur.

'Cobbing' – being beaten by a stockingful of wet sand – was a frequent form of physical abuse. The men's routine sexual needs were usually accommodated in port by allowing prostitutes on board, a practice the vast majority of captains turned a blind eye to, and even regulated to reward the deserving. The cry 'show a leg' in the morning derives from the need to check whether a man or a woman was in a cot, the latter being allowed to sleep on undisturbed. The 'cockpit' of a ship derived its name from the place where the all-too-frequent brawls between the working girls or 'port wives' occurred.

The quality of the food aboard ships of the time has often been commented upon. Much depended on whether the ship was close to port, whether the food was properly stored, the climate and so on. There were certainly abuses, but it must be remembered that these were the early days of food preservation, without refrigeration, canning and the like, and the possibilities for deterioration were much greater. The purser, whose job it was to provide the food, was one of the ship's company, and he too was liable to be judged by his peers.

The rations were the subject of strict written regulations: a packet of biscuits each day for every seaman, which in practice was often sodden and weevil-ridden; and a gallon of small beer, a very weak version of the real drink, no more really than water flavoured with hops. Each seaman was also entitled to 4 pounds of salt beef, 2 pounds of salt pork, 2 pints of peas, 3 pounds of oatmeal, 6 ounces of butter and 12 ounces of cheese a week. Flour, suet, currants and raisins were also issued. Where possible cabbage and greens were provided. Lime and lemon juice had largely conquered the most dreaded disease, scurvy.

Although in practice particular items often went short and food often went bad, these were substantial enough rations – as they had to be to keep the crew strong and able-bodied. The threats to food were legion, according to one purser. Biscuit was endangered

> by its breaking and turning to dust; of butter, by that part next to the firkin being not fit to be issued; of cheese, by its decaying with mould and rottenness and being eaten with mites and other insects; of peas, oatmeal and flour, by their being eaten by cockroaches, weevils and other vermin, and by that part at the top, bottom and sides of the cask being so often damaged, as not being fit to be issued; besides the general loss sustained in all these provisions by rats, which is very great . . .

The beer ration was often changed to a pint of wine or half a pint of rum, the latter usually being mixed with water and called grog, the seaman's favourite drink. Men dined in messes of four to eight on each table.

Cochrane witnessed the first exercise of the lash aboard his uncle's ship. Punishment was a fact of life, but flogging was not all that frequent except on a minority of ships. A typical average was some fifteen floggings in nine months, usually of between twelve and twenty-four lashes, although occasionally far more. This made severe punishment a significant part of navy life, but hardly a daily occurrence.

Captain Frederic Chamier describes the first flogging he witnessed as a young midshipman:

> The Captain gave the order 'Give him a dozen'. There was an awful stillness; I felt the flesh creep upon my bones, and I shivered and shook like a dog in a wet sack. All eyes were directed towards the prisoner, who looked over his shoulder at the preparations of the boatswain's mate to inflict the dozen: the latter drew his fingers through the tails of the cat, ultimately holding the nine ends in his left hand, as the right was raised to

inflict the lash. They fell with a whizzing sound as they passed through the air, and left behind the reddened mark of sudden inflammation . . .

At the conclusion of the dozen I heard the unwilling order, 'Another boatswain's mate!' The fresh executioner pulled off his coat. The prisoner had said nothing during the first dozen, but on the first cut of his new and merciless punisher, he writhed his back in acknowledgement of the pain; the second stripe was followed by a sigh; the third by an ejaculation; and the fourth produced an expression of a hope of pardon. At the conclusion of the dozen, this was granted, and the prisoner released.

Another observer remarked that after two dozen lashes 'the lacerated back looks inhuman; it resembles roasted meat burnt nearly black before a scorching fire'.

This was undoubtedly very harsh, but no more so than many punishments ordinary people could expect on land. Provided punishment was meted out fairly, and not excessively, it was probably supported or at least accepted by the majority of the men, who disliked their fellows getting away with serious offences, particularly major theft, for which the cat-o'-nine-tails was prescribed, or less serious ones, such as malingering.

There were lesser forms of beating for more minor offences – such as minor stealing, always deeply unpopular on board ship, for which a man could be made to walk a gauntlet with his ship-mates hitting him with knittles, small ropes. Liars were publicly humiliated by being made to clean the heads (latrines) for several days. Other punishments included ducking or a public scrubbing – usually for a dirty man – or wearing the cangue, a wooden collar with a cannonball attached, for several hours.

The terrifying ordeal of being flogged around the fleet, applied only in the most serious cases of mutiny, was extremely rare, although performed with sadistic precision to ensure the victim did not die – for example, 200 lashes would be applied at a time on three successive fortnights. Keelhauling, being dragged under the length of the ship, is believed to have died out in the seventeenth century, when it was also extremely rare. About thirty people a year were executed in London and Middlesex, compared with only a dozen executed for desertion at sea over a seven-year period. Only murder, sodomy, and extreme cases of theft were punishable by death. Mutiny was often not punished at all, if non-violent and the purpose was the removal of a hated officer.

Cochrane's first ship was a schooner. This was a plaything compared to the magnificent first-rated three-deckers – which were nevertheless difficult to handle – which provided the admiral and his officers the space to live in state. In 1808 a first 120-gun three-decker was built. There were also 90-gun second-rate three-deckers, the hulls of which were tall and short, and therefore sailed badly; these were being phased out, as were the still more unwieldy 80-gun three-deckers (although 80-gun two-deckers were more manoeuvrable). The bulk of the line-of-battle ships (those which sailed in the traditional line to engage in fleet action bringing all their guns to bear) were, however, 74-gun two-deckers; 65-gun two-deckers were a cheaper version of this, and regarded as very poor quality – they were being phased out by Cochrane's time; 50-gun two-deckers were short, but of slightly better sailing quality.

Frigates, with their speed, manoeuvrability and gunpower, were the real stars, acting in flotillas or single-ship actions. The 38-gun frigate was the most popular of these in Cochrane's time, with some eighty in service compared with the increasingly obsolete 44-gun frigates, the still popular 40-gun frigates and the smaller 28-gun ships.

The cheap, quickly built and even more nimble sloops (of which there were about 200 in 1801) also performed a major role. Bomb vessels had been created to act as mortars capable of firing explosive shells at enemy ports. Brigs (with fourteen 24-pound carronades), schooners (with 4-6 guns), cutters (with ten 18-pound carronades), and gunboats with a single gun made up the complement.

Life aboard the *Hind* for the young Cochrane would have

been concerned with the well-oiled operation of an experienced crew going about routine duties which occupied much of the day. Cochrane himself would have been at a considerable advantage from the start, even for a novice midshipman. He was older, taller and more heavily built than the young midshipmen; as the captain's nephew he would probably have enjoyed some sort of protection from real abuse, if any occurred aboard the ship. He records only one incident of his being disciplined aboard the *Hind*, and then not harshly. When he left his post without authorization on one occasion, he was ordered up the mast by Larmour for several hours.

Cochrane's chief recollection later was of the enormous debt he owed Larmour for teaching him the skills of seamanship; the first lieutenant was in turn astounded that this privileged and titled midshipman should so eagerly seek to learn. For it was much more usual for those from Cochrane's background, knowing that they stood a good chance of being promoted through connection, to disdain the mechanics of sailing the ship. Larmour famously remarked that parliamentary influence never got a ship off a lee shore (one in which the wind is blowing towards the land with the ship dangerously close to the latter). In following his lead Cochrane was already breaking with convention.

To a vigorous young man such as Thomas Cochrane, fulfilling his life's ambition, the discomforts of life on board were compensated for by the excitement of sailing, of experiencing the salt smell of the open sea, the wind lashing his face and the pitching and rolling of the ship for the first time. The young midshipman was first shown the tasks of each man on board: the young, and strong topmen were assigned to the masts, their main job to loose sail or furl it or, more commonly, 'reef' it – shorten it by gathering a section up to the 'yard' and tying it with lengths of ropes sewn into the sail called reef points or let-out reefs. The yard was the spar – the crossbeam – to which the sail was secured.

On the *Hind* there were only two masts, but on a larger ship, such as Cochrane was later to command, three. The sails on the latter were divided into the jibs at the front of the ship, the fore-sails on the foremast, the staysails, also on the foremast but behind them, the mainsails on the mainmast, the staysails also on the mainmast but behind them, and the mizzen sails on the mizzen (rear) mast, with the spanker billowing out behind. In turn, the sails were on three horizontal levels: main, topmast and topgallant. The topmen, whose work was the most dangerous and skilled, were the strongest and bravest of the men, and respected as such aboard ship.

Next in the pecking order came the forecastlemen, who were usually older, often former topmen who had lost their agility. They had charge of the jib sails at the front of the ship as well as the anchor there and the guns. The third group of seamen, also usually older, were the afterguard, handling the spanker, the guns at the stern, and most importantly the braces, the ropes to which all the sails in the ship were attached. The waisters were usually the dullest-minded in the middle of the ship, handling the foresail and mainsail, as well as pumping the bilges. Lowest in the hierarchy were the 'idlers', not because they were idle but because they did menial tasks. They included the carpenter and his mates, the cook and the officers' servants, usually ship's boys. In addition each ship usually had around fifty marines, to fight on land and enforce order.

The men were divided into two watches for each side of the ship, the larboard (the left or, in today's term, port) and starboard (the right). Young Thomas Cochrane would have learnt the inflexible routines aboard ship: the 4 a.m. call with the idlers being called to scrub the decks and prepare the galley, the off-watchmen being woken at around 6 a.m., the stowing of cots and tidying of quarters. Breakfast was at 8 a.m., divisions at 9.30, when the men went on parade, followed by the various ships' tasks and drilling at 10.00. At 11.30 there was a break to 'up spirits' – have a ration of beer or grog – with lunch at noon. After the afternoon work, the day ended at 4 p.m. with another up spirits and evening meal. The two main drills were setting sail, which most well-ordered ships could do all at once in from four to six minutes, a remarkable achievement for around 15,000 square feet of sail in a medium-sized 31-gun frigate, and gun practice.

The young Cochrane would have learnt how the *Hind* would zigzag into the wind or away from it, tacking from one side to the other because it could not sail directly into it, no more in fact than 67.5 degrees on either side of the wind direction. Tacking was a skilful and difficult manoeuvre, which involved briefly facing the wind and risked missing stays and falling astern on the original tack or being unable to catch the wind on either side. The equivalent manoeuvre away from the wind – wearing – was much easier and faster, although more dangerous in heavy seas or before a strong wind because of the speed of the ship. A ship tacking into the wind travelled, of course, much more slowly than one wearing away from it.

Ships would average a speed of around 6 knots, but they could go as fast as 14 knots for short stretches, which was essential when a smaller ship was being chased. There is an account of just such a chase for the very ship Cochrane now sailed for the first time – just three years later, in 1796. James Gardner, a lieutenant aboard ship, described how in a gale and under chase from two French battleships

> We should have been captured for a certainty if the Frenchman had possessed more patience. And so it happened: for a little before six, when he was within gunshot, the greedy fellow let another reef out of his topsails, and just as he had them hoisted, away went his foreyard, jib-boom, foretopmast, and maintopgallant mast . . . We immediately let two reefs out of the topsails, set topgallant sails and hauled the main tack on board, with a jib a third and the spanker. It was neck or nothing. For my part I expected we should be upset and it was with uncommon alacrity in making and shortening sails between the squalls that we escaped upsetting or being taken.

The *Hind* had covered 120 miles in 12 hours before getting away. Upon such superb seamanship as this were ships won or lost.

Brian Lavery describes the subtleties of wind and speed:

According to Admiral Beaufort, a man-of-war in this period needed light airs – perhaps 2 or 3 knots – to give steerage way. When the wind reached about 4 knots (about Force 2 in the Beaufort scale), 'a well-conditioned man-of-war with all sail set and "clean full" would go in smooth water', 1 or 2 knots. A gentle breeze of 7 to 10 knots would give the ship 3 or 4 knots of speed, while a 'moderate breeze' of up to 16 knots would give the ship 5 to 6 knots. In a 'fresh breeze' of 17 to 21 knots, there would be 'moderate waves, taking a more pronounced long form; many white horses are formed. Chance of some spray'. A ship in a chase would still keep all set in these conditions, including royals; but, in other situations, sail would be reduced slightly.

If the wind increased to a strong breeze of over 22 knots, the royals would certainly be taken in, and the topsails and topgallants would be single reefed. Above 22 knots, a 'near gale', 'sea heaps up and white foam from breaking waves begins to be blown in streaks along the direction of the wind'. The topgallants would be furled, and the topsail and jibs would be double reefed. In a gale of 34 to 40 knots, the topsails would be triple reefed, and above that, in a strong gale, the ship would carry close reefed topsails and courses.

A storm of 48 to 55 knots was 'that which she could scarcely bear with close-reefed main topsail and reefed foresail'. By this time, there would be 'very high waves with long overhanging crests. The resulting foam in great patches is blown in dense white streaks along the direction of the wind . . . The tumbling of the sea becomes heavy and shock like'. Sail would be reduced to close-reefed main topsail and reefed foresail, and any idea of making progress to a specific destination would be abandoned.

With winds of 56 to 63 knots, the ship would carry only her storm staysails, and in a hurricane of 65 knots or over, the ship would carry no canvas. In these circumstances, 'The air is completely filled with foam and spray. Sea completely white with driving spray; visibility very seriously affected'. However, practical sailors did not learn these circumstances by rote; they reduced or increased sail according to the feel and performance of the ship, attempting to predict squalls and storms.

Cochrane also engaged endlessly in gun drill. Rarely, though, was powder and shot used in such exercises because captains were anxious to conserve this as they were responsible for its costs.

It is customary in many ships in a general exercise to go through the motions without loading or firing once in a year, and in others to exercise a few guns every day, and seldom to have a general exercise or to fire the guns.

The 28 guns of the *Hind* were on a single deck, and the crew was trained to clear for action in 5 minutes (15 minutes on a ship-of-the-line because the lower deck had to be stripped of more cumbersome material) and fire three broadsides in 90 seconds, although this varied according to the pitch of the sea, because the cannon had to be rolled forward from the recoil. The guns aboard the *Hind* were the smallest large ones, nine-pounders (that is they fired cannonballs (shot) weighing 9 pounds). These went up to 12, 18, 24, 32 (the most common, $9^1/2$ feet long) and 42-pounders (now almost obsolete). Carronades were increasingly in fashion as both shorter and with a larger ball.

The heaviest guns on a battleship were mounted on the lower deck. Doors covered the gunports when not in use, to keep out the sea and seaspray. The guns could be moved slightly to right or left and raised or depressed, but could not be aimed except by judging the roll or pitch of the sea in relation to the enemy ship. The first broadside of all the guns on one side of the ship was usually fired together: then firing was at will, depending on the speed and skill of the gun crews, usually at least eight men.

Cochrane learnt about the types of shot that were used. Round shot was the most common, and was used by the guns on the lower deck against the enemy's hull. Double-headed or chain-shot was used against the enemy's rigging. Grapeshot from the upper deck was used against the men on the enemy's deck. Round shot was extremely effective at close range. A 24-pounder was capable of penetrating a wooden hull 2 feet 6 inches thick. But the ranges fell away sharply. Such a gun had a range of 200 yards, or 2200 yards if elevated although at these distances it would do little damage. A carronade had a range of around 340 yards. The ships thus had to get in close to fire effectively, and sometimes even collided.

Accuracy was extremely limited, rendered more so by the smoke of battle and the effect of reloading under fire. The British were believed to aim during the downroll of the ship at the enemy's hull, to kill their gunners. The French traditionally fired high, to disable the masts and rigging, which would inhibit the enemy's manoeuvring and allow them to move in for the kill, or get away. In practice these decisions were taken on the spur of the moment, as circumstance dictated. The British were certainly much more effective, the number of ships they captured or disabled being vastly higher than the French score.

After each shot the hot gun had to be sponged out to remove debris. A cartridge of powder in cloth was then rammed down, followed by the shot, and then a wad of ripe yarn to fix it. A priming iron was then inserted into the touch-hole on top of the gun along with a quill of powder which was lit by a flammable wick. As a midshipman, Cochrane learnt to supervise the gun crews after the *Hind* steered up the English Channel and turned into the much wider waters of the North Sea.

There were two standard types of small arms: long-barrelled muskets used to fire across at enemy ships, and pistols used in hand-to-hand combat when the ship was boarded. Boarders would be issued with cutlasses. An officer wrote:

According to the custom prevailing from the earliest period of naval history to the present day, in boarding or opposing boarders, the pistol is held in the right hand, and in the attempt to board is fired and thrown away to enable the boarder to draw his cutlass, which yet remains in the scabbard or left hand.

According to another officer:

Eagerness and heat in action, especially in a first onslaught, ought never to be the cause of a man putting himself so much off his guard . . . as to lift his arm to make a blow with his cutlass . . . But on the contrary, by rushing sword in hand straight out and thereby the guard maintained, and watching his opportunity of making the thrust, the slightest touch of the point is death to his enemy.

Pikes and tomahawks were also used, as were hand grenades, smoke bombs and 'stink pots', largely to confuse the enemy.

Most ships had a marine complement. This dated back to 1664, when they had the role of forming boarding parties as a seagoing infantry. However it was later realized that sailors made more skilled boarders. Instead the marines fulfilled two functions: as a kind of military police, separated from the sailors and used to suppress mutinies and be at hand during punishments; and in amphibious operations, when they usually took the lead.

Cochrane learnt the rudiments of signalling and navigation. Under the Howe code then in effect, there were ten numerical flags and a substitute flag, a preparatory flag, and 'yes' and 'no' flags. Each of the numerical flags had its own message. One, for example, meant 'enemy in sight'. The new code of signalling established by Sir Home Popham, which was widely adapted in 1803, was much more sophisticated and complex and thereby liable to misinterpretation. The Popham code in theory could yield 30,000 words. At night, flares, guns and white lights were used to provide limited signalling, up to a total of seventy. Boats carried more specific orders between ships.

Cochrane also acquired his own skills in navigation in the first cruise, learning how to use a compass, how to use seamarks to estimate the position of a ship off the land, as well as the use of long lines – dragged behind the ship – to estimate the ship's speed, and lead lines to work out the depth of the water in dangerous inshore navigation. Although courses were meticulously plotted, as Captain Basil Hall commented, navigation was at best more of an art than a science:

> The ship's place each day, as estimated from the log-board, is noted on the chart; and also the place, as deduced from chronometers and lunar observations. The first is called the place by dead reckoning, the other the true place. The line joining the true places at noon, is called the true track; and that joining the others is called the track or course by dead reckoning. As it happens, invariably, that these two tracks separate very early in the voyage, and never afterwards come together, unless by accident.

The life that beckoned to the boy accustomed to roaming free in a large if shabby country house and a rambling estate was now to be confined, essentially, to four variables for most of the time: the sea; the wind and the sky; the ship; and the crew. The sea was the most unpredictable, and the one that took most getting used to.

Cochrane's first service was on the North Sea, grey, usually choppy, often rough, sometimes extraordinarily so. The disrespect for the sea manifested by those who travel aboard large ships today, or even humble ferries, was never displayed by those in sailing vessels. The construction of these vessels, with their relatively shallow draughts and rounded hulls, which were designed to make them more manageable and manoeuvrable under sail, meant that they were much more sensitive to the movements of the sea than a large ship of today, and finding one's sea-legs took a considerable time for a newcomer aboard. The sea in all its moods provided, day after day, the only scenery for those aboard, always changing, yet always the same.

Similarly, the wind and the sky, of relatively little importance to those on dry land, or even to those who travel aboard any but small vessels today, were a real, menacing presence to those aboard ship in Cochrane's day. Experienced sailors could tell what relatively slight changes in the direction or strength of the wind, or in the height, shape and speed of the clouds overhead, or even in the light, portended. Cochrane, accustomed to the subtle greens, yellows and browns of the Scottish lowlands, would have been both challenged and depressed by the monotony of the combination of sea and sky, day after day.

The ship itself – confined, cramped, creaking, leaking, smelling, uncomfortable, crowded and in constant sickening motion, yet simultaneously home and the very daily means of survival to the crew – loomed large in the lives of those aboard. Although most regarded their tasks as a matter of routine, the furling and unfurling of the sails, the handling of the ship, the navigation with only primitive compasses and leads for sounding depths, the judgment of the winds and sea, the techniques of sailing and tacking all required the constant exercise of skills and seamanship.

Finally, Cochrane would have had to get accustomed to the strains of living so closely to other men in that confined space. It mattered hugely whether one's immediate superior or subordinate or crewmates were pleasant or harsh, fair-minded or vindictive, friends or bullies, cheerful or resentful. To a great extent the intensely formal, layered and disciplined structure of life aboard had evolved to make sure the human parts worked smoothly alongside each other.

The little community of the *Hind* would have been utterly strange and alien to young Thomas at first, at times even alarming and depressing. But it could be exhilarating: for the challenge was the freedom of roaming the whole world, with strange ports and alien cultures as destinations. The boy was simultaneously a confined prisoner aboard ship and had the freedom of the entire globe.

The mission of the *Hind* was thoroughly routine: to ensure that French privateers would not interrupt trade between Norway and Britain. Thomas found the climate, at least, not all that different to his native Scotland. But for a seventeen-year-old with a fairly rudimentary education he now displayed another surprising trait: an acute intellectual curiosity in the makeup of Norwegian society:

> The principal charm was the primitive aspect of a people apparently sprung from the same stock as ourselves, and presenting much the same appearance as our ancestors may be supposed to have done a few centuries before, without any symptoms of that feudal attachment which then prevailed in Britain. I have never seen a people more contented and happy, not because their wants were few, for even luxuries were abundant, and in common use.
>
> Much, however, cannot be said for Norwegian gallantry at that period. On one occasion my uncle took me to a formal dinner at the house of a magnate named Da Capa. The table literally groaned beneath the feast; but a great drawback to our enjoyment of the good things set before us, was that, during a five hours' succession of dishes, the lady of the house stood at the head of the table, and performed the laborious duty of carver throughout the tedious repast. Her flushed countenance after the intervals between the various removes, moreover, warranted the suspicion that the very excellent cookery was the result of her supervision. It is to be hoped that the march of civilisation has altered this custom for the better.

Cochrane described an amusing incident:

> On board most ships there is a pet animal of some kind. Ours was a parrot, which was Jack Larmour's aversion, from the exactness with which the bird had learned to imitate the calls of the boatswain's whistle. Sometimes the parrot would pipe an order so correctly as to throw the ship into momentary confusion, and the first lieutenant into a volley of imprecations, consigning Poll to a warmer latitude than his native tropical forests. Indeed, it was only by my uncle's countenance that the bird was tolerated.
>
> One day a party of ladies paid us a visit aboard, and several had been hoisted on deck by the usual means of a 'whip' on

the mainyard. The chair had descended for another 'whip', but scarcely had its fair freight been lifted out of the boat alongside, than the unlucky parrot piped 'Let go!' The order being instantly obeyed, the unfortunate lady, instead of being comfortably seated on deck, as had been those who preceded her, was soused overhead in the sea! Luckily for Poll, Jack Larmour was on shore at the time, or this unseasonable assumption of the boatswain's functions might have ended tragically.

CHAPTER 2

Lieutenant Cochrane

Returning to Plymouth after six months, Larmour and his young protégé enjoyed a spell of shore leave before entering his uncle's new command, the *Thetis*, a small frigate. This had a more formidable task: to cross the Atlantic to guard the hotly-contested fisheries off Newfoundland from French attack. The first real excitement of the voyage was a sudden and alarming drop in temperature, which the youth was immediately told marked the approach of icebergs. The *Thetis* gave them a safe berth and to Cochrane's astonishment he saw 'ghost ships':

On passing one field of great extent we were astonished at discovering on its sides three vessels, the one nearest to us being a polacca-rigged ship, elevated at least a hundred feet; the berg having rolled round or been lightened by melting, so that the vessel had the appearance of being on a hill forming the southern portion of the floe. The story of two vessels answering the description of Sir John Franklin's ships having a few years ago been seen on an iceberg was scarcely credited at the time, but may receive corroboration from the above incident.

Nothing can exceed the extraordinary aspect of these floating islands of ice, either as regards variety of form, or the wonderful display of reflected light which they present. But, however they may attract curiosity, ships should always give them a wide berth, the indraught of water on their weather side being very dangerous. A singular effect was experienced as we passed to leeward of the field; first, the intense cold of the wind passing over it, and occasionally, the heat caused by the reflection of the sun's rays from the ice whenever the ship came within the angle of incidence.

He evidently performed well, for he was transferred to the *Africa* (which later served at Trafalgar) as an acting lieutenant, where he was put through the daunting experience of being examined by three captains before being appointed a full lieutenant. Passing the technical questions on trigonometry and navigation with ease, he was put through his practical: how would he behave in a series of dangerous sea and weather situations? Thanks to his training by Larmour, he emerged with flying colours. He was now a full lieutenant. He had proved himself in his own right, not through preferment, for the first time.

Pride welled from every pore as he was appointed to Admiral Vandeput's flagship *Resolution*: it was a tremendous recognition of his potential. He was embarrassed when, at his first dinner at the admiral's table, he committed the gaffe of asking whether he could pass a dish to him – to which Vandeput replied that he was perfectly capable of reaching it himself – which showed the rigidness of protocol at the time, Cochrane's morbid sensitivity and the admiral's starchiness. But Cochrane later described him as 'a perfect gentleman and one of the kindest commanders living' although one with 'the habit of showing his worst features first.'

No record exists of Cochrane's impressions as he first glimpsed the New World in 1794. America was to feature but little in his life, although his distinguished uncle, Alexander, was to carve a niche in its history as the man who destroyed the White House and the Capitol. But to a young man of his restless adventurism, the first sight of the dense woods and pleasing contours of New England, beckoning towards a continent of unknown and unexplored vastness beyond, must have been profoundly exciting.

The ship sailed south to Chesapeake Bay, and Cochrane went ashore to spend a happy week on the great continent of America, enjoying the voluminous hospitality, but being chased up a tree on a hunting expedition by a wild boar. He was chided by his young fellow officers for not indulging in their heavy drinking – which was highly unusual and strong-willed for an officer at the time. Life for this fast-promoted lieutenant must have seemed pleasant and relaxed: he spent his spare time reading works of philosophy, again unusual for a naval officer. He also showed the acute political concerns of an intelligent young man – fretting about missing involvement in the real centre of naval action in Europe and commenting on Britain's folly in having lost the American colonies when, as no doubt his American hosts told him, gentler treatment on Britain's part would have kept them.

At the age of twenty-two, in the autumn of 1798, he was ordered away from this peaceful station and back to what he hoped would be action in the Mediterranean. In his absence the great Spithead mutiny and the seizure of Sheerness by the Nore mutineers had occurred. Their chief demands were better pay (which had not been improved for a century) and food. The first uprising was settled amicably, the second amid bloodshed and terrible retribution: the leader of the mutineers, Richard Parker, was hanged, and several were flogged from ship to ship in that slow, terrible ritual, as boats bore the bloodied men around the fleet, drums beating. Some of the mutineers died.

Young Thomas had missed this ghastly demonstration of how far conditions aboard ships fell short of the ideal, and how awful the fate of those who protested about this could be. But the reports he heard of it were to have a profound impression on him. He also missed the defeat of the French fleet by Admiral Howe in 1794, Nelson's spectacular victory off Cape St Vincent, along with his commander John Jervis, soon to be Lord St Vincent, in 1797, and Nelson's astonishing triumph at the Battle of the Nile the following year.

Reaching the great British fortress of Gibraltar in December 1798, Cochrane was once again appointed lieutenant aboard the flagship, this time under a fellow Scot, Admiral Viscount Keith. Gibraltar! That huge rock connected by a tiny ribbon to the

Spanish mainland that provided at once access to the Mediterranean and control of the straits, and a position so defensible that the British, once having seized it, could never be dislodged, even in one of the longest sieges in naval history staged by the Spanish and French a half century before. The Rock enshrined British maritime power as stolidly and immovably as the white cliffs of Dover. A garrison town, it was efficiently ordered, a bustle of resplendent maritime uniforms mingling with deferential local people, a constant buzz of ships coming and going. To Cochrane seeing it for the first time, it must have seemed more a homecoming to Britain than the gateway to the Mediterranean where he was soon to perform some of his most famous feats.

On the Rock, Cochrane was shrewdly assessed by Britain's most powerful naval commander, St Vincent. Small, with an impish, rodent face, leathered by age and experience, he was a ferocious disciplinarian, as well as being aloof and imperious. But no one doubted his ability and seamanship and he had a particular virtue: a granite hatred of the Admiralty corruption that so endangered his men and weakened the British naval effort. By now proud, self-confident and thirsting for action, Lieutenant Cochrane must have felt deeply gratified at the official favours being showered upon him and the grudging approval of this most famous and imposing officer.

To the exasperation of the twenty-three-year-old Cochrane, however, the next few months were to prove uneventful: he still saw no action. Keith transferred his flag to the *Barfleur*, accompanied by his officers. In the boredom of sitting on station off the Rock, Cochrane, still immersed in books, made a first demonstration of his constitutional impatience when he began to complain about the practice of the ship's first lieutenant, Philip Beaver, of storing aboard the rotting but valuable hides of bullocks for resale at home. Beaver was unpopular among his brother officers for his pomposity. As Cochrane described it:

Our first lieutenant, Beaver, was an officer who carried

etiquette in the wardroom and on deck almost to despotism. He was laudably particular in all matters visible to the eye of the admiral, but permitted an honest penny to be turned elsewhere by a practice as reprehensible it was revolting. On our frequent visits to Tetuan, we purchased and killed bullocks on board the *Barfleur*, for the use of the whole squadron. The reason was that raw hides, being valuable, could be stowed away in her hold in empty beef-casks, as especial perquisites to certain persons connected with the flag-ship; a natural result being, that, as the fleshy parts of the hides decomposed, putrid liquor oozed out of the casks, and rendered the hold of the vessel so intolerable, that she acquired the name of 'The stinking Scotch ship'.

Learning of Cochrane's criticisms, Beaver seized the occasion of a late return by his subordinate from shore leave to ask why the latter had not reported to him immediately. Cochrane had been hunting in Tetuan, and was wearing muddy clothes: he had gone down to change before reporting to his senior. Told by Beaver that he had been made to look ridiculous by Cochrane's delay, his subordinate lost his temper and said that he could not help it if Beaver had made himself look ridiculous. Beaver coldly threatened to cancel Cochrane's shore leave, whereupon the latter suggested that 'we will talk of it in another place'. The two clearly detested each other and this was just a minor spark, with Cochrane behaving immaturely.

Instead of turning a blind eye, Beaver took this as a challenge to a duel. While Cochrane clearly should not have been so insolent, Beaver should have let the matter blow over. But he ordered his subordinate to be court-martialled – an extremely grave procedure. Ludicrously, at eight in the morning, with marine detachments assembled and boatswains' pipes playing, the captains of the fleet solemnly assembled aboard the flagship and took their places in the admiral's large cabin. Beaver solemnly called his witnesses and Cochrane, no doubt stunned by the consequences of his minor outburst, wisely refrained from doing likewise. There was no dispute as to the facts; other officers had been present. Keith could not conceal his fury with Beaver:

> I hope this will be a lesson to officers how they apply for courts martial in future, without first speaking to their captains or admirals. The first intimation I had on the subject was from the letter of application for the court martial being put into my hand. Here are all the flag-officers and captains called together, at a time when the wind is coming fair and the ships ought to be under way. I think I am made the most ridiculous person of the whole!

Yet although Cochrane was acquitted, he was reprimanded:

> Lord Cochrane, I am directed by the court to say that officers should not reply sharply to their superior officers, and a first lieutenant's situation should be supported by everyone. A ship is but a small place where six or seven hundred persons are collected together and officers should in every part of it avoid any flippancy.

With that the farce was over. However, it was Beaver, cold, disciplined and unimaginative, who was to be forgiven by the naval establishment and soon promoted captain while Cochrane, a junior who had spoken out against a superior, had blotted his record: subordination was always more important than reason in the Royal Navy at that time. The report of proceedings was sent back to the Admiralty. For the first time, the promising young officer, smoothly promoted lieutenant and then to two flagships, had come to the unfavourable notice of his superiors.

The truth was that Cochrane was bored and frustrated. He had been stuck on blockade duty for a month. This involved sitting off nearby Cadiz, ensuring that the Spanish fleet did not break out and effect a junction with the French, based at Brest. With the winds and seas changing direction, this was not always easy; and the Spaniards made frequent feint sorties which caused the British to engage in pointless manoeuvres to get to windward to engage them. But it was always relentlessly tedious.

Cochrane vented his frustration in a growing lack of respect for his superiors and his resentment towards those, in particular, who had been promoted through parliamentary influence and not seamanship. This was an extraordinary attitude for a young aristocrat, originally preferred himself, and marked a breaking of ranks with his own class. It reflected his own independence of spirit, his confidence in his abilities, and Larmour's training. Unsurprisingly, his dislike was returned, even by Keith, who was a competent sailor but complained of Cochrane in his dispatches back home. The young man appeared to be displaying an unseemly lack of respect towards his superiors and, it had to be admitted, had achieved little so far to justify his own high opinion of himself. Cochrane was cheeky and, although admired by his junior officers, was increasingly regarded as unsociable and impertinent.

His frustration was understandable. In spite of a career which owed a great deal to his own connections initially but had then blossomed because of his skilful seamanship, he had had no opportunity to prove himself in battle after more than six years' service. He appeared headed for an undistinguished career as one of hundreds of mediocre officers jostling for promotion. With his penchant for philosophy, his outspokenness and his restlessness, this tall, gangling figure with the windblown red hair seemed as ridiculous as Lieutenant Beaver.

At last the prospect of action beckoned. The thirty-three-strong French fleet had bolted from Brest, escaping the British blockade, in an effort to rendezvous with the twenty-two-strong Spanish one. Keith manoeuvred his fleet skilfully to prevent the two meeting, while continuing to watch Cadiz. Even more skilfully the French sailed unexpectedly right past him and down through the Straits of Gibraltar, which were now unguarded. At this stage Keith decided to go after the French, instead of continuing to watch Cadiz or keeping guard over the straits. Lord St Vincent, equally unprepared for the bold French move, hastily tried to assemble his ships scattered all over the Mediterranean. Keith almost caught the French as they left Toulon, but St Vincent ordered him back to Minorca. Cochrane reported:

> Shortly afterwards another fast-sailing transport hove in sight, firing guns for Lord Keith to bring-to, which having done, he received peremptory orders to repair immediately to Minorca; Lord St Vincent still imagining that as the enemy had left Toulon they might catch him in Port Mahon; the fact of their having gone to Spezzia, though known to us, being unknown to him. Compliance with this unseasonable order was therefore compulsory, and Lord Keith made the signal for all captains, when, as reported by those officers, his lordship explained that the bearing up was no act of his, and the captains having returned on board their respective ships, reluctantly changed the course for Minorca, leaving the French fleet to proceed unmolested to Spezzia.
>
> On Lord Keith receiving his order, I never saw a man more irritated. When annoyed, his lordship had a habit of talking aloud to himself. On this occasion, as officer of the watch, I happened to be in close proximity, and thereby became an involuntary listener to some very strong expressions, imputing jealousy on the part of Lord St Vincent as constituting the motive for recalling him. The actual words of Lord Keith not being meant for the ear of anyone, I do not think proper to record them. The above facts are stated as coming within my own personal knowledge, and are here introduced in consequence of blame being cast on Lord Keith to this day by naval historians, who could only derive their authority from data which are certainly untrue – even if official. Had the command been surrendered to Lord Keith on his arrival in the Mediterranean, or had his lordship been permitted promptly to pursue the enemy, they could not have escaped.

Both pursuers failed to catch their prey. The French, with another superb display of seamanship, now doubled back again through the still-unguarded straits and joined up with the Spanish, who had bolted Cadiz. Cochrane was probably not alone among the younger officers in seething at the way the British had been comprehensively outwitted. He blamed the elderly St Vincent, whose poor health now compelled him to return to Britain – taking his 110-gun flagship and so depleting the British fleet still further, when a small ship would have done as well for the trip. St Vincent undoubtedly came to hear of Cochrane's views. Later Cochrane attributed his superior's extraordinary vendetta against him to 'the indiscreet plainness with which I have spoken of the manner in which the French fleet had been unfortunately permitted to escape Lord Keith'.

Keith took command of the Mediterranean fleet after St Vincent's departure, transferring his flag to the *Queen Charlotte* and sailing to Naples, where Horatio Nelson was being feted by the Neapolitan court. There the two rival young stars, Beaver and Cochrane, were received by the great naval hero on several occasions, and Cochrane records his single point of advice: 'Never mind manoeuvres: always go at them.' To this Cochrane, with hindsight, appended: 'It has been remarked that Trafalgar was a rash action, and had Nelson lost it and lived he would have been brought to a court-martial for the way in which that action was conducted.' It is not recorded what Cochrane thought of this confused, jumbled, beautiful city, then one of the greatest ports in Europe, nor of the deeply decadent Bourbon court there, to which Nelson had unwisely attached himself.

Still no more than a staff officer leading a life of comfort, naval routine and boredom, on 21 September 1799 Cochrane at last had his first chance of minor action. In two separate boats, Cochrane and Lieutenant Bainbridge were ordered to go to the rescue of a small merchant vessel being attacked by enemy privateers. The young lieutenant brought his boat alongside one and jumped aboard only to find that none of his thirteen-man crew would follow, and he had to leap just as nimbly back. His mortification was increased when he learnt that Bainbridge had successfully boarded his intended victim. The proud Cochrane had been humbled. His only consolation was that his younger brother, Archibald (there were two more), who hero-worshipped the dashing lieutenant, had been allowed to join him as a midshipman.

Nelson gave Cochrane his first big break. The former had discerned a quality of boldness in the young man that his stuffily conventional superiors had not, or found downright distasteful. A 74-gun French ship of the line (battleship), the *Généreux*, had been captured by Nelson between Italy and Sicily; it was in appalling condition, the rigging badly damaged and barely fit for sailing. It needed to be taken to the large British naval base at Minorca for repairs. Keith, on Nelson's advice, gave the task of taking the huge ship to young Cochrane – but there was a further catch. Because of the risk, the admiral decided he could not spare fit men, and gave Cochrane a crew of the sick and infirm taken off all the other ships of the fleet.

As in the dwindling heat of the Mediterranean autumn the young lieutenant was rowed aboard the imposing hulk, he must have felt a sense of awe: to command one of the biggest fighting ships of the time was a huge responsibility. With its two gun-decks, it qualified to fight in the line of battle when refitted and repaired. For a twenty-four-year-old who had never held command, even of a small ship, this was an opportunity indeed.

But it was a poisoned chalice: the crew would barely be able to sail it, and if anything went wrong, it was almost certain to founder, he along with it. As on reaching deck he gazed upon the motley crew of the ailing and infirm lining the battered deck, beneath torn sails and broken spars, Cochrane must have quailed at the impossible task he had been set for his first real test – and wondered whether he had been set up, in fact, to lose.

To execute his mission successfully, he needed calm seas. These he had to begin with. But about half-way along the 500-mile journey a wind rose and the perfectly still waters began to grow choppier with a suddenness that only the Mediterranean displays. Spray began to blow off the top of the waves. The very size of the ship made her almost unmanou-

vrable in the face of the growing wind, and the young lieutenant could only watch in dismay as he realized it was
strengthening to gale force across the path of his
ship. There was little his feeble men could do as the ship
began to lurch dangerously. It was a nightmare come true for
Cochrane – to be in charge of a crew of invalids aboard a
damaged hulk in a gale.

Soon it became obvious that the ship was rolling too heavily
in the mountainous seas, almost being immersed by waves on
the lee side (away from the wind): the trouble lay in the
damaged rigging. When the ship rolled over away from the
wind, the sails drooped; when it rolled back, the wind hit them
with such fury that it threatened to dismast or capsize the vessel
altogether. If dismasted it would have been at the mercy of the
pounding seas broadside (sideways) on, and these were likely to
stave in the gunports – the protective wooden windows on the
two decks where the cannon were drawn up. Then water would
pour in faster than it could be pumped out.

The young commander had been at least partly responsible for
this state of affairs: he had failed to reduce sail as soon as the wind
freshened. The speed with which the gale had arisen – so typical
of the Mediterranean at this time of year – had taken him by
surprise. It now seemed that his first command would end with
the ship foundering with all hands. Looking at his sick crew,
Cochrane knew instinctively what was the only thing that
would give them hope and inspire them to get up and walk.

For the first time showing that his courage matched his
impetuosity, he called his brother and the two started the terrifying ascent of the rigging to the mainmast. There was no
prospect of the crew below being able to work the spars to
which the sails were attached from lines down below in such a
gale. It was dark, and Thomas and young Archibald were
drenched as they reached the slippery spars and began to wrestle
with the ropes and sails.

Below them the fitter men, shamed by the captain's example,
began to follow. As the ship bucked and plunged, the two
Cochranes hung on vertiginously over the boiling seas below,

desperate to keep their hold while working on the huge, unpre-dictable canvas as it lay briefly limp, before flinching back as it billowed out with a force that threatened to kick them into the void. Now reinforced by the other topmen, the task of folding up the whiplashing canvas was accomplished only slowly but, as they began to succeed, the pitching and tossing of the wreck began to slow. After what seemed like hours the crew had won: when the men returned to deck they found they could manoeuvre the ship again. The gale died down after a few more hours, leaving only heavy seas.

When they sailed triumphantly into Port Mahon in Minorca, they learnt that the flagship, the *Queen Charlotte*, had caught fire off the island of Capraia with the loss of 673 men, including its captain, two lieutenants and eighteen midshipmen. Admiral Keith had been ashore at Leghorn, as had Cochrane's rival, Lieutenant Beaver. Fire was one of the greatest possible hazards aboard wooden ships: very few of the men could swim, so they either burnt or drowned. The presence of huge quantities of ammunition made this doubly dangerous (the magazine aboard a ship was carefully lit from behind glass in an adjoining room, and kept dry through the absorption of moisture by charcoal). Had Cochrane been on board the *Queen Charlotte*, he might easily have perished. He was commended for his prompt action in saving the *Généreux*: it had been a first notable display of his mettle.

CHAPTER 3

The *Speedy*

In 1800 at last, in recognition of Cochrane's achievement, the Admiralty decided he could be awarded that most jealously sought after of all promotions for a young officer – his own command. At the last moment, though, Keith decided to prefer the brother of his own secretary to take charge of the corvette destined for Cochrane. Instead the young lieutenant was given charge of a fighting ship barely worthy of the name: a little brig of 158 tons used to patrolling coastal waters in calm seas. It had only 14 guns – tiny 4-pounders that could do little damage even at close range.

Cochrane swallowed his bitter disappointment, and made the ironic discovery that he could carry 114 pounds of shot in his pockets – equivalent to a full broadside. He had command of six officers and eighty-four men. In contrast to his spacious accommodation aboard the flagship, his new captain's cabin was no more than five feet high, and the six-feet-two commander could only shave by poking his head through the skylight. It seemed more a punishment than a promotion. But he had his own ship at last.

Its name was the *Speedy*. Cochrane decided to fit the smallest sail he could find aboard the *Généreux* as a mainsail. He knew he was either still being tested by his superiors, or that they had decided quietly to dispose of him as being too independent-minded – and Cochrane, after so many years as an officer aboard a flagship, had every reason to suspect the latter. They little realized that the tiny craft would soon become as famous as its captain. For the moment Cochrane at least had the satisfaction of no longer being bound by the stuffy protocol of the flagship or kowtowing to men he regarded as incompetent, inferior seamen, lacking in courage.

In the brilliant summer sun off Cagliari in Sardinia, with its picturesque, huddled houses, as the *Speedy* emerged on its first mission to convoy fourteen merchantmen, Cochrane gazed proudly over his ship's company, which included an energetic and able second-in-command, Lieutenant William Parker, and Archibald, still a midshipman. After several hours, one of his lookouts noticed a boat moving in like a shark to pick off one of the stragglers, a Danish vessel, in the now dispersed convoy. Cochrane promptly ordered the *Speedy* to turn around and caught up with the little French privateer, the 6-gun *Intrepid*. Firing a warning shot, the *Speedy* boarded the prize and hauled her in. It had been a battle of pygmies, secured without bloodshed, but Cochrane's first day's fighting had yielded a catch – the first in his career – 'my first piece of luck'.

The long journey to Leghorn proceeded. Four days later five 'sharks' moved in on two stragglers in the convoy and boarded them. Once again Cochrane immediately turned the *Speedy* about and caught up with the two stricken vessels. The five gunboats made off, but were forced to abandon their prize crews. Arriving a week after in Leghorn, Cochrane delivered one prize and fifty French prisoners to Admiral Keith – not bad for a first outing.

Cochrane's tactic was simple: always to go on the offensive. The following month he captured three prizes, and then three more in July. To the young commander, zigzagging across those blue waters at the height of summer, capturing craft with a warning shot and a boarding party, the whole dance seemed unreal and idyllic. He was a man in control of his ship, utterly confident of his seafaring skills and facing little resistance from the small French privateers. He was fishing minnows, although to the captured merchant ships they must have seemed like predators until they were rescued. The impression of the firefly skimming across the waters was captured in the young commander's log:

June 16 – Captured a tartan off Elba. Sent her to Leghorn, in the charge of an officer and four men.

22 – Off Bastia. Chased a French privateer with a prize in tow. The Frenchman abandoned the prize, a Sardinian vessel laden with oil and wool, and we took possession. Made all sail in chase of the privateer; but on our commencing to fire she ran under the fort of Caprea, where we did not think proper to pursue her. Took prize in tow and on the following day left her at Leghorn, where we found Lord Nelson, and several ships at anchor.

25 – Quitted Leghorn, and on the 26th were again off Bastia, in chase of a ship which ran for that place, and anchored under a fort three miles to the southward. Made at and brought her away. Proved to be the Spanish letter of marque *Assuncion*, of ten guns and thirty-three men, bound from Tunis to Barcelona. On taking possession, five gun-boats left Bastia in chase of us; took the prize in tow, and kept up a running fight with the gun-boats till after midnight, when they left us.

29 – Cast off the prize in chase of a French privateer off Sardinia. On commencing our fire she set all sail and ran off. Returned and took the prize in tow; and the 4th of July anchored with her in Port Mahon.

July 9 – Off Cape Sebastian. Gave chase to two Spanish ships standing along shore. They anchored under the protection of the forts. Saw another vessel lying just within range of the forts; out boats and cut her out, the forts firing on the boats without inflicting damage.

19 – Off Caprea. Several French privateers in sight. Chased, and on the following morning captured one, the *Constitution*, of one gun and nineteen men. Whilst we were securing the privateer, a prize which she had taken made sail in the direction of Gorgona and escaped.

27 – Off Planosa, in chase of a privateer. On the following morning saw three others lying in a small creek. On making preparations to cut them out, a military force made its appearance, and commenced a heavy fire of musketry, to which it would have answered no purpose to

reply. Fired several broadsides at one of the privateers, and sunk her.

31 – Off Porto Ferraio in chase of a French privateer, with a prize in tow. The Frenchman abandoned his prize, of which we took possession, and whilst so doing the privateer got away.

August 3 – Anchored with our prizes in Leghorn Roads, where we found Lord Keith in the *Minotaur.*

For the commander of the *Speedy*, life must never have seemed so intoxicating. Not only could he show off his naval skills: the delightful, if occasionally oppressively hot or squally Mediterranean offered a wide range of exotic ports and land-scapes, from the bustle and volubility, fine wines and even better food of a port such as Leghorn to the reserved and sleepy atmos-phere of British-dominated Minorca, Corfu or Malta, to the mutual incomprehension and suspicion experienced by the British in the narrow-alleyed ports of North Africa. Sun-baked, whitewashed one- or two-storey dwellings huddled in the picturesque amphitheatres of northern Mediterranean ports or labyrinthine south Mediterranean casbahs were now Cochrane's playground. It was a heady brew.

Keith ordered Cochrane to the west, to attack enemy ships off the coast of Spain. This was more serious. For the *Speedy*, if she got into trouble, would have no support within striking distance from the British fleet, even at Port Mahon, and there were more likely to be large enemy warships about. But the young commander jumped at the chance, as it gave him a perfect oppor-tunity to improvise and close with the enemy.

Left to his own devices, he adopted an unusual and intelligent tactic – the first real sign that he was not some ordinary if brave young lieutenant, but a commander of real intelligence and ability. He kept well away from the Spanish coast by day, then moved in by night to attack vulnerable and unsuspecting ships. This required total command of his crew, their respect, as well as immensely skilful seamanship, for the dangers of running aground were multiplied at night.

He struck again and again, picking off prizes without resistance;

and as he did so, his reputation grew not only among the British public, but the enemy. The mighty Spanish fleet was increasingly irritated at this gadfly operating off its coast – irked enough to deploy warships to go in chase of it: the *Speedy*, after all, was an insignificant vessel with light armaments operating just under Spanish noses. It was time to swat the insect. But audacity was not Cochrane's only virtue – now, for the first time, he was to deploy another exceptional skill: deception.

As Cochrane buzzed about harassing Spanish merchantmen, he fought no real engagement, instead showing superb sailing skills, mostly at night, to seize his prizes. But the risks were always present, as he well knew. He had his men repaint the *Speedy* in the colours of a Danish ship, the *Clomer*, which he had observed in the area. He recruited a Dane and dressed him up as an officer; he was preparing the ground for the inevitable Spanish counter-attack.

In the blustery, cold winter of that year, on 21 December, he was intrigued that a group of gunboats twice made out of Barcelona to attack him, and then turned tail, challenging him to give chase. This he did. Soon a huge ship appeared. As he approached, broadside, the ship's portholes suddenly opened to reveal that it was bristling with cannon. The trap was deliberate: the Spaniards had caught the fly. They had reckoned without his indifference to intimidation or his brazen resourcefulness. He immediately ran up a Danish flag, as he watched this large Spanish frigate lowering a boatload of men to board him. Cochrane ordered his Danish crewman to parley with them, saying that they were a Danish ship coming from Algeria.

The Spanish boat continued towards them, unbelieving – and then Cochrane raised the yellow flag of quarantine. The Dane explained that the plague was rampant in Algeria, which was true, and that there were cases aboard. The Spanish party was aghast. If this was true, any Spaniard climbing aboard was liable to die. The boat rowed back to the mother ship, preferring to give the Dane the benefit of the doubt. The young lieutenant had bluffed his way through by a whisker. Cochrane wrote afterwards:

By some of my officers blame was cast on me for not attacking the frigate after she had been put off her guard by our false colours, as her hands – being then employed at their ordinary avocations in the rigging and elsewhere – presented a prominent mark for our shot. There is no doubt but that we might have poured in a murderous fire before the crew could have recovered from their confusion, and perhaps have taken her, but feeling averse to so cruel a destruction of human life, I chose to refrain from an attack, which might not, even with that advantage in our favour, have been successful.

Meanwhile the merry chase continued:

December 24 – Off Carthagena. At daylight fell in with a convoy in charge of two Spanish privateers, which came up and fired at us; but being to windward we ran for the convoy, and singling out two, captured the nearest, laden with wine. The other ran in shore under the fort of Port Genoese, where we left her.

25 – Stood for Cape St Martin, in hope of intercepting the privateers. At 8 a.m. saw a privateer and one of the convoy under Cape Lanar. Made sail in chase. They parted company; when, on our singling out the nearest privateer, she took refuge under a battery, on which we left off pursuit.

30 – Off Cape Oropesa. Seeing some vessels in shore, out boats in chase. At noon they returned pursued by two Spanish gunboats, which kept up a smart fire on them. Made sail to intercept the gunboats, on which they ran in under the batteries.

January (1801) 10 – Anchored in Port Mahon, and having refitted, sailed again on the 12th.

16 – Off Barcelona. Just before daylight chased two vessels standing towards that port. Seeing themselves pursued, they made for the battery at the entrance. Bore up and set steering sails in chase. The wind falling calm, one of the chase drifted in shore, and took the ground under Castel De Ferro. On commencing our fire, the crew abandoned her, and we sent

boats with anchors and hawsers to warp her off, in which they succeeded. She proved to be the Genoese ship *Ns. Senora de Gratia*, of ten guns.

22 – Before daylight, stood in again for Barcelona. Saw several sail close in with the land. Out boats and boarded one, which turned out a Dane. Cruising off the port till 3 a.m., we saw two strange vessels coming from the westward. Made sail to cut them off. At 6 p.m. one of them hoisted Spanish colours and the other French. At 9 p.m. came up with them, when after an engagement of half an hour both struck. The Spaniard was the *Ecce Homo*, of eight guns and nineteen men, the Frenchman, *L'Amitié*, of one gun and thirty-one men. Took all the prisoners on board the *Speedy*.

23 – Still off Barcelona. Having sent most of our crew to man the prizes, the number of prisoners on board the *Speedy* became dangerous; we therefore put twenty-five of the Frenchmen into one of their own launches, and told them to make the best of their way to Barcelona. As the prizes were a good deal cut up about the rigging, repaired their damages and made sail for Port Mahon, where we arrived on the 24th, with our convoy in company.

28 – Quitted Port Mahon for Malta, not being able to produce at Minorca various things of which we stood in need; and on the 1st of February, came to an anchor at Valletta, where we obtained anchors and sweeps.

He stayed in Malta to see in the New Year on friendly territory. He dressed up, as a jape, in the clothes of an ordinary seaman for a fancy-dress ball, but was blocked by a group of status-conscious French royalist officers. Cochrane may have been drunk, unusually for him, and he lashed out at one of them. Although it was quickly clear that Cochrane was the audacious young British lieutenant making a name for himself off the coast of Spain, the Frenchman demanded satisfaction.

The two of them went through the absurdities of a duel, Cochrane wounding the other in the leg and being himself hit in the ribs. But the experience shook him: 'It was a lesson to me in future, never to do anything in frolic which might give even unintentional offence.' It was a narrow early escape for the still immature young man; but it also showed him the dangers of taking life too lightly, and of losing his temper – the latter a problem which unfortunately was to dog him for the rest of his career.

A couple of months later he pursued a French brig into Tunis harbour, violating its neutrality and plundering its cargo of ammunition but setting its crew free by ordering that the ship's boat be lowered into the water and left unguarded. Taking his prize back to Port Mahon in mid-March 1801, he suddenly realized he was being shadowed by a large Spanish frigate. Knowing he was no match for her, he flew before the wind at such speed that a sail fell from the mast. As he raced on regardless through the night, he thought he had lost her but in the grey of the morning he saw that the pursuer was still on his heels, although out of range.

He pressed on through the next day, while the frigate, with its superior sailpower, steadily closed on him. By nightfall it was almost within range and Cochrane's crew was exhausted. In a last attempt to escape, Cochrane instructed the ship's carpenter to secure a lantern to the top of a barrel and lower it from the stern, changing direction the moment the barrel was bobbing in his wake. The Spanish frigate bore down on the barrel, all eyes on the single light glowing in the dark, and found that the *Speedy* had disappeared.

It was inevitable, however, that, sooner or later, the daring twenty-five-year-old would be caught. On 5 May 1801, the reckoning came. Almost insolently close to Barcelona, the centre of Spanish naval power in the Mediterranean, Cochrane set off in pursuit of a group of small Spanish gunboats, capturing one and then returning for another among the fishing ships clustered near the harbour the following morning.

From behind those ships there suddenly emerged one of the most powerful Spanish frigates: the gunboats had been deliberately sent out as a decoy to lure Cochrane in. It was the *Gamo*, four times the size of the *Speedy*, carrying 319 men with 32 guns – twenty-two 12-pounders, eight 8-pounders and two 24-pound carronades (among the nastiest of all guns, capable of firing a huge amount of grapeshot). The *Speedy*, by contrast, had only fifty-four men, half of its complement, because so many had been sent off to crew prizes. Its firepower of fourteen 4-pounders could inflict only minimal damage at 50 yards, and none at all at 100 yards.

Cochrane had three possible courses of action. He could surrender; he could make a break for it and run, but the *Gamo*, by far the bigger and faster ship, would overtake him and was already nearly within range; it seemed inevitable that he would be caught. Or he could commit apparent suicide and engage this monster. In what was to become one of the classics of naval engagement between a small ship and a bigger, a David and Goliath, he chose the latter course – perhaps because he realised there was no hope at all in the former, except of surrender.

He sailed straight towards the *Gamo*, placing himself within range of the guns of the latter, although his own puny ones were still out of range. The *Gamo*, astonished, fired a warning shot. Cochrane ran up the American flag to gain time. The Spanish captain, Francisco de Torres, already amazed by the approach of the *Speedy*, was thrown momentarily into confusion: perhaps, after all, this was not the nuisance that had been preying on Spanish coastal shipping for so long, but a neutral. The decision was made not to open fire, partly because the Spaniards now knew that the little ship could not escape.

The guns on all ships at this time were not aimed at specific targets: they were locked into position, and the skill was to open fire when the movement of the sea would place a vessel at the best possible advantage to do damage to its opponent. The *Speedy*, which was to windward of the *Gamo* – the side being struck by the wind, which had the effect of pushing the latter's guns up – made the perfect target, and was within range. Cochrane's objective was to get around to the other side, where the hull was low and the guns would be aiming into the sea. The Spaniard's hesitation allowed him to do just that, and he felt emboldened to run up the British flag. The result was an immediate broadside from the Spaniard which, as he expected, fell short of the *Speedy* and into the sea.

The next British move was more startling still: the *Speedy* moved straight towards the side of the *Gamo* as the other ship rolled back with the sea and reloaded its guns frantically, to get so close that the next broadside would fire harmlessly overhead. It was a matter of seamanship, the movement of the sea itself, and split-second timing: a few seconds too late, and the *Speedy* would have faced a devastating broadside. He succeeded, and the spars of the *Speedy* actually locked with those of the *Gamo*, they were so close, while another large Spanish broadside belched deafeningly forth, to pass way over the smaller ship's decks, which were ten feet below those of the *Gamo*, the shot falling harmlessly into the sea beyond.

What now? The fly seemed merely to have closed with the spider and was easy prey. But Cochrane had made his preparations: like a boxer grappling with his larger opponent at close quarters, preventing him landing a punch, he had ordered his cannon to be 'treble-shotted' and 'elevated' – aiming upwards as far as possible. With the swell tilting his ship sideways so that it aimed up into the *Gamo* (technically he was to leeward), he was able to fire straight up into the other's gun-deck looming overhead.

He was incredibly lucky: the captain, de Torres, was killed in this first devastating broadside from below, which did remarkable damage for such small guns because it was at point-blank range. The little ship was still too close for the *Gamo*'s broadsides to harm it. As Cochrane put it later: 'From the height of the frigate out of the water the whole of her shot must necessarily go over our heads, while our guns, being elevated, would blow up her main deck.'

The two ships now engaged in a bizarre *pas de deux*. Cochrane spotted Spanish marines assembling and preparing to board the little ship just beneath her; he veered away just far enough to prevent this, but not so far as to bring the ship into a position where the Spanish guns could bring their guns to bear. Then he returned to inflict a further upwards broadside. This happened three times during the course of an hour, the precision of sailing involved being extraordinary, because one slip would bring about a collision, or result in boarding, or would have allowed the Spaniards to fire a devastating volley.

Of course, Cochrane in the smaller ship had the advantage of much greater manoeuvrability. But he was locked in: if he bolted, he would be picked off easily. Once again, attack seemed the only option available to him, even against a ship with six times as many men. He told his crew that the Spaniards would give them no quarter if they won, and ordered several to blacken their faces in preparation for boarding. The *Speedy* moved forward to the *Gamo*'s bows and, cutlasses in mouth as though in some old pirate story, some twenty men, including the young Archibald Cochrane, climbed up onto the Spanish ship.

As his advance party climbed the bows, he and Parker led the rest of his men in scaling, from the stern of the *Speedy*, the middle section of the *Gamo*. Only the ship's doctor was left to steer the *Speedy*. By that time the Spaniards were confused and demoralised, having lost their commander, and were uncertain of what to do about the vicious little ship attacking them in defiance of all naval convention and common sense. Cochrane wrote:

> Knowing that the final struggle would be a desperate one, and calculating on the superstitious wonder which forms an element in the Spanish character, a portion of our crew were ordered to blacken their faces, and what with this and the excitement of combat, more ferocious-looking objects could scarcely be imagined. The fellows thus disguised were directed to board by the head, and the effect produced was precisely that calculated on. The greater portion of the Spaniard's crew was prepared to repel boarders in that direction, but stood for a few moments as it were transfixed to the deck by the apparition of so many diabolical-looking figures emerging from the white smoke of the bow guns; whilst our other men, who boarded by the waist, rushed on them from behind, before they could recover from their surprise at the unexpected phenomenon.

In difficult or doubtful attacks by sea – and the odds of 50 men to 320 comes within this description – no device can be too minute, even if apparently absurd, provided it have the

effect of diverting the enemy's attention whilst you are concen-
trating your own. In this, and other successes against odds, I
have no hesitation in saying that success in no slight degree
depended on out-of-the-way devices, which the enemy not
suspecting, were in some measure thrown off their guard.

Minutes later, more were attacking them from behind. In the
confusion they could not know how heavily they outnumbered
the British attackers.

Cochrane yelled at Dr Guthrie, who had been left in charge of
the *Speedy*, to send in the next wave of attackers – although, of
course, there was no one left on board. The startled Guthrie yelled
back that he would. The Spanish officers heard and believed that
another boarding party was on its way. They had been lured into
a trap, believing the *Speedy* to be a small ship with a regular crew:
instead it seemed crammed with attackers – an impression that the
behaviour of the *Speedy* had so far done to dispel.

Cochrane yelled at one of his men to lower the Spanish colours,
which, with remarkable coolness and skill, he did. The leaderless
Spaniards, confused and demoralized, took this to be an order to
surrender; and the battle was over. Fifteen Spaniards, including
the captain, had been killed and forty-one wounded; just three
British seamen had been killed and eighteen wounded, one of
them the valiant Parker, slashed in his leg and wounded by a
musket shot.

Cochrane could not yet pause. Before the 300 or so remaining
Spaniards could realize that a force fewer than a sixth of their
number had taken them prisoner, the fighting captain ordered
them into the hold and ordered the two most powerful guns on
the ship, the carronades, trained down upon them and manned
by British sailors with burning fuses. Cochrane appointed
Archibald to command the giant prize, which the little *Speedy*
proudly led into Minorca.

The fight between the *Speedy* and the *Gamo* was the first of
Cochrane's great naval feats, not just a lucky fluke or an act of
piracy, as later opponents were to dub it. There had been no luck

involved, except in the captain's death, and no piracy in taking on a much larger and more heavily armed vessel. Cochrane had shown a dazzling array of talents as a commander: the first and most important was that his crew were now so accustomed to his natural leadership that they had no hesitation in obeying him when he ordered apparently suicidal tactics; their behaviour was the well-oiled one of men acting perfectly and in co-ordination as a team.

He had behaved with seemingly reckless courage in attacking a much larger ship but for the fact that his subsequent choice of tactics bore out his judgment: it would have been more dangerous and suicidal to run away than to engage. He and his crew had displayed faultless skills that had saved them in an almost impossible situation – in particular those precise movements backwards and forwards from the larger ship to avoid being boarded without bringing them out from under the arc of the *Gamo's* guns. Further, he had displayed great courage in boarding a vessel when his men were so overwhelmingly outnumbered, as well as executing, in the heat of battle, a perfectly co-ordinated plan of attack. His coolness, clear-thinking, and superb tactics under nearly impossible conditions had been extraordinary.

Finally, he had shown the talent for mischievous deception (in hauling up the American colours, in pretending that another boarding party was on the way, in hauling down the Spanish colours) that was to become his trademark. It was, as has been said, an engagement unique in naval history. Nicholas Pocock, the marine artist, painted a famous picture of it when news of the capture of the *Gamo* caught the public imagination. Cochrane became a hero overnight.

Cochrane's astonishing feat did not capture the imagination of the old men in the Admiralty. The real start of the feud between the dashing young commander and his superiors can be dated from this moment – and it was the latter that initiated hostilities. It is far from clear what underlay the Admiralty's vindictiveness. The best guess is simply that, in a service deeply reliant on hierarchy, deference and subordination, Cochrane had refused to play to the rules. He was regarded as insubordinate, and was to be punished accordingly.

When he had been appointed to the command of the insignificant little *Speedy*, his superiors had never envisaged such a triumph as this; their attempt to tame him or relegate him to obscurity had backfired. He had performed spectacularly as an individual commander operating on his own; that grated on men accustomed to co-ordinated team action. He had been continually contemptuous of such men as Lieutenant Beaver, his immediate superior; and he had too full an opinion of himself. The crusty Lord St Vincent, now elevated to First Sea Lord, was not impressed by Cochrane's reputation for insubordination, and possibly even less so by the popular interest his bold action had aroused. The old man had almost certainly come to hear of Cochrane's criticism for the escape of the French fleet in the Mediterranean in 1799.

The system of promotion from lieutenant to post-captain was through political favour, as the Admiralty sought to cultivate peers and MPs; or through coming to the attention of the commander-in-chief, usually by serving aboard his flagship; or, more legitimately, through distinction in action. Cochrane qualified on at least two counts: although the son of a Scottish peer and hence one without parliamentary influence, he had served aboard Keith's flagship and had just won a truly great naval action after dozens of lesser triumphs. He was clearly being victimized.

Cochrane, although formally a lieutenant, was effective commander of the *Speedy* (the title of master and commander having been dropped in 1795), a position equivalent to major in the army. Post-captains were full captains who actually had been granted the title, as distinct from those who were called captains because they had command of a small ship. They took rank from the moment of their appointment, and would qualify for promotion to admiral in order of strict seniority, according to the moment of their appointment. This system of promotion by turn, as opposed to merit, made the timing of appointment as post-captain immensely important.

The young hero, who although critical of his superiors, bore no particular grudge against them and was in the full flush of success, suddenly found himself snubbed by the naval establishment, as though, far from having achieved one of the most spectacular single-ship victories in British naval history, he had committed a major transgression. After a much lesser triumph, it was customary for an officer to be made post-captain (the modern equivalent of captain); this had happened to the obedient, punctilious Beaver soon after his capture of a small gunboat with a superior boatload of armed men. Cochrane was denied this accolade for capturing a ship four times bigger than his own.

It was normal, too, for a warship of such enormity as the *Gamo* to be absorbed into the Royal Navy, with a large part of the prize money being paid to those who had captured her. Instead it was announced by the Admiralty, without explanation, that the *Gamo* would be sold off as a merchantman to the ruler of Algiers, so that there would be virtually no prize money. Most offensively of all, the Admiralty resolutely blocked Cochrane's attempts to secure promotion for his able and courageous second-in-command, Parker, badly wounded in the fighting. Cochrane has been much faulted for his prickliness and insubordination even by sympathetic biographers; but these three actions, which fired in the young lieutenant resentments that until then had only been smouldering, were unprovoked assaults upon him by the Admiralty.

How are they explained? Lord St Vincent, who is usually staunchly defended by naval historians, seems on this occasion to have shown the pettiness that undoubtedly was a feature of his character. Presumably the old disciplinarian could not bear that so junior and independent an officer should achieve such popular fame so quickly. For all his incorruptibility, St Vincent was a deeply unattractive figure, and he was certainly the prime mover in the Admiralty's vendetta against the young lieutenant. But many of Cochrane's own contemporaries disliked him too because he did not play by the rules of preferment, because he believed in sheer ability as the necessary condition of promotion, and had thus in a sense 'betrayed his class', and because, although poor, he was more aristocratic than most of the politicians' friends who were promoted.

On the other hand, Cochrane arguably had shown that he was not prepared to abide by the rules or take slights lying down, and a show of deference might have restored him to official favour. Treated badly by his superiors immediately after so extraordinary a victory, he demonstrated exactly the same fearlessness towards them that he had in attacking the *Gamo* – and the tut-tutting old men of the Admiralty were turned into bitter enemies. But this is to anticipate the story. Meanwhile, he was ordered to go on a routine diplomatic mission to the ruler of Algiers who, ironically, had bought the *Gamo*. Cochrane reported of his visit:

> I was ushered through a series of galleries lined with men, each bearing on his shoulder a formidable-looking axe and eyeing me with an insolent scowl, evidently meant to convey the satisfaction with which they would apply its edge to my vertebrae, should the caprice of their chief so will ... On reaching the presence of the Dey – a dignified-looking and gorgeously attired person, seated cross-legged on an elevated couch in one corner of the gallery and surrounded by armed people of most unprepossessing appearance – I was marched up between two janizaries, and ordered to make three salaams to his highness.
>
> This formality being complied with, he rudely demanded, through the medium of an interpreter, 'What brought me there?' The reply was that 'I was the commander of a [British] vessel of war in the roads, and had been deputed, on behalf of my government, respectfully to remonstrate with his highness concerning a vessel which his cruisers had taken contrary to the laws of nations'. On this being interpreted, the precocious scowls of the bystanders were exchanged for expressions of injured innocence, but the Dey got in a great passion, and told the interpreter to inform me that 'remonstrance came with an ill grace from us, the British vessels being the greatest pirates in the world, and mine one of the worst amongst them', which complimentary statement was acknowledged by me with a formal bow.

'If I did right', continued the Dey, through his interpreter, 'I should put you and your crew in prison, till' (naming a captured Algerine vessel) 'she was restored; and but for my great respect for the [British] government, and my impression that her seizure was unauthorised, you should go there. However, you may go, with a demand from me that the vessel unjustly taken from us shall be immediately restored.'

Disappointed in promotion, he was allowed to resume his raiding career in the *Speedy*, soon capturing a 6-gun Spanish privateer which he put under the command of his brother Archibald and embarking on a raid in conjunction with a bigger ship, the *Kangaroo*, on the Spanish convoy at Oropesa. Cochrane was a strong advocate of raiding along the Spanish coast, but he was one of its few practitioners. It was at this time, as he continued relentlessly capturing prizes, that he began to develop a paranoid hatred of the Admiralty's system for awarding prize money.

Cochrane's obsession with prize money, although driven by a strong mercenary trait in his character, was far from unjustified. It was fashionable in those times for the wealthy landed born to deride those motivated by money; but Cochrane, although of impeccable aristocratic pedigree from one of the most distinguished titled families in Scotland, had no money; he can hardly be faulted, like those without either wealth or title, for seeking to acquire some. The system of prize money, and the possibility that large sums might be obtained thereby even by ordinary seamen, provided the navy with one of its greatest romantic attractions and motivations, as it had since Drake's day.

The pay of able seamen at the time was a derisory 33s 6d a month and for ordinary seamen 25s 6d, and this was usually awarded only when a ship had returned to port after what might be years of sailing on a long posting, and for a ship in port not until six months in arrears to discourage desertions. Sailors often quickly spent this in binges on shore. Prize money offered the temptation of huge potential rewards, however infrequently realized, and was governed by strict naval regulations, which, for example, provided that hatches should be nailed up on captured ships to prevent the holds being raided by the capturing crew. It was also necessary to prove that the ship was indeed an enemy one.

One-quarter of the prize was awarded to the lower ranks; three-eighths went to the captain, and one eighth to the admiral under whose command he sailed. An eighth was awarded to 'captains of marines, land forces, sea lieutenants and masters', to be divided equally among them. An eighth went to 'lieutenants and quartermasters of marines, lieutenants, ensigns and quarter-masters of land forces, boatswain, gunner, purser, carpenter, masters' mates, surgeons and chaplains'. Yet another eighth went to the midshipmen, surgeons' mates, sergeants of marine and various petty officers, while the remaining quarter went to the crew and marines. The hauls could be staggering.

N.A.M. Rodger writes:

Anson's 'lucky hit', the first battle of Finisterre in 1747, gained prizes worth £300,000. His second in command, Rear-Admiral Warren, made over £48,000 in that year, and £125,000 in that war. At the fall of Havana in 1762, the naval and military commanders-in-chief, Admiral Pocock and Lord Albemarle, received £122,697 each. Albemarle's younger brother, Commodore Keppel, the naval second-in-command, received £24,539, and every one of forty-two captains gained £1600. In 1746 Captain Saunders took a single ship which netted him nearly £40,000, and in 1762 the *Active* and *Favourite* shared the capture of the Spanish register ship *Hermione*, worth £519,705 clear of expenses, of which each captain received over £65,000. Augustus Hervey, a favourite of his commander-in-chief and sent on all the best cruises, made £9,000 in the course of 1748.

One abuse resulting from the system was that it rewarded ships for the capture of rich merchantmen, rather than enemy warships (the Admiralty tried to counter this by offering promotions and honours only for naval actions against warships). Another was that port-admirals were handsomely rewarded for doing nothing. The share of the captain was reduced to a quarter after 1808. But Cochrane discerned something far worse: that the Admiralty courts who actually awarded the prize money embezzled much of the haul in an intricate system of fees and charges. As he put it:

> One of the most crying evils of our then naval administration had fallen heavily upon me, though so young in command – viz the Admiralty courts; but for the peculations consequent on which, the cruise of the *Speedy* ought to have sent home myself, officers, and crew, with competence. As it was, we got all the fighting, whilst the Admiralty court and its hungry parasites monopolised the greater portion of our hard-won prize money. In many cases they took the whole and in one case brought me in debt, though the prize was worth several thousand pounds!

Cochrane's success had been startling: by July 1801, after just a year in command of the *Speedy*, he had captured more than fifty prizes equipped with 122 guns and taken 534 prisoners. This meant that his own ordinary seamen were better rewarded than the officers in some other ships – another reason why the crew was so loyal to Cochrane. But in a great many cases the prize money obtained was derisory, and Cochrane felt he had been cheated. His view was that other British commanders did not bother taking prizes simply because there was no money in doing so:

> The amusement of destroying the enemy's trading vessels, even under the excitement occasioned by protecting batteries, ceased to operate as a permanent incentive; and the result, as may be seen by the logs of frigates, etc. stationed at the enemy's coast, was that their commanders avoided the risk of keeping their ships in contiguity with the shore, and adopted the only means of securing a comfortable night's rest by running into the offing. By daylight the coasting convoys got into some port or place of protection. Consequently the British cruisers,

having nothing in sight, their ropes were coiled up, the decks were washed, the hammocks stowed, and at eight o'clock the order was given to pipe to breakfast. In addition to this, the daily journal consisted of little more than the state of the weather, accompanied by the comprehensive remark, 'employed as usual' . . .

If it should be objected that I am deprecating the character of officers, I answer first, that I state only the truth: and secondly that I do not consider such truth as at all derogatory to their character. It is no reflection on their honour, and is creditable to their common sense. They could not reasonably be expected to sacrifice their rest, and to run their ships into danger and themselves into debt, for the exclusive emolument of the courts of Admiralty.

Cochrane's evident concern for his men was a particularly attractive feature of life under his command on the *Speedy*. It was observed from the first how extraordinarily easy it seemed to be for the young lieutenant to get the best out of them, from superb ship-handling to taking exceptional risks. This was no easy task in some ships, where sullen and resentful men would barely do the bidding of their commanders and took recourse in slowness and inefficiency rather than outright insubordination.

Cochrane secured this respect in part because he was as good a seaman as any on board, in part because of his approachability and unfailing courtesy and above all because of his dazzling success. It was exciting to serve under such a commander, and the men would follow him willingly into danger because he had an aura that led them to believe they would emerge unscathed. Cochrane was unfailingly solicitous about the lives of his men; he lost remarkably few because he calculated the odds so carefully in undertaking such apparently suicidal actions as the attack on the *Gamo*. At Oropeso the casualties were all aboard his sister ship; moreover Cochrane did not have command of the operation. Although Cochrane ran his ship efficiently, discipline was not excessive and he never had a man flogged – although he did not express opposition to flogging in principle. It was simply that he had no need to resort to this deterrent. He was a natural-born captain.

Another spectacular joint action followed. At noon on 9 June they attacked a 20-gun xebec accompanied by three gunboats escorting a Spanish convoy. The *Kingfisher* went in to fire at the fort overlooking the town, while the *Speedy* went after the escorting ships. For several hours the ships fired broadsides at each other, until a 12-gun felucca and two more gunboats arrived from Valencia to reinforce the Spaniards. But the *Speedy* gained the upper hand, sinking the xebec and, eventually, all four gunboats.

By now the *Speedy* had used up 1200 shot and the *Kingfisher* had also almost run out of ammunition. Extreme measures were required to finish the action, and Captain Pulling ordered his ship to close on the fort, whose defenders promptly fled, while the *Speedy* sailed straight at the felucca and the other gunboats, which also turned tail. Three merchantmen were captured, three sunk, and four driven on shore, where they were protected by Spanish troops. The *Kingfisher* had nearly been sunk by one of its own cannon, which had broken loose and had bounced down the hatchway into the hold.

The legendary career of the plucky little *Speedy* was brought to an end, fittingly, in one of its most glorious actions. To Cochrane's fury, in the summer of 1801 he was assigned to act as convoy to the mail packet that ran between the British naval base of Port Mahon in Minorca and Gibraltar. This in itself was a glaring example of minor corruption: because the packet ship was barely seaworthy, the mail was transferred to the *Speedy* as soon as the two ships were out of port, and then back aboard the packet as they approached Gibraltar, to give the impression the packet had carried the mail all the way – which meant that the contractor who had provided this unseaworthy boat could pocket the ample fee paid.

Impatient and frustrated, Cochrane cruised along the coast, keeping an eye out for possible prizes. He soon spotted some small merchant ships near Alicante, and got close; the Spaniards aboard ran them aground. Cochrane could not disembark to capture them where they lay beached without risking the flimsy packet boat in his charge, so he fired his cannon at them to set them on fire. One happened to be carrying oil, which blazed fiercely through the night, to Cochrane's satisfaction.

But the flames attracted the attention of three French battle-ships also heading for the Straits of Gibraltar. Cochrane's look-outs spotted the magnificent topsails on the horizon the following morning. As Toulon, from which these warships had emerged, was supposed to be under British blockade, and the Spanish fleet was bottled up in Cadiz, Cochrane concluded that they must be Spanish treasure ships, presenting him with a wonderful opportunity. He had made a fatal mistake. As he sailed towards them, wasting valuable escape time, it gradually became apparent that they were the pride of the French fleet – the *Indomitable*, the *Dessaix* and the *Formidable* – and they were fast closing on the *Speedy*, which was trapped between them and the shore.

Faced with such odds, any other commander would have surrendered at once; there was no chance of escape from the French warships, with their awesome sailpower. Once they came within range, a single broadside by any one of them would be enough to sink the *Speedy*; as there were three of them they could close in on him and block his ways of escape up or down the coast. But he was determined to make a break for it, believing, as with the *Gamo*, in the surprise of so bold a policy on his enemies. He put on all possible sail, dumped his little guns overboard – they would be of no use to him in any action against the overwhelming firepower of the French ships – as well as all other surplus weight, then began to tack as the ships approached so as to ensure that he was never broadside to them.

The French guns in bow and stern managed to damage his rigging, but his bobbing and weaving prevented them concen-trating their fire. He suddenly made a break for it between the *Dessaix* and the *Formidable*. The astonished French, who had expected the *Speedy* to flee at their approach, managed to let off a single broadside as the little ship sped past, but it missed. The

Speedy made it out into the open sea. Captain Christie Pallière of the *Dessaix* turned and went after it.

For a moment it seemed Cochrane had succeeded. But as repeated shots from the Frenchman's bows ripped into the *Speedy*'s canvas, the little ship began to slow and the *Dessaix* caught up after an hour, at last overhauling it. Cochrane takes up the story:

> At this short distance she let fly at us a complete broadside of round and grape, the object evidently being to sink us at a blow, in retaliation for thus attempting to slip past, though almost without hope of escape.
>
> Fortunately for us, in yawing to bring her broadside to bear, the rapidity with which she answered her helm carried her a little too far, and her round shot plunged in the water under our bows, or the discharge must have sunk us; the scattered grape, however, took effect in the rigging, cutting up a great part of it, riddling the sails, and doing material damage to the masts and yards, though not a man was hurt. To have delayed for another broadside would have been to expose all on board to certain destruction, and as further effort to escape was impotent, the *Speedy*'s colours were hauled down.

He was rowed aboard the *Dessaix* and offered his sword to Pallière. 'I will not accept the sword of an officer who has for so many hours struggled against impossibility,' the Frenchman told him chivalrously, in exultation at having at last brought to an end the career of the legendary terror of the Spanish coast and its commander. Cochrane was treated with full courtesy on the remainder of the trip to anchorage at Algeciras near Gibraltar.

CHAPTER 4

Captain Cochrane

After the excitements of the past year, the spell of rest as a French prisoner must have seemed positively enjoyable. Cochrane remarked:

> During this cruise I had ample opportunity of observing the superior manner in which the sails of the *Dessaix* were cut, and the consequent flat surface exposed to the wind; this contrasting strongly with the bag reefs and bellying sails of English ships of war at that period.

When they reached Algeciras, Cochrane was informed of the approach of a squadron of six British warships of 74 guns each under the command of Admiral Sir John Saumarez. Pallière asked him whether they would attack. Cochrane replied:

> An attack will certainly be made, and before night both the French and British ships will be at Gibraltar, where it will give me great pleasure to make you and your officers a return for the kindness I have experienced on board the *Dessaix*.

The French commander ordered his ships to move closer to the protection of the Spanish batteries but, in their haste, the three ships ran aground. As the two men had breakfast the following day a cannonball smashed into the cabin, spraying them with glass from a shattered wine bin nearby. They ran on deck to witness several marines being cut down by intense British fire. Cochrane, not wishing to be killed by his own side, discreetly withdrew to a safe place. He recounted what happened next:

The *Hannibal*, having with the others forged past the enemy, gallantly filled and tacked with a view to get between the French ships and the shore, being evidently unaware of their having been hauled aground. The consequence was that she ran upon a shoal, and remained fast, nearly bow on to the broadsides of the French line-of-battle ships, which with the shore batteries and several gunboats opened upon her a concentrated fire. This, from her position, she was unable to return. The result was that her guns were speedily dismounted, her rigging shot away, and a third of her crew killed or wounded; Captain Ferris, who commanded her, having now no alternative but to strike his colours – though not before he had displayed an amount of endurance which excited the admiration of the enemy.

A circumstance now occurred which is entitled to rank amongst the curiosities of war. On the French taking possession of the *Hannibal*, they had neglected to provide themselves with their national ensign, and either from necessity or bravado rehoisted the [British ensign] upside down. This being a well-known signal of distress, was so understood by the authorities at Gibraltar, who, manning all government and other boats with dockyard artificers and seamen, sent them, as it was mistakenly considered, to the assistance of the *Hannibal*.

On the approach of the launches I was summoned on deck by the captain of the *Dessaix*, who seemed doubtful what measures to adopt as regarded the boats now approaching to board the *Hannibal*, and asked my opinion as to whether they would attempt to retake the ship. As there could be no doubt in my mind about the nature of their mission or its result, it was evident that if they were allowed to board, nothing could prevent the seizure of the whole. My advice, therefore, to Captain Pallière was to warn them off by a shot – hoping they would thereby be driven back and saved from capture. Captain Pallière seemed at first inclined to take the advice, but on reflection – either doubting its sincerity, or seeing the real state of the case – he decided to capture the whole by permitting them to board unmolested. Thus boat by boat was captured until all the artificers necessary for the repair of the British squadron, and nearly all the sailors at that time in Gibraltar, were taken prisoners!

The British sent a boat under a flag of truce to suggest an exchange of prisoners. Pallière refused, but he did agree to parole the young British lieutenant – a great mistake, as subsequent events were to show, but demonstrative of the Frenchman's respect towards his guest-prisoner. Cochrane returned to a hero's welcome at Gibraltar.

It was still a moment of extreme danger and anxiety for the British garrison on the Rock. A Spanish flotilla of six warships was on its way to rescue the three French craft. Saumarez, with only five ships, sailed into the attack as night fell. In the ensuing confusion two of the biggest Spanish warships of 112 guns started firing at one another and destroyed each other, in two spectacular night explosions as their magazines went up, giving the British victory. Cochrane watched the whole show along with the garrison at Gibraltar.

A few days later he was formally court-martialled for the loss of the *Speedy*. Such courts martial, with all their ceremony and pomp, automatically took place on the loss of a ship. At least five, and not more than thirteen, captains were present, the 'prisoner' was represented by counsel, and the judge advocate of the fleet advised on procedural matters; the admiral's deputy usually presided in the great cabin of the flagship. Cochrane was acquitted with honour. The same day Cochrane was promoted to post-captain, reflecting his achievement at last in capturing the *Gamo* – but the appointment was not backdated, so he was left at the bottom of the seniority list, well below many undistinguished colleagues of his own age and with no chance at all of being given a command in view of the huge surplus of officers to ships.

Cochrane's naval uncle, Alexander, and his father lobbied the crotchety old St Vincent on his behalf for a ship. This proved counter-productive. 'The Cochranes are not to be trusted out of sight,' he thundered. 'They are all mad, romantic, money-getting and not truth-telling.' When he was told he must give young Cochrane a ship, St Vincent retorted, 'The First Lord of the Admiralty knows no must.' As another remarked, 'It became almost a point of etiquette with the Earl not to make [Cochrane] a captain [of a ship]'. To Cochrane's former commander, Admiral Keith, St Vincent wrote more reasonably, 'It is unusual to promote two officers [Cochrane and Parker] for such a service – besides which, the small number of killed on board the *Speedy* does not warrant the application.'

Cochrane now himself entered the fray, once again, typically, on behalf of his subordinate Lieutenant Parker, so valiantly injured in the capture of the *Gamo*. Lord St Vincent's reply had been calculated to drive a man of his passion to fury:

> His reasons for not promoting Lieutenant Parker, because there were only three men killed on board the *Speedy*, were in opposition to his Lordship's own promotion to an earldom, as well as that of his flag captain to knighthood, and his other officers to increased rank and honours: for in the battle from which his Lordship derived his title, there was only one man killed on board his own flagship, so that there were more casualties in my sloop than in his line-of-battle ship.

This played on the popular perception that Nelson had won the Battle of Cape St Vincent, while Jervis had watched safely from his flagship. Lord St Vincent was beside himself with this gross impertinence which, however accurate, was extraordinarily ill advised of Cochrane. The naval establishment substituted real spite for its instinctive dislike of the young hero. The unfortunate Parker was dispatched to the West Indies to take command of a ship that mysteriously failed to materialize, and was a broken man on his return home.

Cochrane, a captain without a command, was made doubly redundant by a short outbreak of peace between France and

Britain as a result of the Treaty of Amiens in March 1802, and returned to Britain, where he visited his father whose second marriage to the wealthy Mrs Raymond had given Culross a few more years' lease of life. Astonishingly, he decided to cross the Firth of Forth to go and study moral philosophy at Edinburgh under a famous pedagogue, Dugald Stewart. Cochrane was nothing if not a man of paradox: high intelligence and deep thoughtfulness underlay the popular image of a half-crazed warrior.

It was precisely this acute and overworking mind that led him to his passionate interest in public affairs, in particular the politics of injustice which later got him into so much trouble, where another man of action might simply have rested on his laurels. In addition to his readings aboard ship off Newfoundland, he was taking the opportunity of leisure to make up for his elementary schooling at Culross. Moral philosophy remains an interesting choice for a fighting man, and one can only surmise that he was examining the ethical implications of his own profession. At about that time he first met the Radical leader, William Cobbett, on a visit to Hampshire, as well as another prominent Radical who was to become one of Cochrane's lifelong supporters, Mary Russell Mitford. She gave this description of him:

he was as unlike the common notion of a warrior as could be. A gentle, quiet, mild young man, was this burner of French fleets as one should see in a summer day. He lay about under the trees, reading Seldon on the Dominion of the Seas, and letting children (and children always know with whom they may take liberties) play all sorts of tricks with him at their pleasure.

Dreamy, gentle, philosophical – out of his element at sea, young Cochrane appeared to be more a poet than a warrior, the embodiment of the Romantic movement then so fashionable, except that in reality he was a battle-stained hero, not a dandy, a poet, or a fop.

In March 1803, war was renewed between Britain and France, and Cochrane promptly and predictably applied for command of a ship. He was as promptly and predictably fobbed off. He then compiled a list of all the ships under construction and sent it to the Admiralty. Earl St Vincent replied huffily that they had all already been allocated to other commanders. Cochrane took a coach down to London to see the First Lord in person. Once again the old disciplinarian, after refusing to see him for several days, obstructed him. The incensed young officer played his last and only card, threatening to resign the service. This would have brought a storm of obloquy down upon the Admiralty – Cochrane was one of the few naval commanders with a genuine popular reputation.

The First Lord looked at him with icy thoughtfulness and told him that there was a ship available at Plymouth. Cochrane was exultant, and travelled down on the first available coach. When he arrived at the great dockyard and saw her, his first words were, 'She will sail like a haystack!' HMS *Arab* was a converted collier, a sluggish flat-bottomed hulk with neither speed nor manoeuvrability. He had been outwitted by St Vincent once again.

As soon as Cochrane took to sea with her, he discovered that her greatest problem was that she would not sail against the wind. Ordered to Boulogne, he found it impossible to return:

> With a fair wind, it was not difficult to get off Boulogne, but to get back with the same wind was – in such a craft – all but impossible. Our only way of effecting this was by watching the tide, to drift off as well as we could. A gale of wind anywhere from N.E. to N.W. would infallibly have driven us on shore on the French coast . . . I wrote to the Admiral commenting that the *Arab* was of no use for the service required, as she could not work to windward, and that her employment in such a service could only result in our loss by shipwreck on the French coast.

In a thunderous rage, whether by accident or design, when

Cochrane managed to struggle back across the Channel, he intercepted an American merchant ship, the *Chatham*, on its way to Amsterdam, informing its startled and indignant captain that there was a British blockade of the River Texel. This was news to the Admiralty (as to the Americans) which was unamused. Cochrane was promptly ordered north to protect the Shetland fishing fleet, which was odd, as there was no such fleet. He was in effect in exile for nearly 14 months aboard a wallowing and useless tub, far away from any action; this was

> Literally a period of despair, from the useless inactivity into which I was forced, without object or purpose, beyond that of visiting me with the weight of official displeasure.
>
> I will not trouble the reader with any reminiscences of this degrading command, or rather dreary punishment, for such it was no doubt intended to be, as depriving me of the opportunity of exerting or distinguishing myself.

Cochrane has sometimes been interpreted as the creator of his own problems. In fact, it was the Admiralty which often took the initiative, and he manfully, if unwisely, rose to the bait. In time of war they were wrong to so ill-use one of their best commanders. There was no doubt of his naval skills, as the *Speedy* campaigns had shown, and really good captains were in desperately short supply. Because he had tweaked the noses of naval bureaucrats, challenged their system of preferment and, above all, affronted the First Lord, one of the most exciting British seamen alive was left patrolling the empty northern extremities of Britain in an old collier while the country's very existence was at stake – Napoleon was now preparing to invade. To the impatient young man, his career must have seemed almost over, at the ripe old age of twenty-seven, a commander of brilliance crushed by the system.

Fate is nothing if not ironic, even capricious. Cochrane had secured his initial advancement largely through the connections of his aristocratic, if impoverished family. He had then made his name through superb seamanship and captaincy, excoriating those of lesser talents who had ascended through favouritism, and been obstructed every step of the way. The man who had most come to hate him, Earl St Vincent, was himself a merito-crat who bitterly opposed preferment. The middle-class St Vincent despised Cochrane for his aristocratic hauteur and for his general lack of respect for authority.

Now, with the accession of a new Tory government under William Pitt, a political supporter of his, Henry Dundas, first Viscount Melville, was appointed in St Vincent's place. Melville was political jobbery and corruption personified. He was the political boss of Scotland who could deliver the whole country to Pitt through manipulation and appointment. 'The means by which I govern Scotland cannot be dissolved by the breath of any minister,' he once boasted. He was a bon viveur with a great fondness for wine and huge dinner parties.

As a Scot he took notice of the incestuous lobbying of Scottish families, in particular the Duke of Hamilton, on behalf of young Cochrane; and so the latter's fortunes, ironically, took a new twist. Cochrane was appointed through favour by a corrupt old political boss to be commander of the *Pallas*, a new 667-ton frigate of 38 guns – 12 of them 24-pounders, 26 of them 12-pounders – with a crew of over 200. It was a dream come true, a present from a Tory administration at that. Melville, it seems, had the shrewdness to see that much-needed victories against the French could be won only by appointing the best commanders, however insubordinate, not by exiling them to Shetland. Cochrane, bemused by this astonishing change in his fortunes, was forced to resort to the press-gang to recruit his crew – his old one on the *Speedy* had been dispersed – and he was ordered to attack enemy convoys crossing the Atlantic.

The young captain left Plymouth on 21 January 1805 and after a month's training at sea made his way to the Azores, where he could intercept ships making the Atlantic crossing. On 6 February he reported:

We fell in with and captured a large ship, the *Caroline*, bound from the Havannah to Cadiz, and laden with a valuable cargo. After taking out the crew, we despatched her to Plymouth. Having learned from the prisoners that the captured ship was part of a convoy bound from the Havannah to Spain, we proceeded on our course and on the 13th captured a second vessel which was still more valuable, containing in addition to the usual cargo some diamonds and ingots of gold and silver. This vessel was sent to Plymouth as before. On the 15th we fell in with another, *La Fortuna*, which proved the richest of all.

When *La Fortuna* was taken, its cargo proved to be worth £132,000. Cochrane generously allowed the captain and cargo-manager, much of whose fortune this was, to retain 5000 doubloons each; the crew was consulted and shouted 'Aye aye, my lord, with all our hearts' – as well they might because they stood to gain so much. By the end of March, four major prizes had been sent home.

Then disaster struck in an uncanny repetition of the events that had led to the capture of the *Speedy*. As one of the masts of the *Pallas* poked above a heavy sea mist one morning, the lookout called that he could see three masts approaching. Cochrane himself scrambled up the rigging and immediately recognized them as French ships of the line. He had no choice but to run. Even as the chase began, the wind blew up, the sea grew choppier, and the mist dissipated. The water deepened into the troughs of an approaching gale.

The three ships had much more sail than the *Pallas*, and were soon gaining upon him. But the gale was an advantage to him too: they could not aim their cannon properly as they bucked and surged under the heavy seas. Cochrane recounted:

The *Pallas* was crank to such a degree, that the lee main-deck guns, though housed, were under water, and even the lee quarter-deck carronades were at times emerged.

As the strange ships were coming up with us hand over

hand, the necessity of carrying more sail became indispens-
able, notwithstanding the immersion of the hull.

To do this with safety was the question. However, I
ordered all the hawsers in the ship to be got up to the mast-
heads and hove taut. The masts being thus secured, every
possible stitch of sail was set, the frigate plunging forecastle
under, as was also the case with our pursuers, which could not
fire a gun – though as the haze cleared away we saw them
repeatedly flashing the priming. After some time the line-of-
battle ships came up with us, one keeping on our lee-beam,
another to windward, each within half a mile, whilst the third
was a little more distant.

This was extremely dangerous in a gale, risking the masts snap-
ping or the ship foundering under its own speed in heavy seas.
The ship plunged furiously forward, its bows swamped under
water with each breaking wave. Even so the battleships gained
upon him, two approaching at half a mile's distance on each
side, with one coming up behind.

But Cochrane had trained his men perfectly, and he had a
plan. Ordering his topmen up into the rigging, as the vessel
thundered through the spray and they clung to the spars for life,
he gave them the signal to furl every sail at once. The French
ships ploughing through the waters alongside could not fire
because of the violence of the seas and because they were not yet
within range. At exactly the moment the sails of the *Pallas* disappeared from view, Cochrane's helmsman turned hard over.

For the ship it was a moment of supreme danger. Still moving
fast, but now broadside to the waves in these ferocious seas, the
Pallas could easily have capsized – except that with no sails, as
Cochrane had calculated, the wind would be unable to assist the
sea in turning the ship over. Even so, she 'shook from stern to
stern in crossing the trough of the sea'. In effect, she had stopped
dead in her tracks, and the French ships of the line, their sails
billowing, shot past for several miles downwind, while the *Pallas*
tacked off slowly in the opposite direction, against the wind.

They ran on for several miles before they could shorten sail, or trim on the opposite tack. Indeed, under the heavy gale that was now blowing, even this was no easy matter, without endangering their own masts.

There was no time for consideration on our part, so having rapidly sheeted home, we spread all sail on the opposite tack. The hawsers being still fast to the masts, we went away from our pursuers at the rate of 13 knots and upwards; so that a considerable distance was soon interposed between us and them; and this was greatly increased ere they were in a condition to follow. Before they had fairly renewed the chase night was rapidly setting in, and when quite dark, we lowered a ballasted cask overboard with a lantern, to induce them to believe that we had altered our course, though we held on in the same direction during the whole night. The trick was successful, for, as had been calculated, the next morning, to our great satisfaction, we saw nothing of them, and were all much relieved on finding our dollars and His Majesty's ship once more in safety. The expedient was a desperate one, but so was the condition which induced us to resort to it.

When he reached Plymouth, Cochrane's masthead was adorned with three exquisitely worked golden candlesticks five feet tall taken from a prize. The ship was instantly dubbed the *'Golden' Pallas*. However, customs at Plymouth insisted he pay full duty for them. This was too much for him and they were broken up and admitted as much cheaper 'old gold'.

Basking in this triumph, and the resultant press acclaim, Cochrane was persuaded by his Radical friend William Cobbett to have a stab at entering politics by standing against the ministerial candidate, Cavendish Bradshaw, at the forthcoming parliamentary by-election at Honiton. Cochrane's admirers as a seaman date his self-destruction from this fateful decision: if he had remained pure and aloof, in the profession he knew best, and stayed above the turmoil and corruption of politics, he would have enjoyed an unblemished reputation, they argued.

They missed the point. Cochrane was too intelligent a man to be content with pure seamanship: the restless, inquiring mind inside him constantly sought ways of improving the lot of his fellow man as he fought the complacency around him. The same urge that drove him to his brilliant naval victories deploying unconventional tactics also drove him towards his challenges against the Admiralty and the political status quo. What better way of expressing this than through politics? Cochrane, as we shall see, was not always successful or effective as a politician, but his inner demons left him no choice but to attempt the crusades he undertook.

Once again, his career was steeped in irony. Resolving to fight against Admiralty corruption, he had involved himself in one of the most corrupt boroughs in the country and, in spite of Cochrane's later efforts to cleanse himself of the dirt, there is little doubt he also indulged. 'I always vote for Mr Most,' one voter told him archly, and Cochrane lost resoundingly. He then took the unusual step of paying his own electors ten guineas each – double the amount Bradshaw had provided – for their 'honesty' in having supported him and rejecting the government's bribes, despite the fact that he had lost.

The purpose of this extraordinary exercise was only later to become apparent. It was not to Cochrane's credit. When he ran again the voters assumed he would pay out once more – wrongly, as it turned out, much to their chagrin:

Aware of my previous objection to bribery, not a word was asked by my partisans as to the price expected in exchange for their suffrages. It was enough that my former friends had received ten guineas each after my defeat, and it was judged best to leave the cost of success to my discretion.

My return was triumphant, and this effected, it was then plainly asked, what ex post facto consideration was to be expected by those who had supported me in so delicate a manner.

'Not one farthing!' was the reply.

'But, my lord, you gave ten guineas a head to the minority

at the last election, and the majority have been calculating on something handsome on the present occasion'.

'No doubt. The former gift was for their disinterested conduct in not taking the bribe of five pounds from the agents of my opponent. For me now to pay them would be a violation of my own previously expressed principles.'

Meanwhile, he was back on active service, this time on more mundane duty, escorting one convoy across the North Atlantic and another back. The journeys were uneventful and Cochrane found he had time on his hands. He decided to turn his hand to his father's gift for invention, designing a signal light to guide the merchantmen behind him; all too frequently these badly captained craft would lose the main convoy in the night. He had a friend submit the patents to the Admiralty, which had set up a £20 competition to design such a lamp, and it won. But when the Admiralty learnt who the true designer was, they dropped the idea instantly. Cochrane also took to designing a giant kite to increase the speed of ships, but had to admit defeat:

> A studding sailboom was lashed across a spare flying jib-boom to form the framework, and over this a large spread of canvas was sewn in the usual boy's fashion . . . My spars were of unequal dimensions throughout, and this and our launching the kite caused it to roll greatly. Possibly I might not have been sufficiently experienced in the mysteries of 'wings and tail', for though the kite pulled with a will, it made such occasional lurches as gave reason to fear for the too sudden expenditure of His Majesty's stores.

His return journey was marred by gales of rain and hail. He arrived to learn of the great victory of Trafalgar and the death of Nelson on 21 October 1805. In his thirtieth year, at the full height of his powers, Cochrane was also at last a rich man for the first time in his life. He had brought home some £75,000 in prize money – half of which was immediately seized by the corrupt commander of the port of Plymouth, Admiral Sir

William Young, who had taken the precaution of copying out the Admiralty orders instructing Cochrane and was therefore technically his superior.

Cochrane promptly indulged his gift for invention and spent some of the money on designing a high-speed galley with 18 oars, to go aboard the *Pallas* and thus provide it with the ability to attack while the enemy was becalmed by the wind; it was a simple and brilliant idea:

> She rowed double-banked, and required eighteen hands at the oars, and this together with her beautiful build rendered her perhaps the fastest boat afloat. Escape from such a craft being hopeless, she became so notorious, that the enemy's coasters ran their vessels ashore, and jumping into their boats, thus saved themselves from being made prisoners.

Throughout his life as an inventor, Cochrane was to be preoccupied with the limitations imposed upon the manoeuvrability of sailing ships by the wind.

CHAPTER 5

The Bay of Biscay

Cochrane's new orders were to join up with the fleet under Admiral Thornburgh to harass enemy shipping off the French coast. At last he was back in the thick of the action. Thornburgh, hopeful of securing a share of the prize money Cochrane seemed able to secure with such ease, gave him considerable freedom of movement. Cochrane first intercepted some fishing vessels, confiscating their catch but paying for it, with a touch of gentility; he then relieved a merchantman of a cargo of wine.

He moved south towards the harbour of Les Sables, landing ashore to capture boats run aground. Operating in the Bay of Biscay was very different to his old Mediterranean station. The sea was usually heavy and often dangerously and violently stormy; the huge movement of the tides made that rocky and reef-strewn coast more dangerous still; and the French fleet was of a much higher order to the Spanish, while coastguard defences and signals were similarly far more sophisticated.

None of this daunted the young captain. Reaching the mouth of the river Garonne, he learnt that several French corvettes were sheltering there under the guns of Fort de Royan and Fort du Veron, protected by a guard-ship. He decided to penetrate this stronghold at night. The risks of raiding inland were enormous: he could be bottled up by ships coming in behind him at any time, and the mouth of the Garonne was a treacherous estuary. But Cochrane dispatched the galley with 180 men aboard while he stayed on guard in the *Pallas* at the river-mouth. It was the first of his many 'commando' raids.

After several hours, at 3 a.m., the British sailors climbed aboard the guard-ship, the *Tapageuse*, and after a brief struggle overpowered the startled crew. They then turned her guns on the corvettes she was supposed to be protecting, which had been left with only skeleton crews, destroyed them, and set off back up the estuary to rendezvous with the *Pallas* There, however, Cochrane was growing increasingly impatient. His luck had held while his men were bottled up performing their daring raid. But with only forty men left aboard his ship and only enough crew for two guns, he was desperately vulnerable.

The worst soon materialized along that busy coast. Three sails appeared on the horizon. They were French corvettes, with 50 guns between them and 300 men aboard. Cochrane now resorted to one of the inventive ruses he was capable of in a crisis. He sent his men aloft to undo the complex system of ropes that normally held the sails in place, and instead fixed them in place with thin yarn, which could be easily cut. As the corvettes approached, he gave the orders for these strings to be cut in unison. All the sails fell into place simultaneously – an operation which could only normally be carried out by a full crew.

The corvettes concluded that the ship was fully manned. They turned tail and the *Pallas* set off in pursuit, firing its two forward guns – the only ones that were crewed, but the corvettes had no way of knowing that the ship was not capable of delivering a full broadside. In their headlong flight, each of the corvettes ran aground, either deliberately to avoid capture, or because of the difficulty of navigation in the area. Cochrane's two guns destroyed each sitting duck in turn.

When Cochrane rendezvoused with the captured *Tapageuse* and the galley, the two ships moved north on a daring reconnaissance mission into the treacherous Aix and Basque Roads behind the Isle d'Oléron, which protected the great French naval arsenal at Rochefort, as well as providing a supposedly impregnable anchorage for the French fleet. He cheekily sent in his express galley in a series of 'commando' raids which destroyed five of the chain of signal houses that watched the movements of British shipping along the coast. He also blew up a shore battery. More importantly, he acquired valuable intelligence about the main

French stronghold in the Bay of Biscay. He wrote to Thornburgh:

> The ships of the line have all their topmasts struck and topgallant yards across. They are all very deep, more so than vessels are in general for common voyages. They may be easily burned, or they may be taken by sending here eight or ten thousand men, as if intended for the Mediterranean. If people at home would hold their tongues about it, possession might thus be gained of the Isle of d'Oléron, upon which all the enemy's vessels may be driven by sending fire vessels to the eastward of the Isle of d'Aix . . .

He now decided to try another of his inventions: this was another kite, which was attached to a bundle of propaganda leaflets he had been asked to distribute along the French coast along with a slow-burning match which would eventually consume the yarn that bound them and allow the leaflets to be deposited over land when the wind blew in the right direction.

The value of such leaflets, then as now, was highly questionable – particularly so at a time of low literacy. But the Admiralty had given its orders that they be distributed, and this seemed a more effective way of getting them to the French. Cochrane had no way of verifying whether his kites-and-candles device ever worked.

By May, Cochrane had arrived off the island of Aix again. He embarked on further 'commando' raids to destroy French signal positions:

> The French trade having been kept in port of late, in a great measure by their knowledge of the exact position of His Majesty's cruisers, constantly announced at the signal-posts; it appeared to me to be some object, as there was nothing better to do, to endeavour to stop this practice.
>
> Accordingly, the two posts at Point Delaroche were demolished, next that of Caliola. Then two in L'Anse de Repos, one of which Lieutenant Haswell and Mr Hillier, the gunner, took

in a neat style from upwards of 100 militia. The marines and boats' crews behaved exceedingly well. All the flags have been brought off, and the houses built by government burnt to the ground.

Yesterday, too, the zeal of Lieutenant Norton of the *Frisk* cutter, and Lieutenant Gregory of the *Contest* gun-brig, induced them to volunteer to flank the battery on Point d'Equillon, whilst we should attack in the rear by land; but it was carried at once, and one of fifty men who were stationed to three 36-pounders was made prisoner – the rest escaped. The battery is laid in ruins – guns spiked – carriages burnt – barrack and magazine blown up, and all the shells thrown into the sea.

He spotted a large French frigate, the *Minerve*, with 40 guns, which was twice the size of the *Pallas* nestling under the battery of Aix. This 'large black frigate' had been plaguing the British for some time. In addition, there were three French brigs protecting this predator.

Cochrane nevertheless ordered the *Pallas* to sail straight down the Aix channel towards it. The French, astounded by this medium-sized ship taking on such odds, in their best-protected and most formidable anchorage at that, their equivalent of Plymouth, were stung into action. But by then Cochrane had already put one of the brigs out of action. Tacking backwards and forwards, he managed to avoid the notoriously dangerous shoals of the Aix channel and destroyed another brig, while also doing damage to the rigging of the *Minerve*. The French were unnerved by the rashness of this crazy ship in their midst.

Cochrane sailed the *Pallas* between the *Minerve* and the shore battery, both of which were pounding away ineffectually. He ordered his ship to close with the *Minerve*, in preparation for battle. This was done too sharply: the two ships collided, their masts locking with one another, the guns of the *Pallas*, which had just loosed off a broadside, being knocked back momentarily. Under Cochrane's frantic direction, the British crew recovered far more quickly from the impact of the collision than the French, and let off another devastating broadside at point-blank range.

No more than three solitary pistol shots came back in retaliation. The *Minerve*'s captain, Joseph Collet, had been the only man not to flee below under the onslaught of fire, and he coolly raised his hat in salute through the smoke. Cochrane, only a few feet away, was deeply impressed by his gallantry: when later he found the same officer as a captive in the stable block of Dartmoor prison, he had him moved to better quarters.

Meanwhile the young captain, for all the verve and nerve of his attack, was in greater danger than ever. His own ship was almost as crippled as the *Minerve*; and two French frigates were now bearing down to the latter's help. Fortunately a British ship, the *Kingfisher* under Captain George Seymour, was a little way off. Seymour was regarded as imprudent, and he had orders from Thornburgh not to proceed beyond a lighthouse above Aix. Seeing Cochrane's predicament, however, he decided to ignore these. He sailed south to escort Cochrane out. The two frigates – although each had more guns than the two British ships combined – had seen enough of the danger posed by the British and sheered off to go to the rescue of the crippled *Minerve*.

Cochrane returned to Plymouth a week later even more of a popular hero. His tour in the Bay of Biscay had been a dazzling display of aggression, fearlessness and skill: a single ship had terrorized coastal France. No other British commander had achieved what Cochrane had – taken the fight directly to the enemy – nor had any French commander done the same along the British coast. With his flying galley he had initiated the first 'commando' raids. His punch down the Garonne had intimidated a major French city, Bordeaux, and destroyed its naval defences; he had penetrated the very centre of French naval power at Rochefort, destroying its signals system; and he had crippled a major French ship twice his size and destroyed two brigs. The effect upon French morale was overpowering: nowhere along the coast seemed safe from this marauder. The effect on the British war effort, at a time of despondency, was equally charged: here at last was a sailor worthy to succeed Nelson. In the highest personal compliment of his career following this attack, Cochrane was dubbed by Napoleon 'le loup de mer' – the sea wolf.

Cochrane's performance in the Bay of Biscay, coming after his exploits in the Mediterranean and off the Azores, clearly demonstrated he was the outstanding sea-captain of the time. But he had one defect in the eyes of the Admiralty: he cared not a fig what they thought. So confident was he of his own abilities that he saw no need to ingratiate himself with his superiors or toe the line. After his latest display of seamanship, he felt able to take on his superiors: and that meant immersing himself once again in politics.

Cochrane returned to England after the Bay of Biscay tour flushed with success and ready to take on all comers. His political sponsor was Cobbett, also conceited, but a self-made man who had been a Tory until he had been appalled by the British excesses in Ireland, corruption in general and the attempts to curb his own freedom of speech. He was high-minded to a fault, and perhaps the closest Britain was to having a genuinely revolutionary figure during the fraught days before the Great Reform Act. He was determined to get Cochrane elected.

So also, for entirely separate reasons, was another man who was remarkable in a completely different way: Andrew Cochrane-Johnstone, Thomas's uncle, the younger brother of his father – who was only eight years older than his nephew and had acquired the name Johnstone on his marriage to the daughter of the Earl of Hopetoun. Being almost the same age as Cochrane, he exerted a disproportionate influence on the young man and was to exercise a baleful influence on his life.

According to a local account, on this occasion Cochrane:

. . . set out from the port of Plymouth . . . in a true seaman-like style. He himself, accompanied by a couple of lieutenants and one midshipman all in full dress, as if engaged in actual service, proceeded in one carriage and were followed in another by his boat's crew, new-rigged and prepared for action. On the box sat the helmsman, who wished to regulate the steerage, which he doubtless lamented to see confided to two lubberly landsmen of postilions, with favours in their hats and boots on their legs; while the boatswain, perched on the roof of the carriage with his whistle in his mouth, kept the whole in order, and enabled all to cheer in due time, every blast being accompanied by a long huzza.

This time Cochrane had learnt his lesson: bribery was the key to winning, and he was flushed with prize money. He admitted as much a decade later:

> Though I am conscious that I did wrong, I assure the House that that was the way I was returned. If any member disputes it, I can only say that I am willing to show the bills and vouchers which I had for the money. I have no doubt but that there are very many in this House who have been returned by similar means. My motive, I am now fully convinced, was wrong, decidedly wrong, but as I came home pretty well flushed with Spanish dollars, I found this borough open, and I bargained for it, and I am sure I would have been returned had I been Lord Camelford's black servant or his great dog.

His previous award of ten guineas for every elector who voted for him could be seen as a sweetener – yet in later life he was falsely to claim that he had paid the voters nothing. It was a blot on Cochrane's own career as a scourge of wrongdoing, only mitigated by the fact that these practices were virtually essential to being elected to Parliament at the time. Meanwhile his many local critics forced him to agree to provide a victory dinner, to which he rashly assented, and they had their revenge. After a night of carousing for virtually the entire town of Honiton, the bill was £1200, a staggering sum for a party in those days, which he indignantly refused to pay at first.

Yet he was now an MP and at last had a platform for his views. He bought a house in Dean's Yard, the elegant square by Westminster Abbey just across from the House of Commons. But before it sat he was ordered to sea, perhaps a reflection of Melville's own admiration for him, or perhaps out of Admiralty nervousness about what he might say in the Commons.

PART TWO

Triumph and Disgrace

'He was a sailor every inch of him. He knew a ship from stem to stern, understood the character of seamen and gained their confidence. He was besides a good mechanic, a carpenter, a rope-maker, sail-maker, and cooper. He could hand reef and steer, knot and splice: but he was no orator. He was good tempered, honest and unsophisticated, with a large proportion of common sense and free with his officers.'

Captain Savage, as described by Frederick Marryat in *Peter Simple* (1834)

CHAPTER 6

The Sea Wolf

His new ship was the *Imperieuse*, a 1064-ton frigate, about twice the size of the *Pallas*, and even faster, with 38 guns and 300 men, many of whom Cochrane had arranged to be transferred from the *Pallas*. Among the new recruits was a fourteen-year-old boy, Frederick Marryat, the son of a rich MP and West Indies merchant. Marryat was later to become the first great novelist of the Royal Navy in Napoleonic times, as Captain Marryat. He was vividly to describe his experiences under Cochrane.

The admiral at Plymouth when Cochrane arrived to take up his command in November 1806 was still Sir William Young, who had helped himself to so much of Cochrane's prize money (he was to be dubbed Sir Hurricane Humbug in Marryat's novels). This time he suddenly ordered the *Imperieuse* to sea before she had been properly prepared. Cochrane was furious:

> The alacrity of the port authorities to obtain praise for despatching vessels to sea before they were in fit condition was reprehensible. It was a point in those days for port admirals to hurry off ships, regardless of consequences, immediately after orders for their sailing were received; this 'despatch', as it was incorrectly termed, securing the commendation of the Admiralty, whom no officer dared to inform of the danger to which both ships and crews were thereby exposed.
>
> The case of the *Imperieuse* was very near proving the fallacy of the system. She was ordered to put to sea, the moment the rudder – which was being hung – would steer

the ship. The order was of necessity obeyed. We were therefore compelled to leave port with a lighter full of provisions on one side, a second with ordnance stores on the other, and a third filled with gunpowder towing astern. We had not even opportunity to secure the guns; the quarter-deck carronades were not shipped on their slides; and all was in the utmost confusion.

The result of this precipitation was – for it had no object – that as soon as the land was out of sight, we were obliged to heave-to, in mid-channel, to unstow the after hold, get down the ballast, and clear the decks. Worse still – the rigging had not been effectually set up, so that had a gale of wind come on, the safety of the frigate might have been compromised; or had we been attacked by an enemy – even a gunboat – we could not have fired a shot in return, as, from the powder coming on board last, we had not a cartridge filled.

The weather becoming thick on the following day, no observation could be taken. The consequence was, that from the current and unknown drift of the frigate whilst hove-to, to set up the new rigging, secure the masts, and stow the hold, we drifted towards Ushant, and in the night struck heavily three or four times on a shelf, but fortunately forged over into a deep pool.

Marryat recorded more graphically:

The signal for sailing was enforced by gun after gun; the anchor was hove up and with all her stores on deck, her guns not even mounted, in a state of confusion unparalleled from her being obliged to hoist faster than it was possible she could stow away, she was driven out of harbour to encounter a heavy gale. A few hours more would have enabled her to proceed to sea with security, but they were denied. The consequences were appalling; they might have been fatal. In the general confusion some iron too near the binnacles had attracted the needle of the compasses; the ship was steered out of her course.

At midnight, in a heavy gale at the close of November, so dark that you could not distinguish any object however close, the *Imperieuse* dashed upon the rocks between Ushant and the Main. The cry of terror which ran through the lower decks; the grating of the keel as she was forced in; the violence of the shocks which convulsed the frame of the vessel; the hurrying up of the ship's company without their clothes; and then the enormous wave which bore her up and carried her clean over the reef will never be effaced from my memory.

Cochrane immediately ordered an anchor dropped so that the ship would not be carried onto other reefs. As the storm subsided, Cochrane carefully inched his ship out of the rocky trap into which she had blundered, his headsman shouting out the depths so that she would not strike. It had been a very narrow escape.

Cochrane took to raiding the French coast once again, capturing ship after ship with a languid professionalism that deeply impressed the young Marryat:

The cruises of the *Imperieuse* were periods of continual excitement, from the hour in which she hove up her anchor till she dropped it again in port; the day that passed without a shot being fired in anger was with us a blank day; the boats were hardly secured on the booms than they were cast loose and out again; the yard and stay tackles were for ever hoisting up and lowering down. The expedition with which parties were formed for service; the rapidity of the frigate's movements day and night; the hasty sleep, snatched at all hours; the waking up at the report of the guns, which seemed the only key note to the hearts of those on board; the beautiful precision of our fire, obtained by constant practice; the coolness and courage of our captain, inoculating the whole of the ship's company; . . . when memory sweeps along those years of excitement, even now my pulse beats more quickly with the reminiscence.

Cochrane embarked on another of his spectacular raids inshore, against a French convoy guarded by small warships south of the Gironde. The convoy was protected by the formidable guns and defences of Fort Roquette. The French, hearing of his approach, had ordered the soldiers from the fort down to the beach. As they waited for the expected attack, Cochrane landed a raiding party further up which attacked the almost undefended fort, destroying its guns and blowing up the arsenal. On hearing the explosion the French soldiers on the beach ran in the direction of the attack, abandoning the ships. Cochrane's boats silently pounced upon them, setting fire to seven merchant ships and gunboats. In the space of only 12 weeks, he destroyed or captured fifteen ships.

Returning to the fleet, which was anchored off Rochefort, he encountered the *Atalante*, a battered British sloop which had been on station blockading the port for eight months. Its captain appealed to him: she could barely stay afloat, she was leaking so badly, taking 20 inches of water an hour. The pumps could only just expel this. Cochrane protested to the commander of the squadron, Keats, who did nothing, and then to the authorities at Plymouth on his return there. In any gale, he declared, the *Atalante* was certain to sink. Soon enough word came that just this had happened – as well as the demise of the similarly unseaworthy *Felix*, whose commander had been similarly rebuffed by the ruthless Captain Keats. Cochrane now saw the corruption, jobbery and indifference of the mediocre naval establishment in a different, more sinister light.

In May 1807 a fresh general election had been called. Cochrane, campaigning against naval corruption, could not contest Honiton again where he was much disliked. But his Radical sympathies were stronger than ever. His friend Cobbett suggested he try for one of the few genuinely popularly elected constituencies in the country, the City of Westminster, which at the time comprised most of central London. The current members were the playwright Richard Brinsley Sheridan and Samuel Hood. Sheridan was by now a hardened alcoholic, consuming up to six bottles of wine and one or two bottles of brandy a day.

The favourite for the seat was another Radical, the wealthy Sir Francis Burdett, married to the daughter of the banker Thomas Coutts, who had a splendid house on Piccadilly and two fine country estates. Cobbett's motive was undoubtedly to get Cochrane in as a counter to the lordly Burdett, a man of admirable sentiments and eloquence, who was not always personally courageous.

To get elected for one of the two Westminster seats was one of the few real tests of public opinion in the early nineteenth century, and it was a measure of Cochrane's fame that he soon became one of the principal candidates. He campaigned with gusto, composing an election ditty:

All hail to the hero – of England the boast,
The honour – the glory – the pride of our coast;
Let the bells peal his name, and the cannons' loud roar,
Sound the plaudits of Cochrane, the friend of her shore.

Of one of his opponents he asked:

Do you think that a creature whose whole time almost is employed in making a noise at the head of his horses, and grinning to please the ladies; or, when he is displeased himself, breaking the heads of beasts by the hand of a brute – is such a man fit to represent you?

Cochrane came second with 3708 votes to Burdett's 5134 and Sheridan's 2645. When Cochrane took his seat, he immediately made himself unpopular in the House by launching into a demand for an inquiry into the sinecures held by MPs, which he claimed were worth £180,000 for eighteen placemen alone. This was blocked on procedural grounds by experienced older hands. He pressed for papers relating to the loss of the *Atalante* and the *Felix*. In both he was frustrated. The veterans at Westminster regarded him as a minor nuisance they could swat effortlessly aside. Anyway he belonged to a party with only a handful of MPs. Cochrane's political philosophy was sea-breeze straightforward:

> It had become unmistakeably manifest that the two great factions into which politicians were divided had no other object than to share in the general plunder, and, as a first step to this, to embarrass the government of the 'ins' by the factious opposition of the 'outs'. Indeed, so obvious had this become, that the appellations of Whig and Tory were laid aside by common consent, and the more descriptive names of 'outs' and 'ins' substituted in their stead. My election had no doubt been secured by the emphatic declaration, that I would belong to neither party, supporting or opposing either as in my judgment might seem conducive to the national good.
>
> The animosity of these respective parties against each other was favourable to such a course. Each accused the other of grasping at offices for the sake of personal or dependent advantage, and averred that the aim of their opponents was neither the administration of government – which, as has been seen, was left to administer itself in its own way – nor the good of the country, but the possession and distribution of the public money. So virulent did these mutual recriminations become, that it cannot be wondered at if people took the disputants at their word; the more so as the moment either party was in power they threw aside the principles which had gained momentary ascendancy, and devoted their sole attention to their former practices, knowing that, as their possession of office might be short, a tenure so uncertain must be made the most of. Statesmanship amongst such people was out of the question. Neither party could even foresee that the very disgust which their scramble for office was exciting in the public mind must one day overthrow both factions.

The Admiralty ordered him back to the *Imperieuse*, anxious to be rid of his embarrassing public demands. His electors gave him leave to do so. Cochrane was ordered to the Mediterranean to serve under Admiral Lord Collingwood, who sensibly respected his independence and sent him to command the Corfu squadron, patrolling the Ionian Islands. After a disturbing incident in which four of Cochrane's men were killed trying to board a pirate boat near Malta, he engaged in an angry argument with a British officer licensing contraband vessels in the Adriatic.

Collingwood, an exceptional and enlightened commander who had banned the use of flogging aboard his ships, then appointed him to harass the enemy of France and Spain. Cochrane resumed his old activities along the Spanish coast with gusto. As in *Speedy* days he found it almost too easy – and he was now commanding a much bigger and better ship.

On 17 February, the *Imperieuse* spotted a convoy some 8 miles west of Cartagena and pursued the ships along the shore. It veered away when it spotted four gunboats, anchoring out of sight of land, and waiting for these to leave their anchorage just after sunset. The predatory *Imperieuse* suddenly moved in among them, firing broadside after broadside, sinking two with all hands and boarding a fourth gun vessel. The fourth escaped to Cartagena, where the Spanish fleet was at anchor and Cochrane prudently decided not to pursue it.

From the captured prisoners, he learnt that a large French ship filled with munitions was at anchor in the Bay of Almeria, and he decided to 'cut her out' – take her at anchor. The *Imperieuse* hoisted American colours, sailed in close to the French ship and sent out two boats with boarding parties. The French opened fire, but were successfully boarded although the leader of the boarding party, Lieutenant Caulfield, was killed as he jumped aboard. However, the wind suddenly died away, leaving the *Imperieuse* and its prize becalmed under a heavy fire from shore batteries just half a mile away. The battery damaged the hull of the prize, which Cochrane had skilfully placed between the *Imperieuse* and the enemy guns, and at 11 a.m. a light breeze took them out of range – not a moment too soon, as a Spanish ship of the line had arrived to help. The *Imperieuse* was, however, the faster ship, and got away.

After securing a number of prizes laden with wine, the

Imperieuse ran into a gale and was compelled to seek the nearest safe anchorage – under a cliff dominated by an enemy barracks. The troops there opened fire, but broadsides from the *Imperieuse* demolished the barracks. Near Majorca, Cochrane landed a party to blow up the battery of Jacemal. But he was running short of food and water. He landed a force nearby, which captured some sheep, bullocks and pigs, and then landed a boat to forage water near Blanes. A large body of troops appeared, but as they fired their muskets, the *Imperieuse*'s cannon, a quarter of a mile off, responded, and they fled back into the woods.

On 20 May a convoy of eight boats was spotted, escorted by four gunboats. These ran close inshore, firing briskly, and three of them grounded. Keeping up a hail of musket-fire, Cochrane's men soon compelled the crews of two of them to abandon their vessels, and captured the third whose wounded captain had refused to strike his colours. As the wind got up suddenly, Cochrane decided to set the two grounded ones on fire, while managing to get one off as a prize.

But the *Imperieuse* herself was now in deadly danger, in only four fathoms of water as a gale blew up. Luckily the wind veered away from off the sea and blew from the land and the *Imperieuse* was able to sail off by nine o'clock. In the course of the night the Spanish captain died. 'Every attention possible was paid to the poor fellow, from admiration of his gallantry, but anything beyond this was beyond our power. On the following morning we committed his remains to the deep, with the honours of war.'

CHAPTER 7

The First Commando

In June 1808, after a rest in Gibraltar, he put to sea again facing a radically altered political situation. In the celebrated uprising of 2 May the Spanish people had risen in revolt against Napoleon's occupying forces, and the British could now count on the support of the people of the peninsula. As Cochrane passed Algeciras this time he hoisted both British and Spanish colours, and was delighted to witness the enthusiasm of the people on shore. At Cartagena the same happened. At Barcelona he taunted the French-manned shore batteries by sailing just out of range while they wasted shot, sending up spectacular plumes of water just before him. He was scathing about French atrocities:

We then bore up along the coast, and when clear of the enemy's lines, a number of boats came off complaining bitterly of the French troops, who were burning their towns on the least resistance, or even pretended resistance, and were permitted by their officers to plunder and kill the inhabitants with impunity. Perhaps it would be more in accordance with military justice to say, that with the ideas of equality and fraternity then prevalent amongst the soldiers, their officers had no control over them . . .

On the 8th we were becalmed close to several villages, one of which had been nearly destroyed by the French on pretence of some trifling resistance. A deputation from the inhabitants of one village came off, and informed us that their church had been plundered of everything, and that forty-five houses had been burned to the ground. A wretched policy truly, and one which did the French great harm by the animosity thus created amongst the people, who were treated as rebels, rather than in the light of honourable adversaries.

Cochrane, observing the enemy's dispositions from the shore, realized that the entire French army in this sector was supplied along the single coastal road. If he could but disrupt movement along the route or block it, he could inflict weeks of delay upon the French.

The nature of these operations will be readily comprehended by the statement that a considerable portion of the main road ran along the face of the precipitous rocks nearest the sea. By blowing up the roads themselves in some places, and the over-hanging rocks in others, so as to bury the road beneath the debris, it was rendered impassable for cavalry or artillery, whilst removal of the obstructions within reasonable time was out of the question – indeed, so long as the frigate remained in the vicinity, impossible, as any operation of the kind would have been within reach of our guns.

The latter, desperate to keep the road open against constant harassment from Spanish guerrillas, had resorted to extreme brutality, destroying villages, raping the women and filling holes made by the guerrillas in the road with the possessions of local people.

The coast of Catalonia at that time comprised a succession of small, pretty fishing ports in picturesque bays and inlets with beaches rimming the intense blue of the sea. At the small town of Mataro, Cochrane went ashore, blew up the road in several different sectors, and threw the 24-pound guns of the local battery over a cliff – collecting them at the bottom the next day by boat. The French troops stationed at the nearby town of Canette had rushed towards his position, but he sailed across to their now abandoned one and found still more cannon, winching them with hawsers from the cliff edge to his frigate, while he blew up the road in more than six different places.

At Mongat, between Barcelona and the French border, Cochrane learnt that General Duhesne, having successfully defeated the Spanish at Gerona, was on his way back to Barcelona. He had sent an advance force to occupy the fortress at Mongat. That night, two massive explosions took place on either side of the fortress, and the occupiers found that the roads leading up to the fort and away from it had been blown up. The French were cut off, and a small army of Spanish guerrillas was advancing towards them. Meanwhile the *Imperieuse* opened up on the fortress from the sea. After a couple of broadsides, the French garrison signalled its surrender.

The Spanish rushed the position – but the French fought back. They had surrendered only to the British – understandably, in view of the Spanish thirst for retaliation after the atrocities committed against them. The 100 or so French defenders had to be protected by a British escort as they were marched through lines of Spaniards baying for their blood. The coast road was now blocked. Duhesne, abandoning his artillery, had to struggle through to Barcelona by other routes a month later.

As Cochrane continued his raiding along the coast, at little cost to himself, he wrote:

It is wonderful what an amount of terrorism a small frigate is able to inspire on an enemy's coast. Actions between line-of-battle ships are no doubt very imposing, but for real effect I would prefer a score or two of small vessels well handled to any fleet of line-of-battle ships.

He wrote archly of the Catalans:

The Catalans made capital guerrilla troops, possessing considerable skill in the use of their weapons, though previously untrained. A character for turbulence was often attributed to them; but in a country groaning under priestcraft and bad government the sturdy spirit of independence, which prompted them to set the example of heroic defence of their country, might be, either mistakenly or purposely – the latter the more probable – set down for discontent and sedition. At any rate the descendants of men who, in a former age, formed the outposts of the Christian world against Mahomedism in no way disgraced their ancestors, and became in the end the terror of their enemies. One quality they predominantly possessed, patience and endurance under privation; and this, added to their hardy habits and adventurous disposition, contributed to form an enemy not to be despised – the less so in that they were in every way disposed to repay the barbarities of the French with interest.

Cochrane moved up to the French side of the border, with another objective: to destroy the signal stations that reported upon both French and enemy troop movements. He struck against the first on 16 August, and two more the following morning after a gruelling trek by his men under fire through the boggy Rhone estuary.

On the 24th he sent in three boats to attack a French signal station called St Maguire. While still 10 yards off the beach, however, they were greeted by volleys of grapeshot, and retreated out of range. During the night, his favourite time for attack, he landed and blew up a signal station amid a hail of ill-directed French musketry. Then his raiding party made for a battery and attacked, the French soldiers there fleeing in confusion. They tried to secure two guns, but a signal from the *Imperieuse* alerted them to the fact that a force of French cavalry was assembling on the top of the hill. Cochrane hastily blew up the guns and the battery and returned to the boats, as the cavalry attacked, injuring just one sailor as they pushed off. With breathtaking perseverance, day after day, Cochrane's policy of sea-to-shore harassment continued, plunging the whole coastline from Toulon to Catalonia into a state of alarm.

He engaged in a piece of early counter-espionage. He had the enemy code-books carefully copied, and half-burnt so as to convince the French that they had not been read. He forwarded the copies to Admiral Collingwood, who was now able to read the signals without the French suspecting, or altering their codes. Sir Walter Scott wrote:

> Lord Cochrane during the month of September 1808, with his single ship, kept the whole coast of Languedoc in alarm – destroyed the numerous semaphoric telegraphs, which were of the utmost consequence to the numerous coasting convoys of the French, and not only prevented any troops from being sent from that province into Spain, but even excited such dismay that 2000 men were withdrawn from Figueras to oppose him, when they would otherwise have been marching farther into the peninsula. The coasting trade was entirely suspended during this alarm; yet with such consummate prudence were all Cochrane's enterprises planned and executed that not one of his men were either killed or hurt, except one, who was singed in blowing up a battery.

Cochrane joined up with Jahleel Brenton, another young captain who had commanded the *Speedy* before him. The two performed a magnificent *pas de deux* along the coast of Vendres – which contradicted the view that Cochrane was an impossible man to work with. Of them Collingwood wrote:

> The activity and zeal of those gallant young men keep up my spirits, and make me equal to bear the disagreeables that happen from the contentions of some other ships. Those who do all the service give me no trouble; those who give the trouble are good for nothing.

One searing Mediterranean summer's day the two ships, the *Imperieuse* and the *Spartan*, had all their ships' boys dressed in scarlet marines' uniforms. Boats were lowered, and these were rowed towards the Spanish side of Port Vendres. Ashore, French cavalry posted to deter an attack by Cochrane were watching: seeing the boatfuls of 'marines' setting off they galloped to intercept them. As soon as the French cavalry was out of sight, Cochrane and Brenton brought their ships rapidly in under the

French batteries, to a point beneath the arc of their cannon range, and bombarded the town. Their real marines were sent in, landing unopposed, and took possession of the French batteries, destroying them.

The cavalrymen meanwhile had reached the spot where they expected the marines to disembark, then discovered that the boats were filled with excited ships' boys. Realizing they had been tricked, they galloped back to intercept Cochrane's and Brenton's raiding parties. As they did so they had to cross a stretch of shoreline where they were exposed to the sea. Cochrane was waiting for them. With extraordinary precision he let loose a broadside of grapeshot and cut down the entire detachment, leaving a few men and horses scrambling to their feet after the smoke had cleared. He directed the operation from the masthead, not the quarterdeck, with uncanny accuracy.

Cochrane also attempted to live off the land, rather than return to Gibraltar for supplies, which wasted time. This had mixed results. He sailed up the Rhone on one occasion to collect river water, using his fire pump to fill huge bags improvised out of sails; but his attempt to capture a herd of cattle grazing ashore failed. He was forced to return to the Rock for supplies and refitting, eventually returning to the Catalan coast in late November for his last, and greatest, Mediterranean exploit.

Gibraltar was in fact the biggest of the British overseas bases (the others being Halifax, Jamaica and Antigua, soon joined by the Cape, Mahon and Bermuda). These overseas bases lacked the facilities of the home dockyards. Gibraltar had the disadvantage of southerly winds. The dockyard boasted a commissioner, storekeeper, master shipwright and master apprentice as well as 170 craftsmen and labourers in 1814. This was considerably more than Port Mahon in Minorca, where there was 'convenience for careening three ships at a time, and much more could be made of the port as might be required. There is plenty of water at St John's . . . The arsenal is small but sufficient for the supply of a fleet of twelve sail of the line and frigates and proportion.' On average, ships had to put in for major servicing once every three or four years; with the introduction of coppering the bottoms, the regular cleaning of the ships' hulls every four months or so was a thing of the past. But Cochrane's visit was for relatively light repairs, and also for revictualling because of the difficulty of obtaining supplies in hostile territory.

As Cochrane laid anchor in the beautiful bay off the town of Rosas, he learnt that a column of 6000 French soldiers and tens of thousands of Italians was marching into Catalonia. Captain John West of the *Excellent*, a ship double the size of the *Imperieuse*, had already occupied two strongpoints: the citadel of the town and the crumbling fortress just outside, Fort Trinidad. But he had decided to abandon the latter as impossible to defend, and his successor, Commodore Richard Bennett, was no more impressed by its strategic potential. The citadel and its Spanish defenders were already under fire from advance French batteries.

When the *Imperieuse* arrived, Cochrane ordered fire upon the French positions, hindering their operations. His practised eye surveyed the scene. He decided that a stand could, after all, be made at Fort Trinidad which was being shelled from the higher French position on a hill opposite. The fort, he observed, had:

walls some 50 feet high. Behind this and joined to it rose another fort to the height of 30 or 40 feet more, the whole presenting the appearance of a large church with a tower 110 feet high, a nave 90 feet high, and chancel 50 feet. The tower having its back to the cliff as a matter of course sheltered the middle and lower portions of the fortress from a fire of the battery above it.

The French had blown a hole in the tower 'as large as the Great West Window at Westminster Abbey'; but Cochrane realized that because of the elevation of the French guns, they could not be depressed any lower to make a breach at the base of the fort. Usually French guns would pound away at the same spot until it collapsed and infantry would swarm up to it before the defenders had time to repair it. If the French tried to climb through the breach they had made, they would be at least 50 feet above ground, just above a large stone arch.

Cochrane led his men into the fort and they promptly set about booby-trapping the arch. He built

a huge wooden case, exactly resembling the hopper of a mill – the upper part being kept well greased with cooks' slush from the *Imperieuse*, so that to retain a hold on it was impossible. Down this, with the slightest pressure from behind, the storming party must have fallen to a depth of fifty feet and all they could have done if not killed would have been to remain prisoners at the bottom.

Cochrane also planted explosives in the tower itself, so that when the British had to abandon it and retreat to the inner fortification, they could blow up the French who had swarmed inside. In addition the gap between the outer and inner tower had ships' chains embedded with fish hooks pulled across it in order to impale those attempting to get through – an early, if rather crude and giant-sized version of barbed wire. Meanwhile, with his men, some Spanish guerrillas and a group of Irish mercenaries, he settled down to wait for the inevitable attack.

It was a nerve-stretching ordeal. From just 300 yards away, 24-pound cannonballs battered the fortress every few minutes. On 25 November no fewer than 300 hit the fortress. Conditions inside were appalling. As Marryat, who had accompanied Cochrane, reported, 'We all pigged in together. Dirty straw and fleas for our beds; our food on the same scale of luxury.' There were days when Cochrane's small force was cut off by French fire from supplies from his ship and had almost nothing to eat; but the two ships also lobbed shots into the French positions. This was not enough to deter the French from entering the town and laying siege to the citadel of Rosas. Cochrane admired their gunnery:

The practice of the French when breaching the walls of Rosas was beautiful. So skilfully was their gunnery conducted that, to use a schoolboy similitude, every discharge 'ruled a straight line' along the lower part of the walls. This being repeated till the upper portion was without support, as a matter of course the whole fell in the ditch, forming a breach of easy ascent.

After four days of such barely endurable punishment, with the French cannonade growing in intensity, Cochrane ostentatiously walked out of the fortress to where the Spanish flag from the tower had just been shot down. The cannonballs went well overhead, but shrapnel from the wall they hit fell all about him. With elaborate slowness he picked up the flag and walked back to cheers from his men. It was a display of bravado so typical of the man – but as a demonstration of fearlessness it was certainly effective for the morale of his men.

Soon afterwards, he was taught his lesson. When he was gazing across at the French positions, a shot crashed into the wall near him, sending up a spray of stone splinters, and Cochrane staggered back. His nose had been broken by one such splinter, which had penetrated the roof of his mouth. His eyes were also blackened, although fortunately not injured. The pain must have been intense, but he showed no sign of acknowledging it, even though he could breathe only through his mouth.

A day later the town of Rosas fell, just a few hours before a column of 2000 Spaniards arrived in an attempt to relieve it. The citadel still held out. The French offered Cochrane the chance of surrender under a flag of truce. Cochrane twice refused. The gunnery resumed, with many more batteries now added to the French side.

On 30 November, after nine days' siege, Cochrane awoke before dawn. He wrote:

The dawn of the 30th might have been our last, but from the interposition of what some persons may call presentiment. Long before daylight I was awoke with an impression that the enemy were in possession of the castle, though the stillness which prevailed showed this to be a delusion. Still I could not re-compose myself to sleep, and after lying for some time tossing about, I left my couch and hastily went on the esplanade of the fortress. All was perfectly still, and I felt half ashamed of having given way to such fancies.

A loaded mortar, however, stood before me, pointed, during the day, in such a direction that the shell should fall on the path over the hill which the French must necessarily take whenever they might make an attempt to storm. Without other object than that of diverting my mind from the unpleasant feeling which had taken possession of it, I fired the mortar. Before the echo had died away, a volley of musketry from the advancing column of the enemy showed that the shell had fallen amongst them just as they were on the point of storming.

Rushing on, their bullets pattered like hail on the walls of the fort. To man these was the work of a moment; for, as may be supposed, our fellows did not wait for another summons, and the first things barely discernible amidst the darkness were the French scaling ladders ready to be placed at the foot of the breach, with an attendant body of troops waiting to ascend, but hesitating, as though the unexpected shell from our mortar rendered them uncertain as to our preparations for defence. To the purposeless discharge of that piece of ordnance we owed our safety, for otherwise they would have been upon us before we even suspected their presence; and so exasperated were they at our obstinate defence, that very little attention would have been paid to any demand for quarter. The French deserved great credit for a silence in their movements which had not even attracted the attention of the sentries on the tower.

The then sixteen-year-old Marryat had a slightly different story:

The Captain came out and asked me what I was looking at. I told him I hardly knew; but there did appear something unusual in the valley, immediately below the breach. He listened for a moment, looked attentively with his night-glass, and exclaimed in his firm voice but in an undertoned manner, 'To arms! They are coming.' In three minutes every man was at his post; and though all were quick there was no time to spare, for by this time the black column of the enemy was distinctly visible, curling along the valley like a great centipede; and, with the daring enterprise so common among the troops of Napoleon, had begun in silence to mount the breach.

Cochrane was deeply impressed by the disciplined order in which the long column of Frenchmen trekked down from the hill opposite and up the path to reach the great jumble of broken masonry below the break in the outer tower. He ordered his men to open fire, but the French marched inexorably on, placing their scaling ladders on the rubble and climbing up to the great breach in the wall.

As they came through they encountered the first of Cochrane's booby-traps. They tried to descend the slippery surface below, and found themselves falling to their deaths. The few that survived ran on to the chains and fishhooks, and were impaled, providing easy targets for Cochrane's marksmen. The pressure of the men coming up behind through the breach was such that those in front were pushed down the deadly ramp.

Cochrane ordered his men to open fire on those coming up into the breach. He spied the officer leading the French standing on the rampart, looking down into the terrible pit and resolved not to shoot him, telling him he could retreat. The officer 'bowed as politely as though on parade, and retired just as leisurely'. Meanwhile the French came on to be shot down as they were silhouetted against the sky or to slide to their deaths.

Cochrane lit the fuse of a huge mine he had placed just under the rubble outside the wall. It exploded, with devastating effect among the Frenchmen trying to climb into the tower. Marryat wrote: 'up they went in the air, and down they fell buried in the ruins. Groans, screams, confusion, French yells, British hurrahs, rent the sky!' Around 100 Frenchmen had been killed, while

Cochrane had lost one of his own men and two Spaniards.

Having been driven off, the French continued to fire into the citadel of Rosas. The Spanish there, under intense bombardment, sued for peace on 4 December. Cochrane, with his usual decisiveness, decided to evacuate Fort Trinidad before the French could muster their full firepower against him. In a spectacular display of efficient evacuation he signalled the *Imperieuse* and the *Excellent*, now joined by the *Magnifique*, to launch a major bombardment of the French-held town while he dangled rope ladders out the seaward side of the fort and his men climbed down the cliff towards safety.

The last to leave were Cochrane himself and a gunner who had lit the fuses for the two great explosions prepared for the fort. The French were wary of entering after they had seen the British withdraw, learning from their last experience of Cochrane's penchant for booby-traps: the main tower went up in a dazzling display of firepower which, however, wrecked the fuse for the second explosion. Meanwhile, every one of Cochrane's surviving men had got safely away. Altogether three of Cochrane's men had been killed and seven wounded.

What had the action achieved? The young captain had delayed the main French thrust into Catalonia, blocking their lines of communication for a fortnight. He had certainly delayed the taking of Rosas. He had given the hard-pressed Spanish forces a reprieve – and a huge propaganda fillip. From then on, Cochrane became a Spanish national hero. But above all he had demonstrated the damage that even a small British naval force could inflict on French lines of communication into Spain.

Cochrane had already established himself as the master of 'cutting out' – taking ships from under the enemy's noses. Now he had shown himself to be a brilliant 'commando' and amphibious commander – capable both of co-ordinated land and sea tactics. Unfortunately, with the intellectual curiosity, self-righteousness and utter lack of fear that were his hallmarks, he proceeded to add the high command of the British army to his list of enemies.

He used his reconnaissance knowledge of the islands off the Bay of Biscay coast to urge their seizure by the British, for use as bases to stage harassing raids across the French lines of communication with Spain. He believed this to be a far quicker way of choking off the French expeditionary force in Spain than the launch of a major expeditionary army into Portugal under Sir Arthur Wellesley – the tactic espoused by the British army establishment.

The recipient of Cochrane's memorandum was none other than the First Secretary to the Admiralty, William Wellesley-Pole, brother of Sir Arthur. There were many who agreed with Cochrane. The *Naval Chronicle* argued that:

Seeing what Lord Cochrane has done with his single ship upon the French shores, we may easily conceive what he would have achieved if he had been entrusted with a sufficient squadron of ships, and a few thousand military, hovering along the whole extent of the French coast, which it would take a considerable portion of the army of French to defend.

The Tory Sir Walter Scott wrote:

The event might have been different had there been a floating army off the coast – the whole of the besieging force might then have been cut off. Of the errors which the British government committed in the conduct of the Spanish war, the neglect of this obvious and most important means of annoying the enemy and advantaging our allies is the most extraordinary. Five thousand men, at the disposal of Lord Cochrane or Sir Sidney Smith, or any of those numerous officers in the British Navy who have given undoubted proofs of their genius as well as courage, would have rendered more service to the common cause than five times that number on shore, because they could at all times choose their points of attack, and the enemy, never knowing where to expect them, would everywhere be in fear and everywhere in reach of the shore in danger.

The Peninsular War was intensely controversial in its day, criticized as being strategically inept and painfully bloody. As the long-drawn-out campaign was ultimately successful, its advocates felt vindicated. But if Cochrane was right in his judgment thousands of lives might have been spared if a less costly alternative had been adopted. There can be no way of knowing.

Cochrane remained on station for a few more months. His most spectacular further raid was against an army of 5000 advancing along the coastal road, which he drove into the hills under heavy bombardment. On his return he alerted the press to his newfound strategic conviction:

> My chief motive for wishing to return to England was that during our operations against the French on the Spanish coast I had seen so much of them as to convince me that if with a single frigate I could paralyse the movements of their armies in the Mediterranean – with three or four ships it would not be difficult so to spread terror on their Atlantic shores as to render it impossible for them to send an army into Western Spain.

He later claimed:

> Had this permission been granted, I do not hesitate to stake my professional reputation that neither the Peninsular War nor its enormous cost to the nation from 1809 onwards would ever have been heard of.

Of this only history can be the judge. He was far too junior an officer, in spite of his public profile, for his argument to count for much. Meanwhile Collingwood, his superior and admirer, bombarded the Admiralty with dispatches in favour of Cochrane: 'Captain Lord Cochrane maintained himself in possession of Trinity castle with great ability and heroism . . . His resources for every exigency have no end.'

The depressing riposte was an official Admiralty reprimand to Cochrane for 'excessive use of powder and shot' in defending

Fort Trinidad, as well as for the costs of refitting the *Imperieuse*. As Cochrane put it: 'In place of approbation I was reproached for the expenditure of more sails, stores, gunpowder and shot than had been used by any other captain in the service.'

The dislike within the naval establishment for Cochrane had by now passed reasonable limits. This was no longer a matter of a junior officer who was a member of the 'awkward squad'. At Rosas Cochrane had performed an act of valour that had earned him the plaudits of the press and the public, as well as of his immediate superiors and his more able brother officers. This had been no mere routine effort, but an act of heroism on land of a kind of which only a few British commanders, such as Clive and Wolfe, had shown themselves capable.

The very ease with which Cochrane had collected prizes, first in the Mediterranean, then the Atlantic, then the Bay of Biscay, and now the Mediterranean again, masked his professionalism. No other British commander, perhaps since the days of Henry Morgan, had been able to claim such spectacular results. It was perhaps the single most attractive characteristic of Cochrane as a commander that for all the risks and dangers, hardly any of his crews were killed – which helped to explain the attachment of his men to him. The captain and writer, Edward Brenton, wrote of him:

No officer ever attempted or succeeded in more arduous enterprises with so little loss. Before he fired a shot he reconnoitred in person, took soundings and bearings, passed whole nights in the boats, his head line and spy glass incessantly at work. Another fixed principle of this officer was never to allow his boats to be unprotected by his ship, if it were possible to lay her within range of the object of attack. With the wind on shore he would veer one of his boats in by a bass hawser (an Indian rope made of grass, which is so light as to float on the surface of the water). By this means he established a communication with the ship, and in case of reverse the boats were hove off by the capstan, while the people in them had only to attend to the use of their weapons.

Brenton had been the biographer of St Vincent, and might have been expected to have taken against Cochrane. His brother Jahleel, past commander of the *Speedy* and Cochrane's companion in the Mediterranean, was even more outspoken:

> Bold and adventurous as Lord Cochrane was, no unnecessary exposure of life was ever permitted under his command. Every circumstance was anticipated, every caution against surprise was taken, every provision of success was made; and in this way he was enabled to accomplish the most daring enterprises with comparatively little danger and still less actual loss.

Marryat was yet another witness:

> I never knew anyone so careful of the lives of his ship's company as Lord Cochrane, or any who calculated so closely the risks attending any expedition. Many of the most brilliant achievements were performed without the loss of a single life, so well did he calculate the chances; and half the merit he deserves for what he did accomplish has never been awarded him, merely because, in the official despatches, there has not been a long list of killed and wounded to please the appetite of the English public.

Yet there was absolutely no recognition from the Admiralty, only resentment because he would not conform to its ways. Cochrane had treated the system with contempt, and the compliment was exchanged, however astonishing his exploits and courage. If he had shown the slightest respect, he might instantly have ascended to the pinnacle of national life.

CHAPTER 8

The Battle of Aix Roads

Cochrane now entered the defining moment of his career: a naval battle which was only less decisive than Trafalgar because of the actions of other men, but which ended by almost destroying him. The drama that follows is one of the epics of British naval history – and is still barely known, even less understood.

The Admiralty disliked Cochrane, yet it could hardly dispense with his services. There were few able commanders at this time, still fewer like Cochrane who had the confidence of their men, were widely popular, and were prepared to take huge risks. The French fleet had escaped in a gale from the British blockade of Brest, when the British ships had been blown out to sea. On 21 February 1809 the enemy had seized their chance. Eight battleships under Admiral Willaumez and several frigates had escaped into the Atlantic.

When Rear-Admiral Stopford, with seven ships, encountered the French fleet in the Bay of Biscay, they withdrew to the Aix Roads. The anchorage there seemed impregnable and the British commander who had presided over the fiasco at Brest, Admiral Lord Gambier, on being advised by the Admiralty that he should attack the French with fireships as the only means of getting at them, was deeply equivocal:

A trial was made six years ago, when a Spanish squadron lay at the same anchorage, but without effect. The report of it you will find in the Admiralty . . . The enemy's ships lie much exposed to the operation of fireships, it is a horrible mode of warfare, and the attempt hazardous, if not desperate; but we should have plenty of volunteers in the service. If you mean to do anything of the kind, it should be done with secrecy and quickly, and the ships used should be not less than those built for the purpose – at least a dozen, and some smaller ones.

The danger was that the French fleet, reinforced by the ships already at Aix Roads, might slip away and attack the British in the West Indies.

It was vital to stop them, but Gambier was a cautious man. An Admiralty bureaucrat of the kind that Cochrane most despised, he had spent seventeen of his twenty-two years in the navy behind a desk, his connections with the Pitt family ensuring his promotion. He had been commander of the seventeen-strong fleet when the British had bombarded Copenhagen in 1807 with appalling results for that beautiful city (which Nelson had spared in his famous 1801 battle). Although the attack was not well executed nor even particularly necessary, the Danish fleet had surrendered after this punishment, which had earned him command of the Channel fleet as well as his title.

Gambier was a dedicated tractarian Christian who distributed fundamentalist pamphlets to his crew, fiercely opposed alcohol, and refused the common practice of allowing women on board in port. He was known as 'dismal Jimmie' by his men. He was fully in the tradition of St Vincent, a new type of Admiralty bureaucrat, determined to bring greater morality on board ship, espousing middle-class values and despising old-style aristocratic pretensions, the kind Cochrane personified. Gambier's religious concerns seemed doomed from the start. As one contemporary chaplain wrote:

Nothing can possibly be more unsuitably or more awkwardly situated than a clergyman in a ship of war; every object around him is at variance with the sensibilities of a rational and enlightened mind . . . The entrance of a clergyman is, to a poor seaman, often a fatal signal . . . To convert a man-of-war's crew into Christians would be a task to which the courage of Loyola, the philanthropy of Howard, and the eloquence of St Paul united, would prove inadequate.

Cochrane observed:

The fact was, that the fleet was divided into two factions, as bitter against each other as were the Cavaliers and Roundheads in the days of Charles I . . . The tractarian faction, consisting for the most part of officers appointed by Tory influence or favour of the Admiral, and knowing my connection with Burdett and Cobbett, avoided me; whilst the opposite faction, believing that from the affair of the tracts I should incur the irreconcilable displeasure of Lord Gambier, lost no opportunity of denouncing me as a concocter of novel devices to advance my own interests at the expense of my seniors in the service.

Gambier's religion made him a close friend of the great anti-slavery campaigner, William Wilberforce, also a zealous Christian. The poet Thomas Hood mocked him:

Oh! Admiral Gam – I dare not mention bier,
In such a temperate ear;
Oh! Admiral Gam – an Admiral of the Blue,
Of course, to read the Navy List aright,
For strictly shunning wine of either hue,
You can't be Admiral of the Red or White.

Gambier's intense religious beliefs did not of course prevent him being a good commander, but as he so patently was not – he was cautious and indecisive, the legacy of his long years away from action – they merely grated on the officers beneath him, none more so than Admiral Eliab Harvey, the celebrated captain of the *Fighting Témeraire* at Trafalgar. Harvey detested his superior. The bad blood between these two senior commanders of the fleet further demoralized it.

With Gambier in a mire of uncertainty off Aix Roads, the Admiralty, which so disliked Cochrane, conceived of an extraordinary idea. It was vital that the French fleet not be allowed to escape again, yet it seemed equally likely that they would. The one officer with close knowledge of Aix Roads from his tour of duty three years before was Thomas Cochrane, who had long suggested invading the anchorage with fireships. Here at last was a use for this tiresome but fearless seaman. If Cochrane perished the Admiralty would be well rid of him, if he succeeded, they could claim the credit.

Cochrane had no sooner arrived in Plymouth than he was ordered immediately to report to Whitehall. Where once Cochrane had striven desperately to gain an audience with St Vincent, he was now received warmly, even effusively, by the new First Sea Lord, Lord Mulgrave, a red-faced Tory just appointed to office, who was a connoisseur of the arts and displayed an enviable unflappability towards all events, good and bad. Mulgrave was to the point, welcoming him and informing him that in spite of Gambier's reservations, twelve transports were being converted for use as fireships:

> You were some years ago employed on the Rochefort station and must to a great extent be acquainted with the difficulties to be surmounted. Besides which, I am told that you then pointed out to Admiral Thornburgh some plan of attack, which would in your estimation be successful. Will you be good enough to detail that or any other plan which your further experience may suggest?

Cochrane was immediately interested, and launched into his own pet project for building 'explosion ships' to add to the fireships. Even Cochrane was taken aback by how seriously, he, a mere captain, was being taken by the First Sea Lord. Now came the shock: Mulgrave told Cochrane that he was to command the expedition.

At this Cochrane was aghast: he knew the fury that giving command of so major a venture to so junior a captain would arouse not just in Gambier, but all the senior captains serving with him. He was deeply cynical of the Admiralty's motives:

> It was now clear to me why I had been sent for to the Admiralty, where not a word of approbation of my previous services was uttered. The Channel fleet had been doing worse than nothing. The nation was dissatisfied, and even the existence of the ministry was at stake. They wanted a victory, and the admiral commanding plainly told them he would not willingly risk a defeat. Other naval officers had been consulted, who had disapproved of the use of fireships, and, as a last resource, I had been sent for, in the hope that I would undertake the enterprise. If this were successful, the fleet would get the credit, which would be thus reflected on the ministry; and if it failed, the consequence would be the loss of my individual reputation, as both ministry and commander-in-chief would lay the blame on me.

Mulgrave brushed aside his objections:

> The present is no time for professional etiquette. All the officers who have been consulted deem an attack with fireships impracticable, and after such an expression of opinion, it is not likely they would be offended by the conduct of fireships being given to another officer who approved of their use.

Cochrane argued that any senior officer could command the expedition as effectively as he:

> The plan submitted to your Lordship was not an attack with fireships alone, and when the details become known to the service, it will be seen that there is no risk of failure whatever, if made with a fair wind and flowing tide. On the contrary, its success on inspection must be evident to any experienced officer, who would see that as the enemy's squadron could not escape up the Charente, their destruction would not only be certain but in fact easy.

Mulgrave promised to think the matter over. The following day
he summoned Cochrane:

> My Lord, you must go. The Board cannot listen to further
> refusal or delay. Rejoin your frigate at once. I will make you
> all right with Lord Gambier. Your confidence in the result
> has, I must confess, taken me by surprise, but it has increased
> my belief that all you anticipate will be accomplished. Make
> yourself easy about the jealous feeling of senior officers. I will
> so manage it with Lord Gambier that the amour propre of the
> fleet shall be satisfied.

To Gambier and the officers of the fleet, a single instruction was
sent selecting Lord Cochrane 'under your Lordship's direction
to conduct the fireships to be employed in the projected attack'.
For once, operational considerations had overridden political
ones in the Admiralty.

Cochrane's head was swimming with the opportunity offered as
his carriage galloped back with all speed to Plymouth to join the
twelve transports and to meet up with William Congreve, the
inventor of a new type of explosive rocket, who was to take part
in the attack. They set off to join the Channel fleet where
Cochrane went aboard Gambier's flagship to witness an extraordinary scene.

Harvey, incensed by news of Cochrane's appointment, was
giving vent to his spite. As the embarrassed young Cochrane
stood by, the veteran seaman hurled a stream of invective
upon the self-righteous admiral. Cochrane recalled that
Harvey's

> abuse of Lord Gambier to his face was such as I had never
> before witnessed from a subordinate. I should even now hesi-
> tate to record it as incredible, were it not officially known by
> the minutes of the court-martial in which it sometime after-
> wards resulted.

The young captain stood by in embarrassment and afterwards sought out Harvey to apologise to him:

> Harvey broke out into invectives of a most extraordinary kind, openly avowing that 'he never saw a man so unfit for the command of the fleet as Lord Gambier, who instead of sending boats to sound the channels, which he [Admiral Harvey] considered the best preparation for an attack on the enemy, he had been employing, or rather amusing himself with mustering the ships' companies, and had not even taken the pain to ascertain whether the enemy had placed any mortars in front of their lines; concluding by saying, that had Lord Nelson been there, he would not have anchored in Basque Roads at all, but would have dashed at the enemy at once.
>
> Admiral Harvey then came into Sir Harry Neale's cabin, and shook hands with me, assuring me that 'he should have been very happy to see me on any other occasion' than the present. He begged me to consider that nothing personal to myself was intended, for he had a high opinion of me; but that my having been ordered to execute such a service, could only be regarded as an insult to the fleet, and that on this account he would strike his flag so soon as the service was executed'. Admiral Harvey further assured me that 'he had volunteered his services, which had been refused.'

That provoked this exchange. Cochrane began:

> The service on which the Admiralty has sent me was none of my seeking. I went to Whitehall in obedience to a summons from Lord Mulgrave, and at his Lordship's request gave the board a plan of attack, the execution of which has been thrust upon me contrary to my inclination, as well knowing the invidious position in which I should be placed.

Harvey replied:

> Well, this is not the first time I have been lightly treated, and

that my services have not been attended to in the way they deserved; because I am no canting Methodist, no hypocrite, nor a psalm singer. I do not cheat old women out of their estates by hypocrisy and canting. I have volunteered to perform the service you came on, and should have been happy to see you on any other occasion, but am very sorry to have a junior officer placed over my head.

Harvey was soon afterwards removed from command for using 'grossly insubordinate language' towards Gambier. He was court-martialled and dismissed from the service. But he was an immensely popular figure, one of Nelson's most famous commanders and was reinstated the following year, although he was never given a command again.

Cochrane, assured by Harvey that he had no personal grudge against him, went off to the *Imperieuse* to make preparations. He wrote directly to Mulgrave in response to his request to detail his original plan of attack, dating from Thornburgh's time:

My Lord – Having been very close the Isle d'Aix, I find that the western wall has been pulled down to build a better. At present the fort is quite open, and may be taken as soon as the French fleet is driven on shore or burned, which will be as soon as the fireships arrive. The wind continues favourable for the attack. If your Lordship can prevail on the ministry to send a military force here, you will do great and lasting good to our country.

Could ministers see things with their own eyes, how differently would they act; but they cannot be everywhere present, and on their opinion of the judgement of others must depend the success of war – possibly the fate of England and all Europe.

No diversion which the whole force of Great Britain is capable of making in Portugal or Spain would so much shake the French government as the capture of the islands on this coast. A few men would take Oléron; but to render the capture effective, send twenty thousand men who, without risk, would find occupation for the French army of a hundred thousand.

The Admiralty took no notice.

Cochrane supervised the conversion of the transports into fireships as they arrived from England. The construction of fireships was an old technique. Five large trails of gunpowder were laid criss-cross on the deck. Wood and canvas were stretched between them. Up above, tarred ropes dangled down from sails also covered in tar. Chains were fixed to the sides with grappling hooks so that it would be difficult for a ship which a fireship drifted against to detach itself. Resin and turpentine were poured all over the fireship to help it to burn. Finally huge holes were made in the hull so as to help suck in air and feed the flames after the ship began to burn.

With the arrival of a further nine fireships from England, Cochrane now had twenty-one under his command. But he was busier still on his own invention: explosion ships. The French would be prepared for fireships, but they would have no understanding of his new secret weapon, just approved by the Admiralty. The preparations for these were more elaborate still:

The floor was rendered as firm as possible by means of logs placed in close contact, into every crevice of which other substances were firmly wedged so as to afford the greatest amount of resistance to the explosion. On this foundation were placed a large number of spirit and water casks, into which 1500 barrels of powder casks were placed, several hundred shells, and over these again nearly three thousand hand grenades; the whole, by means of wedges and sand, being compressed as nearly as possible into a solid mass.

Admiral Willaumez had been replaced by Vice-Admiral Allemand, who had anchored his ships in an apparently impregnable position. They were drawn up in two lines, between two small islands, the Ile d'Aix and the Ile Madame, which dominated the approaches to the river Charente. There were gun batteries on the Ile d'Aix and the Ile d'Oléron, a large spur of land to the west, as well as on the mainland.

Cochrane had already personally observed that the battery on Aix was in a poor state of repair, and its firepower grossly exaggerated. Moreover his earlier reconnaissance had led him to discover a remarkable thing. The only clear line of attack upon the French would have to be between a large reef, around 3 miles wide, called the Boyart Shoal, which was uncovered at low tide, and the Ile d'Aix. Cochrane, crucially, had found out that:

> From previous employment on the spot on several occasions I well knew there was room in the channel to keep out of the way of red-hot shot from the Aix batteries even if, by means of blue lights [flares] or other devices, they had discovered us. The officers and crews of the line-of-battle ships would be impressed with the idea that every fireship was an explosion vessel, and that in place of offering opposition they would, in all probability, be driven ashore in their attempt to escape from such diabolical engines of warfare, and thus become an easy prey.

In other words, the fort providing protection for the French fleet was no use at all. Even if the Admiralty ignored his recommendation that they seize the bases on Aix and Oleron, the 'lethal' fire of their guns could not reach the British ships if the latter stuck to the right-hand side of the channel. The Aix guns were 36-pounders manned by 2000 men, but these were raw recruits and the guns themselves were in a state of disrepair. There was no threat from this quarter, which Gambier persisted in regarding as extremely dangerous. 'Dismal Jimmie' had written to the Admiralty just a few days before:

> The enemy's ships are anchored in two lines, very near each other, in a direction due south from the Isle d'Aix, and the ships in each line not farther apart than their own length; by

which it appears, as I imagined, that the space for their anchorage is so confined by the shoaliness of the water, as not to admit of ships to run in and anchor clear of each other. The most distant ships of their two lines are within point-blank shot of the works on the isle d'Aix; such ships, therefore, as might attack the enemy would be exposed to be raked by red-hot shot, etc, from the island, and should the ships be disabled in their masts, they must remain within range of the enemy's fire until they are destroyed – there not being sufficient depth of water to allow them to move to the southward out of distance.

Having thus set out the dangers of an attack in alarmist tones, Gambier then typically reached an ingratiatingly ambiguous conclusion:

I beg leave to add that, if their Lordships are of the opinion that an attack on the enemy's ships by those of the fleet under my command is practicable, I am ready to obey any orders they may be pleased to honour me with, however great the risk may be of the loss of men and ships.

What neither Gambier nor Cochrane knew was that the French had their own secret defence – a 900-feet-long boom made of wooden trunks held together by chains and anchored to the sea floor. Allemand had also taken other precautions: he had stationed four frigates along the boom, as well as some seventy smaller boats whose purpose was to tow the fireships away from the main fleet should they succeed – which seemed unlikely – in breaking through the boom. The ten French battleships in the front line had lowered their sails in order to lessen their chances of catching fire.

On the morning of 10 April Cochrane went to Gambier to seek formal authorization to put his plan into action. To his astonishment, Gambier refused, citing the danger to the crews of the fireships: 'If you choose to rush on to self-destruction that is your own affair, but it is my duty to take care of the lives of others, and I will not place the crews of the fireships in palpable danger.' Depressed and frustrated, Cochrane returned to the *Imperieuse*. The following day the wind got up from the west and a heavy sea began to run. Far from being deterred by this, Cochrane saw that it presented an opportunity: the sea would favour the British, especially as the tide came in, and the French would be less on their guard, thinking the conditions too dangerous · for an attack. Of course, the swell would make navigation much trickier in the treacherous channel.

Gambier, meanwhile, had had time to reflect. His explicit orders were to allow Cochrane to make the attack. He could not continue to refuse him authority without risking injury to his own reputation. Cochrane returned on board the flagship to ask for permission. This time it was grudgingly given.

His ships would attack in three waves. The first would be his three explosion ships, the foremost of which he, never reluctant to place himself in intense danger at the front of the fighting, would command. The second wave would consist of the twenty-one fireships. Behind them were three frigates, the *Pallas*, the *Aigle* and the *Unicorn* – accompanied by HMS *Caesar* to pick up the returning crews of the explosion vessels and fireships, although they would not come close to the action at this stage.

There were two sobering thoughts. First, the French understandably regarded fireships as a barbaric instrument of war, and would execute anyone they caught that could be identified as crewing them. The sailors were instructed to say, if caught, that they belonged to victualling ships nearby. Second, although the flood-tide to shore in this heavy swell favoured the fireships' approach, it would make it very difficult for their crews, now in small boats, to go out against the flow and regain the safety of the rescue ships. Of Gambier's great fear, Cochrane had nothing but contempt:

A more striking comment on the 'red-hot shot', etc, of which

Lord Gambier made so much in one of his letters to the Admiralty, could scarcely be found. Of course, had a red-hot shot from the batteries on Aix reached us [in his explosion ship] – and they were not half-a-mile distant – nothing could have prevented our being 'hoist with our own petard'. I can, however, safely say, that such a catastrophe never entered into my calculations.

Gambier, astonishingly, anchored his fleet 9 miles away. It was such a distance that it could only be supposed he wanted to be able to make a break for it and escape if the French fleet came out after him – the reverse of virtually all British naval tactics for a century or more, which were based on carrying the fight to the French. The fleet would be too far to exercise the slightest influence on the initial action and, worse, it was impossible for him to see what was really going on; even signals were liable to be misinterpreted at that distance.

Cochrane floated in on the flood-tide aboard the foremost explosion vessel – itself a desperately dangerous venture, as he and his men were sitting on top of tons of explosive; one lucky shot from the French and they would be annihilated. Besides Cochrane and Lieutenant Bissel of the *Imperieuse* were four seamen. Behind him a second explosion ship followed with Midshipman Marryat on board, commanded by a lieutenant. Cochrane had no idea there was a boom but his ship navigated successfully down the channel at dead of night, in spite of the heavy swell, approaching as close to the distant huddle of the French fleet as he dared. Then he lit the 15-minute fuse of the explosives aboard. He was certainly very close to the boom when he did so; his men had already climbed aboard the getaway gig.

As soon as he jumped aboard, they rowed for all they were worth away from the explosion ship in the pitch darkness. According to press accounts Cochrane, hearing barking, saw a dog aboard – the ship's mascot – and rowed back to fetch it. Certainly something delayed his departure, and the fuse, for some reason, went off after only 9 minutes. Cochrane's boat had barely managed to get clear of the ship again when it went up. He was saved by his failure to get further. If he had not gone back he would have been on the receiving end of the shower of debris that soared overhead and landed in an arc in the sea just beyond. The explosion was awesome. Cochrane vividly described the scene:

> For a moment, the sky was red with the lurid glare arising from the simultaneous ignition of 1500 barrels of powder. On this gigantic flash subsiding, the air seemed alive with shells, grenades, rockets, and masses of timber, the wreck of the shattered vessel; whilst the water was strewn with spars shaken out of the enormous boom, on which, on the subsequent testimony of Captain Proteau, whose frigate lay just within the boom, the vessel had brought up before she exploded. The sea was convulsed as by an earthquake, rising in a huge wave on whose crest our boat was lifted like a cork and as suddenly dropped into a vast trough, out of which, as it closed on us with a rush of a whirlpool, none expected to emerge. The skill of the boat's crew however overcame the threatened danger, which passed away as suddenly as it had arisen, and in a few minutes nothing but a heavy rolling sea had to be encountered, all having become silence and darkness.

The boom now lay shattered. The second ship passed through its broken fragments some 10 minutes later, and the decision was taken to detonate it and abandon ship in the same way. Another tremendous explosion shattered the peace of the night sky. The third explosion ship had, however, been pushed away from the scene by the *Imperieuse* because a fireship had come too close, and there was a risk of all three blowing up together. Marryat was ordered to go aboard the fireship and steer it away, a heroic action – after which Cochrane asked him laconically whether he had felt warm.

To Cochrane's disappointment the fireships were badly

handled. As he rowed back to the *Imperieuse*, three or four passed him, being towed by small rowing boats towards their destination. But the towing boats of some seventeen others had abandoned them about 4 miles out to sea, judging the risk too great, and most drifted harmlessly ashore.

The whole spectacle had been enough to cause havoc among the French fleet. Their first experience of the attack had been the ear-shattering explosion and conflagration aboard Cochrane's ship, followed by another even closer to hand. Then the night sky had been lit up by the spectacle of twenty blazing vessels, some close, others out to sea, in a massive attack to destroy the French fleet.

Their first assumption was that the fireships coming towards them were also explosion vessels, and in the small space of water of the Aix anchorage, the French ships of the line manoeuvred desperately to avoid them, while both wind and tide drove them relentlessly towards the shore. The flagship *Ocean* was the first to run aground. According to one of its officers:

At 10.0 we grounded, and immediately after a fireship in the height of her combustion grappled us athwart our stern; for ten minutes she remained in this situation while we employed every means in our power to prevent the fire from catching the ship; our fire engines and pumps played upon the poop enough to prevent it from catching fire; with spars we hove off the fireship, with axes we cut the chains of the grapplings lashed to her yards, but a chevaux de frise on her sides held her firmly to us. In this deplorable situation we thought we must have been burned, as the flames of the fireship covered all our poop.

Two of our line-of-battle ships, the *Tonnerre* and *Patriote*, at this time fell on board of us; the first broke our bowsprit and destroyed our main chains. Providence afforded us assistance on this occasion. At the moment the fireship was athwart our stern, and began to draw forward along the starboard side, the *Tonnerre* separated herself from us, and unless this had happened the fireship would have fallen into the angle formed

by two ships and would infallibly have burnt them. The fireship having got so far forward as to be under our bowsprit, we
left it there some time to afford the two ships above
mentioned time to get far enough away to avoid being
boarded by this fireship. While this fireship was on board of
us we let the cocks run in order to wet the powder, but they
were so feeble that we could not do that.

Some fifty of the *Ocean*'s men fell into the water and drowned.
In the confusion the French ships made towards the coastal
mud-flats and the Palles Shoal off the Ile Madame; they got too
close. The tide was on the turn and now ebbing fast. The *Ocean*
was joined ashore by the *Aquilon*, *Tonnerre*, *Ville de Varsovie* and
Calcutta; soon there were seven, with their hulls stranded like
ducks' bottoms out of the water.

As the first streaks of light illuminated the morning sky,
Cochrane looked on the scene with deep satisfaction. His
victory had been far from perfect. He had been forced to blow
up the explosion ships before they could reach the fleet but they
had destroyed the boom that protected the French. The fireship
attack had almost been a disaster, but the confusion sown by the
first two explosion ships and the four fireships that had reached
the French had been enough effectively to disperse the fleet, run
most of it aground, and place it at the mercy of the British.
Complete victory lay in the offing, thanks to his imagination,
and the bravery of his crews.

At 5.48 a.m., at first light, he signalled triumphantly to the
flagship, the *Caledonia*, some 9 miles away: 'Half the fleet to
destroy the enemy. Seven on shore.' Gambier signalled back
with the 'answering pennant' – a bare acknowledgment.
Cochrane, just outside the Aix channel, watching the floun-
dering French fleet, waited for Gambier's ships to approach and
give him the signal to attack with his small flotilla of frigates. He
wondered why there was no movement by Gambier's ships, but
watched delightedly through his telescope as four more French
ships were beached.

At 6.40 he reported this to the *Caledonia*. The answering pennant was hoisted and Gambier made no move. Cochrane's notoriously short fuse was now burning to explosion point. He had just taken in a ship laden with explosives at enormous personal risk to himself, narrowly escaped with his life, rowed back against a surging flood-tide and taken action to save his ship from a rogue fireship. He had seen his attack effectively incapacitate the entire French fleet. It was impossible for beached ships to fire broadside, indeed any guns at all. Now that they could be picked off at will, Gambier and his huge fleet were still hesitant to come in and finish them off.

An hour later, at 7.40, Cochrane sent off another signal: 'Only two afloat.' The reply was the answering pennant again and the fleet made no move. Whatever the explanation he gave at the subsequent court martial, Gambier's motives in refusing to attack the beached French fleet were probably mixed. He had been witness to the amazing fireworks of the night before. He heartily disapproved of the whole tactic of sending in explosion ships and fireships, and disliked the impulsive and reckless Cochrane. His captains had been almost mutinous about Cochrane's appointment.

How could the commander-in-chief even be sure that Cochrane was telling the truth and not seeking to entice the fleet into a dangerous engagement from which it might emerge badly damaged? His duty was the protection of the fleet, and he could not put it at risk on the word of an impertinent young captain. He decided, first, not to risk his ships in the confined waters of the Aix-Boyart channel under the guns of enemy batteries; and, second, to teach Cochrane a lesson and show who was in command. The Admiralty had ordered him to support Cochrane's flagship attack. It had not insisted that he risk any of his own ships.

This was to be one of the most contemptible acts of any commander-in-chief in British naval history, far eclipsing Admiral Byng's realistic decision to surrender Minorca only half a century before – for which he had been shot. The ideal chance to move in and destroy the beached French fleet would be short-lived. The British ships would have the perfect chance to come in on the flood before the French ships floated once again. It was a small window of opportunity.

Cochrane fumed in an agony of frustration and impotence. He signalled at 9.30: 'Enemy preparing to move.' Gambier was later to claim that 'as the enemy was on shore, [I] did not think it necessary to run any unnecessary risk of the fleet, when the object of their destruction seemed to be already obtained'. There is a small possibility that he was telling the truth – in other words that he believed the French ships to have been incapacitated by their grounding – although any sailor with more experience than Gambier would have realized that a ship beached by a tide was perfectly capable of floating off with little damage done.

But if so this misreading of Cochrane's signals was a terrible mistake. It is true that there was a slight element of ambiguity in the first three signals – but only to the most obtuse commander. Cochrane claimed later that he then sent another signal 'the frigates alone can destroy the enemy' – which allowed of no ambiguity, but was clearly impertinent. It was not, however, logged aboard the flagship. But after his 9.30 signal even Gambier could have harboured no illusions that the enemy was destroyed.

At 11.00 a.m. the admiral ordered his captains aboard to confer – itself a time-wasting procedure. He at last ordered his ships inshore – and then, to Cochrane's astonishment, the fleet stopped some 4 miles out. Cochrane watched in utter disbelief: victory was ebbing away with the incoming tide. As he wrote:

> There was no mistaking the admiral's intention in again bringing the fleet to an anchor. Notwithstanding that the enemy had been four hours at our mercy, and to a considerable extent was still so, it was now evident that no attack was intended, and that every enemy's ship would be permitted to float away unmolested and unassailed! I frankly admit that this was too much to be endured. The words of Lord Mulgrave rang in my ears, 'The Admiralty is bent on destroying that fleet before it can get out to the West Indies.'

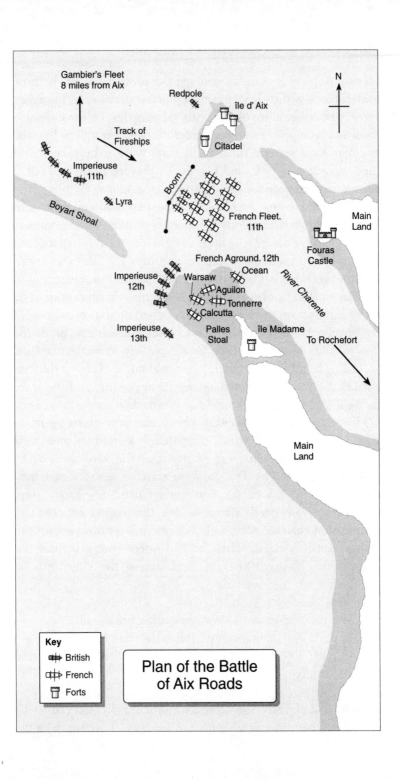

Plan of the Battle of Aix Roads

Having displayed so much courage the previous night, he now took what is said to have been the bravest decision of his entire career, because it involved both defying his commander-in-chief and taking on alone the French fleet – although to him the risk may have seemed small as the ships were at his mercy. But they were floating off, and Gambier's prevarications had left it almost too late even for him to attack successfully.

He decided to raise anchor aboard the *Imperieuse* and drift, stern foremost, down the perilous Aix channel – that is, with his vulnerable rear exposed to enemy fire – straight into the midst of a dozen warships. This required superb seamanship. The idea was not to let Gambier see what he was doing until the last moment, and to be able to claim that he had floated accidentally with the tide. The shore batteries on the Ile d'Oléron opened up, but the shells fell reassuringly far from the ship – as Cochrane had always predicted they would. The ones on the Ile d'Aix were so ineffectual that, according to a British gunner, 'we could not find above thirteen guns that could be directed against us in passing; and these we thought so little of that we did not return their fire'.

However, the huge flagship *Ocean* was now afloat again, as were four other ships, which immediately turned tail and made for the safety of the Charente estuary upon the *Imperieuse*'s backwards approach. The French were now so demoralized they were not prepared to take on even Cochrane's single ship. Cochrane wrote later, 'Better to risk the frigates or even my commission than to suffer such a disgraceful termination [of the engagement]'. At last, when he had safely emerged from the channel, he unfurled his sails, signalling at the same time to Gambier:

1.30 p.m. The enemy's ships are getting under sail.
1.40 p.m. The enemy is superior to the chasing ship.
1.45 p.m. The ship is in distress, and required to be assisted immediately

Thus he had cleverly outwitted his admiral. He could claim that he had not been responsible for the *Imperieuse*'s approach to the

French fleet, and it was unheard of for a commander not to come to the help of one of his ships in distress, thus forcing Gambier's hand.

By two o'clock the *Imperieuse* was close enough to deliver a broadside into the 50-gun French magazine ship, the *Calcutta*, while her forecastle guns fired upon the *Aquilon* and her bow guns fired on the *Ville de Varsovie* – three ships at the same time. Captain Lafon of the *Calcutta*, fearing that his explosive-laden ship would blow up, climbed understandably but ignominiously out of his stern cabin window and ran away across the mud – for which he was later shot by the French.

The *Imperieuse* itself came under fire. Marryat recalled graphically how a seaman in the forecastle was decapitated by a cannonball, and how another was blown in two while the spine still attached the two parts: the corpse, its reflexes still working, jumped to its feet, stared at him 'horribly in the face', and fell down. In fact only three members of the crew were killed and eleven wounded throughout the whole engagement – another example of this 'reckless' man's meticulous care for the safety of his men. The *Calcutta* surrendered at 3.20 and Cochrane's men took possession.

Behind him, Gambier had at last been goaded into action. He sent in two battleships, the *Valiant* and *Revenge*, along with the 44-gun *Indefatigable*, described by Marryat:

> She was a beautiful ship, in what we call 'high kelter'; she seemed a living body, conscious of her own superior power over her opponents, whose shot she despised as they fell thick and fast about her, while she deliberately took up an admirable position for battle. And having furled her sails, and squared her yards, as if she had been at Spithead, her men came down from aloft, went to their guns, and opened such a fire on the enemy's ships as would have delighted the great Nelson himself.

The *Revenge* fired at the *Calcutta* before realising she had already been occupied by Cochrane's sailors. The *Aquilon* and the *Ville de Varsovie* surrendered at 5.30. The *Caesar*, under Rear-Admiral Stopford, had also joined the battle by then. At 6 p.m. the crew of the *Tonnerre* abandoned ship and set fire to her; it blew up an hour later, as did the *Calcutta*, which had been set alight by Cochrane's men, at about 9 p.m. Six of the French ships, however, had escaped up the Charente. Stopford sent in hastily converted fireships after them, but these were unable to prevail against the wind, and he used them instead against other, lesser vessels.

The fighting raged on through the following night. At 4 a.m., however, Gambier hoisted three lights aboard his flagship as a signal for the recall of the British ships. The two ships Cochrane had captured, the *Aquilon* and the *Ville de Varsovie*, were set alight by *Stopford* – although Cochrane had hoped to bring them back as prizes. As the *Indefatigable* sailed past, Cochrane tried to persuade her captain to join him in a final attack on the French flagship, the *Ocean*, but he refused. So Cochrane set off in pursuit, accompanied by a flotilla of small boats. Gambier thereupon sent him an astonishing letter, which had to be rowed all the way to his ship:

You have done your part so admirably that I will not suffer you to tarnish it by attempting impossibilities, which I think, as well as those captains who have come from you, any further effort to destroy those ships would be. You must, therefore, join as soon as you can, with the bombs, etc, as I wish for some information, which you allude to, before I close my despatches.

PS: I have ordered three brigs and two rocket vessels to join you, with which, and the bomb, you may make an attempt on the ship that is aground on the Palles, or towards Ile Madame, but I do not think you will succeed; and I am anxious that you should come to me, as I wish to send you to England as soon as possible. You must, therefore, come as soon as the tide turns.

Cochrane replied curtly:

I have just had the honour to receive your Lordship's letter. We can destroy the ships that are on shore, which I hope your Lordship will approve of.

For four hours now Cochrane and his little boats had engaged the mighty *Ocean*, convinced that further successes could be obtained. But at 5 a.m. a further letter arrived from Gambier unambiguously relieving Cochrane of his command:

It is necessary I should have some communication with you before I close my despatches to the Admiralty. I have, therefore, ordered Captain Wolfe to relieve you in the services you are engaged in. I wish you to join me as soon as possible, that you may convey Sir Harry Neale to England, who will be charged with my despatches, or you may return to carry on the service where you are. I expect two bombs to arrive every moment, they will be useful in it.

At last, after nearly 36 hours of exhausting battle, Cochrane obeyed orders and returned to the flagship. The battle-stained and exhausted young captain confronted the impeccably dressed and pompous non-combatant admiral who had done so little to help him, and had turned what should have been an over-whelming victory into half of one. Cochrane:

begged his lordship, by way of preventing the ill-feeling of the fleet from becoming detrimental to the honour of the service, to set me aside altogether and send in Admiral Stopford, with the frigates or other vessels, as with regard to him there could be no ill-feeling: further declaring my confidence that from Admiral Stopford's zeal for the service, he would, being backed by his officers, accomplish results more creditable than anything that had yet been done. I apologised for the freedom I used, stating that I took the liberty as a friend, for it would be impossible, as matters stood, to prevent a noise being made in England.

Gambier replied huffily, 'If you throw blame upon what has been done, it will appear like arrogantly claiming all the merit to yourself.' Cochrane retorted: 'I have no wish to carry the despatches, or to go to London with Sir Harry Neale on the occasion. My object is alone that which has been entrusted to me by the Admiralty – to destroy the vessels of the enemy!'

Cochrane was peremptorily ordered to depart for England the following morning, arriving at Spithead six days later. Even the French acknowledged the magnitude of the victory:

> This day of the 12th was a very disastrous one: four of our ships were destroyed, many brave people lost their lives by the disgraceful means the enemy made use of to destroy our lines of defence.

The planned French expedition to Martinique had been completely destroyed.

CHAPTER 9

Court Martial

Gambier's dispatch to the Admiralty about a victory most of which he had witnessed at 9 miles' distance made astonishing reading. It began well enough:

> Sir, the Almighty's favour to His Majesty and the nation has been strongly marked in the success He has been pleased to give to the operations of His Majesty's fleet under my command . . . I cannot speak in sufficient terms of admiration and applause of the vigorous and gallant attack made by Lord Cochrane upon the French line-of-battle ships which were on shore, as well as of the judicious manner of approaching them, and placing his ship in a position most advantageous to annoy the enemy and preserve his own ship.

But he made no mention of the fatal hesitation that had allowed so many ships to get away. Nor did the dispatch refer to Cochrane as having led the attack of the explosion ships and fireships, referring only in passing to 'some vessels filled with powder and shells, as proposed by his lordship, with a view to explosion'. Indeed, according to Gambier, the initial attack had been led by Captain Woolridge of the *Mediator* fireship – which was palpably false as the explosion ships had gone ahead of the fireships.

As to the delay of around 10 hours before Gambier responded to Cochrane's increasingly frantic signals, the admiral claimed to have 'immediately' proceeded to destroy the French ships at 5.38 a.m. – a straight lie, but an admission that Cochrane had been right to summon Gambier at that time. In an obvious attempt to soothe the ruffled feelings of his senior officers, he contended that other commanders would have performed just as well as Cochrane. Gambier soon afterwards wrote a new dispatch giving no credit to Cochrane at all.

But the press had already made Cochrane a hero in Britain. A ballad was composed for him, whose first verses ran:

> We poured in our shot and our rockets like hail,
> Till at length that their courage began for to fail,
> Some were taken and destroyed, and some got on
>   shore,
> The rest ran up harbour and would fight no more.

> *Chorus:*
> So success to our sailors that sail on the sea,
> Who with Cochrane undaunted, whenever they're
>   wanted,
> They'll fight till they die, or gain the victory.

> So now, Master Bonyparte, cease for to brag
> Till you build some more ships for to hoist your
>   white flag
> Which so often had been beat by the lords of the
>   main;
> And if they dare face them, they'll serve them so
>   again.

Cochrane was awarded the prestigious Order of the Bath. Yet news was beginning to leak that the great victory was not all it seemed, as other ships and their crews returned to port. One officer wrote:

> I well remember the indignation which pervaded the whole fleet in witnessing the total want of enterprise, and even of common sense of duty, which permitted so many of the enemy's ships to escape when they were entirely at our mercy.

A leader in *The Times* thundered:

> Lord Cochrane's signal, as we learn from the [*Naval*] *Gazette*, to the Admiral of the Fleet, was that 'seven of the enemy's ships were on shore, and might be destroyed'. The question which hereupon naturally suggests itself to the mind is, 'Why, then, if seven might be destroyed, were there only four?'
>
> The despatch proceeds: 'I immediately made the signal for the fleet to unmoor and weigh'. Indeed! Had Admiral Lord Gambier to unmoor at the time he received this intelligence? Did he not expect this might be the case? Or with what view was Lord Cochrane sent up the Roads?

It was proposed that Parliament award a vote of thanks to Gambier, as had happened to Howe after the Glorious First of June and Nelson after the Battle of the Nile. This was too much for Cochrane. Not only had Gambier spent most of the battle 9 miles away, and never closer than 4 miles, but he had played no active part in it and frustrated its most important attack. The angry captain went to see the jovial First Lord, Mulgrave:

> In my capacity as one of the members for Westminster, I will oppose the motion, on the ground that the commander-in-chief has not only done nothing to merit a vote of thanks, but has neglected to destroy the French fleet in Aix Roads, when it was clearly in his power to do so . . .
>
> I told his lordship that . . . feeling conscious that I had not been enabled satisfactorily to carry out the earnest wishes of the Admiralty by the destruction of the enemy's fleet, as impressed on me by his lordship before accepting the command with which I had been entrusted. I nevertheless begged his lordship to consider that in my professional capacity as a naval officer, I neither did offer nor had offered, any opinion whatever on Lord Gambier's conduct, but that my position as member of Parliament for Westminster forbade my acquiescence in a public misrepresentation.

Mulgrave was aghast. Britain was in deep need of a victory in the Napoleonic wars and Aix Roads had undoubtedly been that, although it could have been a much bigger one. Now Cochrane proposed to tarnish the achievement in an act of insubordination without precedent by publicly exposing his commander-in-chief as, in effect, a coward and a liar. Mulgrave resorted to every trick in the book to make Cochrane desist from his threat. First there was intimidation:

> Such a course will not only prove injurious to the Government, but highly detrimental to yourself, by raising up against you a host of enemies.

Then he offered to include Cochrane's name in the vote of thanks. Cochrane replied:

> Speaking as a member of the House of Commons, I do not recognise Lord Gambier's services at all, for none have been rendered. As for any thanks to myself, I would rather be without them.

Mulgrave pointed out that the public would not view him as a Member of Parliament performing his duty, but as an insubordinate junior naval officer. He resorted to threats again. The government was 'highly dissatisfied' with his conduct and he would feel their 'huge displeasure'. Cochrane replied:

> The displeasure of the government will not for a moment influence my parliamentary conduct, for which I hold myself answerable to my constituents.

Finally there came a whopping bribe – everything Cochrane could have dreamed of in a command:

> If you are on service, you cannot be in your place in parliament. Now, my lord, I will make you a proposal. I will put under your orders three frigates, with carte blanche to do

whatever you please on the enemy's coasts in the Mediterranean. I will further get you permission to go to Sicily, and embark on board your squadron my own regiment, which is stationed there. You know how to make use of such advantages.

Cochrane replied:

Were I to accept this offer, the country would regard my acquiescence as a bribe to hold my peace, whilst I could not regard it in any other light. Self-respect must, therefore, be my excuse for declining the proposal.

Lord Mulgrave could do no more. In retrospect this was certainly the turning point in Cochrane's career, the moment he ascended from being a major irritant in the side of the Admiralty, but a containable one, to becoming an enemy who must be destroyed. Cochrane was faulted by many of his own admirers for his stubbornness in the matter. For example, Ian Grimble's usually highly sympathetic biography (1978), written with the Dundonald family's authorization, spoke of this as being

the most tragic error of judgment in Cochrane's long and varied life . . . It is one of the anomalies of Cochrane's character that he could assess a situation with such lightning clarity when his feet were on a quarterdeck, yet could not now perceive how false his stance was on land: that he thought he could accept service in a department of the government and then attack its administration in a different capacity.

Did Cochrane's understandable anger after his amazing performance at Aix Roads and the way in which near defeat was snatched from victory by Gambier combine with his bitterness at the latter's attempt to take the credit and the official cover-up to harden his usual good judgment into bitterness and arrogance of a kind that sought to undercut his country's navy? Was he giving comfort to the enemy by challenging the official version that a great victory had been won? Certainly the view of Cochrane as a great but flawed man, of a brilliant commander brought low by his egotism, prickliness and refusal to listen to reason or to share the glory with others, dates from this period.

This question needs to be answered at several levels. First, was he indeed guilty of Grimble's charge – effectively of insubordination? As a junior officer did he not have a duty to support his commander, even in the House of Commons? It is easy to answer yes. Membership of the House, although the sovereign body in the land, did not automatically confer supremacy over all other stations in life, in particular one's duty as a serving officer at a time of national peril: for example the need to preserve secrecy in a military operation in which lives could be endangered might override the need for a member to point out incompetence in the course of that operation.

But this depends on the circumstances. The Aix Roads operation was already past. Cochrane was acting to expose a huge deception being practised as to the conduct of that operation on the public. It was surely in the public's interest to know the details, and as he had been in the thick of the fighting, he had every reason to reveal them – if only so that the same mistakes would not be made again. This was not giving comfort to the enemy. The French were only too well aware of the extraordinary British mistake that had allowed several of their vessels to escape.

Only in the narrow sense that British public opinion needed a boost, and that the Battle of Aix Roads had provided one – which its exposure as only half a victory would undermine – was this prejudicial to the British cause in the war. But the reality had long since been leaking out. The background was that the government needed a victory, however dubious, to survive.

Cochrane could have been held to allow his subordinate status in the navy to override his duty as an MP only if it was in the national interest to do so, which in this case it was not. Men such as Gambier needed exposure and removal before they did more harm. Discipline had already been undermined by the

Admiralty itself in the decision to send so junior a captain as Cochrane to command the fireships under the noses of Gambier and his senior officers.

If Cochrane can be absolved of the charges of insubordination and lack of patriotism, the question remains: did he display that fatal lack of judgment in this crucial case of which he is so often accused? The answer to that may be yes, as far as his own interests were concerned. For to defy the full weight of the naval establishment and a corrupt government when he was so clearly and unequivocally warned off, and to reject a command which would have led to an even more glorious naval career was professional suicide, even for a man who so regularly defied the odds as Cochrane. The radical politician, it seemed, had taken over from the great seaman, and so wrecked his career in the Royal Navy just as he achieved his greatest triumph after a thoroughly remarkable spell as Britain's greatest sea captain.

Against that, it should be remembered exactly what he was being asked to swallow by his superiors, under a mixture of threats and bribes: to keep quiet as the man responsible for the near-frustration of a great sea victory was given the highest accolade his country could offer, while Cochrane, the author of that victory, was to be relegated to a minor role. Even for a man less self-assertive and more self-effacing than Cochrane that would have been a bitter pill to swallow.

Was he guilty of mere wounded vanity and bitterness that someone else had stolen his thunder (a frequent accusation in war as in life)? It is impossible to say how much his bruised feelings in the aftermath of a traumatic battle may have warped his character. But it bears repeating that he was the injured party, that the British had been cheated of a truly spectacular victory by one officer's incompetence, and that it was certainly in the national interest for this to be exposed.

There now followed one of the greatest courtroom scandals of British military history, which held the nation in thrall for several days, and was to be debated for years deep into the Victorian era. Gambier insisted on being exonerated of the charges Cochrane had brought against him, and demanded a court martial for himself:

> Feeling that even a doubt upon such a subject cannot be entertained consistently with my reputation as commander in chief, I request that you will be pleased to move the Lords Commissioners of the Admiralty to direct a court martial to be assembled as early as possible, for the purpose of enquiring into my conduct as commander in chief.

This apparently brave gesture was in fact a clever procedural tactic, for if Gambier was the one to be court-martialled, he would be able to provide a full defence of his actions, whereas Cochrane would simply be a witness, called upon to answer a few selected questions like any other. He would not be able to state his own side of the case in any detail.

Cochrane also now made a tactical blunder. Asked by the Admiralty to produce written details of his accusations, he refused to do so in order not to be labelled the accuser of his senior officer. He naïvely said that the log-books would reveal the truth. These in fact were contradictory, as between Gambier's and his own, and he had passed up the chance to highlight the sections of his own logs that would support his case. The charge was limited to just one:

> It appears to us that the said Admiral Lord Gambier, on the 12th day of the said month of April, the enemy's ships being then on shore, and the signal having been made that they could be destroyed, did, for a considerable time, neglect or delay taking effectual measures for destroying them.

The court was chosen with exquisite care. Its president was Admiral Sir Roger Curtis, commander-in-chief at Spithead and Portsmouth – an old and close friend of Gambier. His deputy was none other than Sir William Young – the corrupt admiral formerly in charge at Plymouth who had secured a large cut of Cochrane's prize money by copying out Admiralty orders, and who had ordered Cochrane out in the *Imperieuse* before she was ready, which had nearly resulted in the shipwreck off Ushant. Admiral Sir John Sutton, although intensely able, was an old sparring partner of Cochrane. He had refused to recall the unseaworthy *Atalante*, which had resulted in the loss of the ship and its unhappy crew. Sir John Duckworth, Gambier's second-in-command, was required to sit in judgment on his superior. He was well known as a stern disciplinarian, who had once condemned a man to be hanged on Christmas Day and ordered a flogging of 500 lashes and two of 300 on Boxing Day for a relatively minor act of insubordination. There were three other admirals unconnected with either Gambier or Cochrane sitting in judgment.

The next proceeding was the careful selection of witnesses: Captain (later Admiral Sir) Frederick Maitland, who had supported Cochrane's version of events, was dispatched abroad. Captain (later Admiral Sir) Francis Austen was not called, but was later to provide an account of what he would have said if he had been. He wrote to Cochrane:

> I must in conscience declare that I do not think you were properly supported, and that had you been the result would have been very different. Much of what occurred I attribute to Lord Gambier's being influenced by persons about him who would have been ready to sacrifice the honour of their country to the gratification of personal dislike to yourself, and the annoyance they felt at a junior officer being employed in the service.

Austen faulted Gambier for not proceeding to a position just beyond the range of the Aix guns and so witnessing the battle, instead of remaining miles out to sea. Other witnesses favourable to Cochrane were usually kept to brief statements and question-and-answer sessions. Captain William Broughton of the *Illustrious*, for example, argued that

It would have been more advantageous if the line of battleships, frigates and small vessels had gone in at half flood, about 11 o'clock . . . There were nine sail ashore, and if the British ships had been ordered in, it would have been more advantageous. I told Sir Henry Neale on board the *Caledonia*, when the signal was made for all the captains in the morning, that I thought 'they were attackable from the confused way in which the French ships were at the time'.

I heard my Lord Gambier the same morning say (at this council) it had been his intention to have gone against the batteries I now speak of, but as the enemy were on shore he did not think it necessary to run any unnecessary risk of the fleet when the object of their destruction seemed to be already obtained.

Broughton further discovered a point that was soon to become crucial – that there were no rocks obstructing the Aix-Boyart channel. He had soundings taken so as to ensure the safe passage of his ship. Captain (later Admiral Sir) Pulteney Malcolm argued that Gambier's decision to delay sending in his ships actually increased the danger to them, as it allowed the French to float off:

The risk was then small and of course I would have sent them in instantly . . . I saw the enemy's three-decker [the flagship] on shore. Till about noon she was heeling over considerably, and appeared to me to be heaving her guns overboard. She got off about two o'clock. All the ships got off except those that were destroyed. Had it appeared to me that there was no other chance of destroying those ships but by such an attack, I certainly think it ought to have been made.

The charge was thus that Gambier was endangering his own ships and men by acting so cautiously and sending them in so late. Captain (later Admiral Sir) George Seymour, Cochrane's friend and closest supporter in the engagement, also argued strongly that the fleet should have gone in earlier:

I think the ships might have floated in sooner; that they might have come in on the last half of the flood-tide.

President: How much sooner would that have been than the time they actually did go in?

Seymour: At eleven o'clock.

President: What time did the line-of-battle ships go in?

Seymour: Within a short time after two o'clock.

Seymour's questioning was, however, cut short.

But several of Gambier's other captains, most of whom had witnessed the engagement from their vantage point several miles away, supported him – some because of their resentments at being superseded in command of the night attack by so junior a captain, others simply with a wary eye out to their own interests. Gambier and the naval establishment were unlikely to look favourably upon any officers who supported Cochrane in court.

Cochrane himself proved a poor witness. Always curiously shy and reticent, even nervous as a public speaker, he was quickly flustered and even lost his temper in court – in the face of relentless hostile questioning. He was asked to explain why he had engaged the enemy without orders from his commander-in-chief – an offence for which he could be court-martialled. He admitted this was 'my own act'. Why had he signalled he was in distress when he was not? It seemed at times that Cochrane, not Gambier, was being court-martialled. He replied he had signalled for assistance, which was the same signal as that for distress. He went on:

> Had the attack been made in the morning, it is my opinion that seven sail of the enemy, including the three-decker, might have been destroyed with facility, by two sail of the line, assisted by the frigates and smaller vessels; and that after the hour of half past eleven . . . the frigates alone, assisted by the smaller vessels, might have destroyed the whole of the above-mentioned ships.

The President of the court, Sir Roger Curtis, interrupted:

Really, I very humbly beg your pardon, but I do not see how this can be an answer!

Cochrane persisted:

I consoled myself with the supposition that his lordship intended a grand blow on the island and on the ships at once, although I thought this highly unnecessary and imprudent. I could not in any other way account for a proceeding, which thus enabled the helpless French ships to endeavour to escape undisturbed into the river Charente. Twelve o'clock arrived; no signal was made to weigh. Half past twelve, still no signal –

Admiral Young interrupted:

This is very improper. This is no answer to the question. It is only calculated to make an unfavourable impression against the prisoner.

Cochrane burst out:

I am bound to tell the truth, the whole truth and nothing but the truth, and with submission to the court, if I am not permitted to state the circumstances upon which my opinion is grounded, it is impossible I can give a full answer to the question and until the court hears the whole of my answer, it is not possible that they can form any correct judgment upon it, and must remain in ignorance of the fact.

Young retorted coolly:

Lord Cochrane, you are bound to give a direct answer to the question, and not to state that which the court are decidedly of the opinion is wholly irrelevant.

After a further interruption by Young, Cochrane burst out:

If a question is put by a person ignorant of the whole proceedings, and which does not lead to get the truth and the whole truth, I hold that I am to give the whole truth.

In the stodgy, grandiose surroundings of HMS *Gladiator*, moored in Portsmouth Harbour, looking across to Spithead, with the seven admirals in their full dress uniforms and the scene watched over by impeccably dressed Royal Marine guards, Cochrane's answer was regarded as impertinent, insubordinate and insolent towards the court. There was a gasp. The court was cleared: Cochrane was officially reprimanded by the President:

It was in no small degree, indecorous to the court, to make use of such an expression.

Later, however, Cochrane indulged in another outburst.

I have felt if I had answered yes or no to all the questions which have been put to me, I ought to be hung; and that if a court martial was held upon me, and only the answers yes or no appeared to those questions, I should be hung for them!

Yet it was not Cochrane who was on trial. The issue was completely straightforward. Had Gambier's conduct prevented an overwhelming British victory at Aix? To defend himself against this charge, Gambier made a string of excuses in what had become a personal contest between him and Cochrane. Gambier insisted that it would have been 'preposterous and impracticable' to send in the fleet:

I am firmly persuaded that the success attending this achieve-ment would have proved more dearly bought than any yet recorded in our navy annals.

The principal points of his defence were the following. Cochrane's explosion vessels had not damaged the French boom, which was anyway not a strong one, but that this had been done by the leading fireship. The Aix channel was too narrow for Gambier to risk his ships. The channel was exposed to devastating fire from the Aix battery and a dangerous shoal existed in the channel which would have sunk his ships.

It is worth examining all four points as they were presented at the court martial. The first was clearly an attempt by Gambier to diminish Cochrane's achievement. Subtly, Cochrane's detractors found a letter written by a French officer which stated:

> The boom is composed of strong cables of the smaller kind and is floated by large logs of wood and other materials; it is held by strong anchors.

From this, ridiculously, it was alleged that the boom was in fact a flimsy structure (not a double one moored with 100 anchors) and Gambier claimed that Captain Woolridge of the foremost fireship, the 800-ton *Mediator*, deserved the credit for breaking through it. Cochrane asserted that he had deduced his explosion ship had destroyed the boom from the huge amount of wreckage floating in the water at daylight – although some of this, of course, came from the fireships and the explosion ships themselves and, in any case, would have been visible if Woolridge had broken it.

Still, it was possible that the *Mediator* did the damage – but only if the boom was a very light one and Cochrane was indeed exaggerating its strength. Yet it seems unlikely that the French would have gone to the trouble of setting up a boom expressly designed to stop fireships so ineffectual that the first would have got through – or at any rate less likely than that Cochrane's two explosion ships, with their tremendous destructive power, did the damage. There can be no certainty, only a strong probability that Cochrane was right on this issue.

What is beyond dispute – and was not challenged by Gambier – was that the explosion ships and the fireships caused havoc among the French ships. As only four of his fireships reached their destination, it can be asserted that the real terror of the

French were the explosion ships, which many enemy officers also took the fireships to be.

Cochrane was vigorously criticised for his assertion that the fireships were mostly abandoned by their crews too far out, as a disgraceful slur on the brave crews of these ships. Yet it is hard to disagree when no fewer than seven ended up grounded far from the battle zone. Certainly, however, Captain Woolridge, who was badly burnt in the action, and his crew performed heroically in staying with the ship for so long, as did those in the three others that reached their destination.

The evidence as to the size of the Aix channel came in charts provided by the Admiralty. Thomas Stokes, master (chief navigator) of Gambier's flagship, the *Caledonia*, and thus a biased witness, and Edward Fairfax, Master of the Fleet, had drawn these up. Fairfax claimed to have made soundings himself but only as far as the Boyart shoal. Stokes had not got so close: 'It cannot be expected that from the opportunities I had of sounding in this place, I could accurately point out the distance between the sands.'

However he said he had based his observations on a chart taken from the French ship, the *Almide*, which had been captured in 1806. Cochrane had used charts taken from the *Neptune Française*, the standard work for French ships, for his attack on Aix Roads, plus his own observations from his previous visit. This showed the Aix channel to be some 2 miles wide, not 1 mile as Stokes and Fairfax asserted.

Cochrane had just sailed down the channel himself, as he had twice before, while the two navigators had no direct experience of it. A channel only a mile wide would have made a full-scale attack by British ships much more difficult, if not impossible. But this also touched on the third point: British ships would inevitably have come too close under the guns of Aix. Cochrane regarded the threat from these guns as almost non-existent. One made a hole in the topmast of the *Indefatigable* about 7 inches in diameter, and an officer of the *Revenge* later said that a 42-pound shot had hit her bowsprit, with the quarterdeck beam being shot away. Five men aboard were killed and one wounded.

Although this damage was not insignificant, it hardly bore out Gambier's contention that the Aix battery represented a serious threat. Eight other British ships eventually sailed past her in both directions unscathed. If Cochrane was right that the channel was 2 miles wide, the British ships had for the most part sailed out of the range of its guns, down the south side of the channel; Gambier's ships had sensibly fired upon workmen constructing a battery on the south side several days before the battle.

The charts drawn up by Stokes and Fairfax revealed the existence of a further obstacle: a reef of rocks 12 to 16 feet below the water at low tide that blocked the channel almost completely for ships with a deep draught. In such circumstances it would indeed have been folly for Gambier to order in British battleships with some 22 feet of their hulls below the waterline – although at high (spring) tide the depth would rise to between 33 and 42 feet.

If these calculations were correct, Gambier would have had every reason for hesitation. But the key point was that he indeed did send in several battleships regardless – although much too late, when the tide was on the turn and the water level was dropping. As observed, the *Revenge, Valiant, Caesar, Theseus, Indefatigable, Pallas, Unicorn* and *Aigle* were all sent in after 4 p.m., encountering no shoal of hidden rocks. According to Captain Bligh of the *Valiant* (his evidence was intended to support Gambier) his ship was in a 'very perilous situation – nothing but the wind shifting and blowing her out could have saved her from being wrecked'.

But all four ships floated as soon as the tide allowed, and Admiral Stopford was able to lead them out in the early morning of 13 April without difficulty, while the *Imperieuse*, the *Pallas*, a small mortar ship, the *Etna*, and the schooner from which Congreve was experimenting with his rockets, were able to remain. Gambier's defence made little sense. If it was too dangerous to send in the ships on the morning of 12 April because of the narrowness of the channel, the guns on Aix and the hidden reef, why was it acceptable to do so in the afternoon?

Cochrane, as a mere witness, was not given access to the Stokes–Fairfax charts until thirty years later, and was unaware of the grounds they gave – which the court martial found convincing – for acquitting Gambier. When he did see them, he pronounced them forgeries. He wrote:

A chart of Aix Road based on a modern French chart has recently been shown me, as on the point of being issued by the Board of Admirals, on which chart the main channel between the Isle d'Aix and the Boyart sand is laid down according to charts copied from fabricated charts produced on Lord Gambier's court martial, and not according to the hydrographic charts of the *Neptune Français*. The comparatively clear anchorage shown in the new chart is also filled with Mr Stoke's imaginary shoals! The result being that no British admiral, if guided by the new chart would trust his ships in Aix Roads at all, though both under Admiral Knowles, and at the attack of 1809, British ships found no difficulty whatever from want of water, or other causes when once ordered in.

Cochrane may have been right. Certainly Stokes and Fairfax had no obvious grounds for knowing better than Cochrane, who was on the spot. When they had at last sailed in to attack the French, the British ships had encountered no hidden shoal and sailed in and out, suffering negligible damage from the guns.

In fairness to Stokes and Fairfax, the French charts may have been a forgery of the French themselves, to deceive the British into thinking that their anchorage was unassailable. But Gambier's own decision to send in the battleships eventually anyway completely refuted his contention that it was too dangerous to do so. If it was too dangerous earlier, it was surely too dangerous later when the tide had ebbed.

One of Gambier's supporters, Captain Poo Beresford, said reverently:

> Lord Gambier seemed to be most anxious to act with his fleet, but that if he had sent them in there, it clearly appeared that few would have returned, if any, were I think my expressions and that it would have been madness to have done it. His Lordship [Lord Cochrane] said that three sail-of-the-line might have been lost, which in his opinion did not signify. My reply was, that even one sail-of-the-line being lost would have been a disgrace to the enterprise and to England.

This exchange reflects the most extraordinary thing about the whole battle: not only had Gambier stayed between 4 and 9 miles out to sea during most of the action, he appeared unwilling to risk any of his big ships in combat at all, until Cochrane forced his hand. This was in startling contrast to the old Nelson adage of taking spectacular risks which might lose ships in order to inflict a decisive defeat. The French fleet had been at their mercy, but half of it had been allowed to get away.

In spite of itself the battle had been decisive. The two 74-gun battleships and a 56-gun magazine ship as well as a frigate had been destroyed. Two more 74-gun battleships had been damaged beyond repair. Two other ships had been saved, along with the two battleships. The French fleet had been irreparably damaged and the Basque Roads blockade could be lifted. The French threat to the West Indies was no more: Guadelupe and Martinique, the two prize spice islands, were soon to fall into British hands. Years later Napoleon, in exile in St Helena, had the last word. Cochrane, he said:

> could not only have destroyed them . . . but he might and would have taken them out, had your admiral supported him as he ought to have done.... The French admiral was a fool, but yours was just as bad.

> I assure you that, if Cochrane had been supported, he would have taken every one of those ships. They ought not to

have been alarmed by your *brulots*, but fear deprived them of their senses, and they no longer knew how to act in their own defence.

Gambier brought the proceedings complacently to a close at his trial:

Some positions laid down by two of these witnesses have been so completely refuted by other evidence brought forward, that I feel myself more and more confirmed in my opinion, that the measures pursued for the attack of the enemy were those best calculated for the object in view.

The result was a foregone conclusion:

The charge has not been proved against the said Admiral the Right Honourable Lord Gambier . . . His Lordship's conduct on that occasion, as well as his general conduct and proceedings as Commander-in-Chief of the Channel Fleet . . . was marked by zeal, judgment, ability, and an anxious attention to the welfare of His Majesty's service . . . the said Admiral the Right Honourable Lord Gambier is hereby most honourably acquitted.

Gambier's sword was returned to him. Soon afterwards the parliamentary vote of thanks to Gambier was passed in January 1810 by 161 votes to 39, with Cochrane and his Radical friends bitterly but ineffectively opposing it; even so the size of the minority vote came as something of a surprise. The outcome of the court martial in no way affected the popular perception of Cochrane as the real hero of the Battle of Aix Roads.

However, the whitewash of the man who had never fought in the battle was complete. Worse, the actual victor of the great and controversial battle was, to all intents and purposes, officially disgraced. This had two dramatic effects on Cochrane's subsequent career. It meant that a large and dangerous part of the establishment was now determined to ruin the man who had challenged them and proved so dangerous to their interests, and it deeply embittered Cochrane himself. From now on his natural boldness and insubordination was to be transformed into a streak of foolhardiness and even quixotic eccentricity. It was the turning point of his life.

CHAPTER 10

The Radical

What had Cochrane achieved in his seventeen years at sea? His had been perhaps the most spectacular career of any individual sea captain in Britain's long naval history. It had begun with his exploits aboad the tiny, ill-armed, but legendary *Speedy*, which had brought terror to Spanish and French shipping in the western Mediterranean. Like a dragonfly skimming across the deep blue waters, he had sailed with speed, courage, and unnerving skill.

His engagement with the *Gamo* was one of the greatest David-and-Goliath confrontations in naval history, executed with skill and improvisation. His range of tricks and deceptions created a new precedent – at moments of crisis he never seemed stuck for a ruse or a hoax, from raising flags of quarantine to dropping lanterns in barrels during the night. The *Speedy*'s very demise – running directly at three French battleships in a bid to get away – had been a fitting end to that vessel's career.

His spell aboard the *Pallas* was another *tour de force*, marked by spectacular prize-catching in the much rougher water of the Atlantic and the astonishing race with the three battleships – which this time he won. His third great tour of duty along the western coast of France had also been characterized by an aura of impregnability that had inspired terror along the shoreline.

His fourth, back in the Mediterranean aboard the *Imperieuse*, had been crowned by two extraordinary amphibious operations at Mongat and Port Vendres. It had culminated in the spectacular defence of Fort Trinidad, with its aura of dash and adventure – establishing Cochrane as a formidable land commander as well as a sea one, and, taken together with his raiding operations off the coast of France, Britain's first 'commando' chief.

Finally, the Battle of Aix Roads had been one of the decisive engagements of the Napoleonic Wars, accomplished by Cochrane's leadership in the teeth of the obstinate caution of his commanding officer. Now his country was to dispense with his services for the remainder of the Napoleonic Wars.

Cochrane was ordered to take the *Imperieuse* to join the long-standing blockade of Toulon. He refused.

I beg permission to say that I have got some objects of moment to bring forward in Parliament, and that as there is no enterprise given to the *Imperieuse*, I have no wish that she should be detained for me one moment.

The Admiralty twisted the knife: they wanted to be:

distinctly informed whether or not it is your Lordship's intention to join your ship as soon as Parliament shall be prorogued. I shall be much pleased to receive an answer in the affirmative because I should then entertain hopes that your activity and gallantry might be made available for the service.

Cochrane was faced with the choice of either going with his ship on a routine mission and giving up his seat in Parliament, or giving up his command. He chose the latter.

Cochrane had only been prevented by the court martial from sailing with the *Imperieuse* on the great Walcheren expedition launched under Admiral Sir Richard Strachan, a fine seaman, and the Earl of Chatham, William Pitt's elder brother, and an appalling and inexperienced general. It was as well for his reputation that he did so. With no fewer than 40,000 troops, thirty-five ships of the line, two 50-gun ships, three 44-gun ships, eighteen frigates and 200 smaller vessels, the objective had been to seize three arsenals and dockyards at Flushing, Terneuse and Antwerp, as well as to destroy the French fleet at the Scheldt.

Cochrane was certain long before the expedition set out that the wrong targets had been chosen. He wrote:

> Had one half of the troops been placed, as suggested in my letter to Lord Mulgrave, on the islands of the French coast, and had one half of the frigates alone been employed as had been the *Imperieuse* and other vessels in the Mediterranean, not a man could have been detached from Western France in the Spanish peninsula, from which the remaining position of the British Army might have driven the French troops already there.

As it was, Wellesley was in the process of winning the prolonged and bloody battle of Talavera, but had to retreat to Portugal. His progress in the Peninsular War was painfully slow. The attempt to capture the island of Walcheren in the estuary of the Scheldt proved to be one of the most expensive and wretched fiascos in British military history. Only Flushing was taken, while 14,000 British soldiers fell sick, some 3000 dying in the swamp marshes. A famous ditty of the time ran:

> Lord Chatham, with his sword half-drawn,
> Stood waiting for Sir Richard Strachan.
> Sir Richard, longing to be at 'em,
> Stood waiting for the Earl of Chatham.

As a result of this debate, the government of the Earl of Portland fell, to be replaced by that of Spencer Perceval in October 1809. It was a dismal moment for British politics, an interlude of deep mediocrity after the great Pitt–Fox duels. Both court and parliament lapsed into a contest for place between reactionary and corrupt figures representing rotten boroughs, while outside the new age of a deprived working class was dawning, posing a potentially revolutionary challenge. The worst of it all was that the war effort against Napoleon after the dismal fiasco at Walcheren had degenerated into a single hope: Wellesley's plodding, bloody progress up the Iberian peninsula, which had been saved from fiasco by the quality of his generalship.

By this time, the Prince Regent, later George IV, had more or less secured the reins of monarchy from his father, George III, who had at last descended into final madness. The Prince had secretly married a Catholic, Mrs Fitzherbert (which technically barred him from the succession) in a union that was bigamous to that of his hideous cousin Queen Caroline, with whom he quarrelled frequently.

His next brother, William Duke of Clarence, openly lived with his own mistress, Mrs Jordan, and their children. He made public speeches in favour of the slave trade, by which he was almost certainly paid, in opposition to William Wilberforce's efforts to ban it. However, he was relatively well regarded by the public as a seaman of ability. Another brother, the Duke of Cumberland, was alleged to have had a child by his sister, to have attempted to rape the wife of the Lord Chancellor and to have murdered his valet. The Hanoverian dynasty had never been in a lower state of public repute and, together with the inertia of the political system and the social upheaval generated by the industrial revolution, there was a real danger of open revolution more than at any time in British history. The unlikely protagonists of this revolutionary expression were the Radicals outside both the Tory and Whig parties, led by the voluble but ultimately self-seeking and shallow plutocrat, Sir Francis Burdett; the sincere, self-made William Cobbett; and Cochrane himself – the rich dilettante, the tireless reformer and the aristocratic and impetuous naval hero. All three were fast becoming popular heroes in a climate of repression and a faltering war effort.

The spark of revolt was, as always, an unlikely one. Typically the House of Commons decided to hold its inquiry into the fiasco of the Walcheren expedition in February 1810 in secret. John Gale Jones, a veteran and professional Radical who was probably slightly off his head, put up a poster denouncing this 'outrage'. Charles Yorke, former First Lord of the Admiralty and a veteran of the cabal of die-hards in the cabinet, promptly inflated the whole affair into a breach of the House of Commons' privileges. Jones was thrown into Newgate jail without a trial.

Burdett tabled a motion for his release, which was crushingly defeated. The Radical leader, Cochrane's own fellow member for Westminster, wrote a stinging denunciation of parliament, accusing it of indulging in arbitrary practices of the kind which the Tudors and Stuarts had practised, and witheringly labelling his parliamentary colleagues 'as part of our fellow subjects collected together by means which it is not necessary for me to describe', an allusion to the bribery and purchase of rotten boroughs and the unrepresentative nature of most MPs.

Indignantly, the government held a vote, which, by 189 to 152 votes, narrowly found Burdett guilty of breach of privilege and in medieval fashion ordered his committal to the Tower of London. The size of the minority was in fact a triumph for Burdett, but the vote had to be acted upon. The serjeant-at-arms, Francis Colman, was dispatched to Burdett's sumptuous house at 78 Piccadilly, but found that the Radical leader was not there. Burdett, from hiding, proclaimed the warrant illegal and said he would submit only to overwhelming force. Popular agitation spread in Burdett's defence. Soon tens of thousands had taken to the streets, spreading across London in what seemed the prelude to a general insurrection.

On the night of 7 April the mob occupied the main approaches to the Tower. Small boats were also blocking the river approach. The crowds outside 78 Piccadilly, where Burdett had now taken refuge, continued to grow, spreading into Albemarle Street, Berkeley Square and St James's Square. Violence erupted and windows were smashed in the houses of such leading political figures as Charles Yorke, Spencer Perceval and Lord Chatham, some of the houses being broken into and furniture carried off. Anyone who passed Burdett's house and refused to raise his hat and shout 'Burdett for ever' was pelted with mud.

The authorities responded by sending in the troops. The Horse Guards were ordered out to charge the demonstrators, while the Foot Guards and Light Dragoons attacked demonstrators by hitting them with the flats of their swords. Batteries of artillery were erected in St James's Park, Berkeley Square and Soho Square – and fortified. The moat of the Tower was flooded, the guns there were prepared for action, and all troops within 100 miles of London were recalled to the capital. It was suggested that Wellington himself should be recalled from the Peninsular War to take charge. To the nervous minor politicians running Britain, there were echoes of the tumbrils, the Bastille and the guillotine.

The Life Guards charged the demonstrators, who fled into the side streets down Piccadilly. As the cavalry regrouped, enterprising rioters seized ladders which they pulled suddenly across as barricades when the cavalry charged again, forcing their horses to shy away under a hail of stones and mud. The demonstrators kept up a torchlight vigil outside Burdett's house long into the night. The authorities could not approach through the crowds.

The following day, 8 April, the tall, distinguished figure of the hero of Aix Roads, arrived by coach. To the crowd's delight he rolled out a barrel of gunpowder, which he took into the house, busily knocking holes in the wall to accommodate charges, so that he could threaten a massive explosion if the house were raided.

Even by Cochrane's standards this was extreme. He was crossing the fine dividing line between legitimate parliamentary protest and initiating a revolution that could result in violence and bloodshed. Nothing in his previous or subsequent career suggested that he was wedded to the cause of violent revolution as the solution for the country's many abuses (indeed he was later to help defuse the growing surge of popular anger in Britain), nor had he ever articulated any theory of revolution. Was this simply the act of a crank or a crackpot, someone whose mind had been unhinged by the Gambier affair?

The answer is probably less dramatic. Cochrane was first and

Cochrane in his prime:
  skilled and fearless.

Implacable persecutor:
  Earl St Vincent.

The *Speedy* and the *Gamo*: David and Goliath, 5 May 1801.

Recruiting poster of 1804.

THE SEVERE
SENTENCE
ON

LORD COCHRANE & OTHERS,

STAND IN THE PILLORY,

IN THE FRONT OF THE

Royal-Exchange,

FOR

A CONSPIRACY,

TO RAISE, BY FALSE REPORTS, THE PRICE OF THE PUBLIC FUNDS;

As pronounced by Sir Simon Le Blanc,

IN THE COURT OF KING'S-BENCH,

ON TUESDAY, the 21st of JUNE, 1814.

"That you, Sir Thomas Cochrane, commonly called Lord Cochrane,* and that you, Richard Gathorne Butt, do pay a fine of one thousand pounds to the King; and that you, John Peter Holloway, having also benefited from this infamous conspiracy, do pay a fine of five hundred pounds to the King.

"That you, the six several Defendants, Sir Thomas, commonly called Lord, Cochrane, Richard Gathorne Butt, John Peter Holloway, Charles Random De Berenger, Henry Lyte, and Ralph Sandom, be severally imprisoned in the custody of the Marshal of the Marshalsea of this Court for the term of twelve calendar months, and that,

* Member of Parliament for the City of Westminster, and late Captain of his Majesty's Ship Imperieuse.

during that period, you, Charles Random De Berenger, you, Sir Thomas, commonly called Lord, Cochrane, and you, Richard Gathorne Butt, be set in and upon the pillory in the front of the Royal-Exchange, for the space of one hour, between the hours of twelve at noon and two in the afternoon.

"And that, you, Sir Thomas, commonly called Lord, Cochrane, Richard Gathorne Butt, and John Peter Holloway, be further imprisoned until your several fines be paid."

The other two persons found guilty of the said Conspiracy, namely, Andrew Cochrane Johnstone and Alexander M'Rea did not appear in Court, consequently judgment was not pronounced upon them.

Published by John Fairburn, 2, Broadway, Ludgate-Hill.

Disgraced: the broadsheet announcement of Cochrane's sentence.

Even in the stocks, routing his enemies (G. Cruikshank, 1814).

Cochrane's talented admirer:
Maria Graham.

Courage to match her beauty: Kitty Cochrane with Tom.

Destruction of the French fleet: Aix Roads, 12 April 1809.

Cochrane unbowed in old age (he died in 1860).

foremost a man of action and a fighter. The first course that would come into his mind when the threat of force was proposed against his fellow Radical MP for Westminster was to set up defences which could not be crossed, and defy the authorities to do so. They would surely back down. If they used force first, and the house was blown up, the responsibility would be theirs. Mining the house was not, in itself, an offence.

It is unlikely that he thought through the consequences of his actions. If violence did break out and half the façades of Piccadilly were blown up, along with countless soldiers and demonstrators, it could be classed as open insurrection and terrorism. He would then have no alternative but to lead the revolution, or be brought to the gallows. Inside, Burdett and the brilliant Radical tailor, Francis Place, a pioneering advocate of universal suffrage, education and contraception, were aghast at Cochrane's plans. Place summed up the argument: 'It will be easy enough to clear the hall of constables and soldiers, to drive them into the street or to destroy them, but are you prepared to take the next step and to go on?'

Cochrane was overruled. 'The gallant Tar then retired, apparently much disconcerted, and he was particularly required to take away with him the cask of gunpowder.' Meanwhile Place set about trying to raise a force of peaceful volunteers to defend Burdett and to steward the unruly mob. There were encouraging reports of disaffection among the troops. Place was told that 'the Foot Guards and the 15th Light Dragoons were much more disposed to fight the Life Guards than they were disposed to obey an order to attack the people'.

It all came to naught. On the morning of 9 April, an enter-prising constable climbed through an open back window of the house, followed by several colleagues. They found Burdett teaching the Magna Carta to his son at breakfast. He was seized, smuggled out and put in a coach, which was escorted by cavalry on a roundabout route to the Tower.

The authorities hesitated to inflame popular passion by taking action against Cochrane, who had come so close to an act of revolutionary violence but not actually broken the law. The popular naval hero became the focus of agitation for Burdett's release, frequently being carried shoulder-high to the House of Commons to present petitions while MPs debated whether or not to expel him.

After two months Burdett was released upon the prorogation of parliament, the government hesitating to turn him into a martyr. Although Place had organized a triumphal procession for him, he slipped away from the Tower by boat and the half-idiot 'Citizen' Jones took his place on a coach ranting at the awaiting crowds.

Although this particular protest fizzled out, Cochrane's reforming zeal did not. Having wildly overreached himself, and infuriated the government, he now demonstrated real qualities of depth and weight as a reformer in parliament. He chose the subject in which he was most expert: naval corruption and reform. In a series of devastating interventions, he made his mark as a serious politician – even if his efforts were initially crowned with failure and only served to expose the depth of animosity felt towards the naval establishment and its allies.

Cochrane was guilty of two profound errors in this campaign. Never a good judge of character, having crossed swords early in his career with St Vincent, he failed to appreciate that on the issue of naval corruption the two men stood on the same side. Furthermore, he had been taken in by John Wilson Croker, one of the most sinister and corrupt men ever to run the Admiralty as its secretary, made more dangerous because he was genuinely intelligent and able.

Lord St Vincent, against whom Cochrane conducted such a public vendetta, had written as far back as 1797, 'you may rest assured, the civil branch of the navy is rotten to the very core'. Four years later he toured the naval dockyards as First Sea Lord, and was appalled by what he found. He wrote to the Prime Minister, Addington: 'We find abuses to such an extent as would require many months to go thoroughly into, and the absolute necessity of a commission of enquiry to expose them appears to the Admiralty board here in a much stronger light than ever.'

Addington agreed to set up a naval commission of inquiry, which issued fourteen damning reports. It was discovered that 300 men could build seven ships a year in private dockyards – ten times fewer than were necessary to repair the same number of ships in Admiralty shipyards. Two 74-gun warships and one 64-gunner had sunk because a contractor had secured their timbers with only the tops of nails so as to cream off a little extra profit. Children of nine or ten worked in the dockyards for as little as £5 a month. Anchor cables were sometimes as much as 90 feet short. It was reckoned that fully a third of the cost of the navy could be saved through a few elementary reforms.

Lord St Vincent's reports succeeded in driving the corrupt First Lord, Lord Melville, from office, but he failed to make much of a dent in the system and was himself eventually driven from office. Meanwhile Cochrane had bitterly continued his misguided campaign against his old enemy. In 1807, for example, he had attacked the shortages in naval hospitals:

Mistaken economy has even reduced the quantity of lint for the purpose of dressing wounds. To the ships there is not half enough allowed. This lint has been cut off by a person worthily employed in the late administration as commander-in-chief. [I do] not know whether it [is] regular to mention his name in the House [a cry from several parts of the House – Name! Name!] [I have] no hesitation in naming Lord St Vincent. Unworthy savings [have] been unworthily made, endangering the lives of officers and seamen. Indeed, the grievances of the navy are so severe, through rigour and mistaken economy, that I can see nothing more meritorious than the patience with which those grievances have been endured.

Lord St Vincent retorted cholerically that a bill should be brought in to disqualify any officer under the rank of rear-admiral to sit in the House of Commons; while a little drunken, worthless jackanapes is permitted to hold seditious language in the presence of flag officers of rank, you will require a man of greater health and vigour than I possess to command your fleets.

Cochrane had meanwhile met Croker in 1806 and initially taken a liking to him. Anglo-Irish, smooth, cold, soft-spoken, he had already made a reputation as an acerbic literary reviewer. His feline criticism, it was later said, hastened the death of the greatest poet of the time, John Keats. Byron had written of this episode: 'Tis odd the soul, that very fiery particle, should let itself be snuffed out by an article'. Cochrane wrote:

This gentleman had an invitation to my table as often as he might think proper, and of this – from a similarity of taste and habit, as I was willing to believe – he so far availed himself as to become my daily guest; receiving a cordial reception, from friendship towards a person of ardent mind who had to struggle as I had done to gain a position.

A year later Croker was promoted secretary to the Admiralty, his Tory patrons being the influential Wellesley brothers. He was to hold the job for twenty years. When Croker met Cochrane again one day, the latter asked why the former had not picked up some excellent wine the *Pallas* had taken from a prize off France:

Nor did I by any chance meet him till, some time afterwards, we encountered each other by accident near Whitehall. Recognising me in a way meant to convey the idea that he was now my master, our relations were slightly altered. I asked him why he had not sent for his wine. His reply was: 'Why really, I have no use for it, my friends having supplied me more liberally than I have occasion for.'

As Admiralty secretary Croker, like the Wellesleys, was now

the fighting captain's sworn enemy and the man who conspired most assiduously at the Admiralty in Cochrane's downfall.

One of Cochrane's Radical friends, Samuel Bamford, gave a vividly contemptuous picture of the House of Commons at about this time:

At the head of the room, or rather den, for such it appeared to me, sat a person in a full loose robe of, I think, scarlet and white. Above his head were the royal arms, richly gilded; at his feet several men in robes and wigs were writing at a large table on which lamps were burning, which cast a softened light on a rich ornament like a ponderous sceptre of silver and gold, or what appeared to be so.

Some of the members stood leaning against pillars with their hats cocked awry; some were whispering by half dozens; others were lolling upon their seats; some with arms-a-kimbo were eye-glassing across the house; some were stiffened immovably by starch, or pride, or both; one was speaking or appeared to be so, by the motion of his arms, which he shook in token of defiance, when his voice was drowned by a howl as wild and remorseless as that from a kennel of hounds at feeding time. Now he points menacing to the ministerial benches – now he appeals to some members on this side – then to the speaker; all in vain. At times he is heard in the pauses of that wild hubbub, but again he is borne down by the yell which awakes on all sides around him.

Some talked aloud; some whinnied in mock laughter, coming like that of the damned, from bitter hearts. Some called 'order, order', some 'question, question', some beat time with the heel of their boots; some snorted into their napkins; and one old gentleman in the side gallery actually coughed himself from a mock cough into a real one and could not stop until he was almost black in the face.

When Croker proposed the vote on the naval estimate in May,

Cochrane rose to deliver the single most powerful speech of his career, for once without anger and bolstered by excellent research: his targets were naval sinecures as compared to the compensation awarded ordinary seamen and their families:

> An admiral worn out in the service is superannuated at £410 a year, a captain at £210, a clerk of the ticket office retires on £700 a year. The widow of Admiral Sir Andrew Mitchell has one-third of the allowance given to the widow of a commissioner of the navy . . .
>
> Thirty-two flag officers, twenty-two captains, fifty lieutenants, 180 masters, thirty-six surgeons, twenty-three pursers, ninety-one boatswains, ninety-seven gunners, 222 carpenters, and forty-one cooks, in all 774 persons, cost the country £4028: less than the net proceeds of the sinecures of Lords Arden, £20,358 – Camden, £20,536 – and Buckingham, £20,693. All the superannuated admirals, captains and lieutenants put together have but £1012 more than Earl Camden's sinecure alone. All that is paid to the wounded officers of the whole British Navy, and to the wives and children of those dead or killed in action, do not amount by £214 to as much as Lord Arden's sinecure alone: that is, £20,358. What is paid to the mutilated officers themselves is but half as much.
>
> I find upon examination that the Wellesleys receive from the public £34,729, a sum equal to 426 pairs of lieutenants' legs, calculated at the rate of allowance of Lieutenant Chambers' legs. Calculating for the pension of Captain Johnstone's arm – that is £45 – Lord Arden's sinecure is equal to the value of 1022 arms. The Marquess of Buckingham's sinecure alone will maintain the whole ordinary establishment of the victualling department at Chatham, Dover, Gibraltar, Sheerness, Downs, Heligoland, Cork, Malta, Mediterranean, Cape of Good Hope, Rio de Janeiro and leave £5460 in the Treasury.
>
> Even Mr Ponsonby, who lately made so pathetic an appeal to the good sense of the people of England against those

whom he pleased to call demagogues, actually receives, for
having been thirteen months in office, a sum equal to nine
admirals who have spent their lives in the service of their
country; three times as much as all the pensions given to all
the daughters and children of all the admirals, captains, lieutenants and other officers who have died in indigent circumstances or who have been killed in the service.

From the minute expenses noticed in the naval estimate,
viz for oiling clocks, killing rats, and keeping cats, I suppose
that great care has been taken to have everything correct. It
was, therefore, with great surprise that I found the name of
my worthy and respected grandmother, the widow of the
late Captain Gilchrist of the navy, continuing on the list as
receiving £100 per annum, though she ceased to exist eight
years ago!

It was brilliant stuff. He was taking on the most powerful
dynasty in the land, for the Wellesley brothers had amassed a
huge swathe of power and wealth for themselves in Ireland,
India and Spain. The eldest brother, the Marquess of Wellesley,
had made his fortune in India. His abuses had earned him the
condemnation even of his brilliant younger brother, Sir Arthur,
who said he deserved to be constrained. But the family closed
ranks against this attack from Cochrane. William Wellesley-
Pole rose to answer in tones full of menace:

Let me advise him that adherence to the pursuits of his
profession, of which he is so great an ornament, will tend
more to his own honour and to the advantage of his country
than a perseverance in the conduct which he has of late
adopted, conduct which can only lead him into error, and
make him the dupe of those who use the authority of his
name to advance their own mischievous purposes.

These were threats not to be taken lightly. The establishment
had shown it was capable of fighting back, viciously. In June
1810 the courageous Cobbett, who had written an article

attacking the flogging of four militiamen who had objected to their low pay, was brought to trial by the ferocious Lord Eldon, the Lord Chancellor, a judge who specialized in intimidating those he disliked in court – in particular, reformers of any kind. Cobbett was sentenced to a draconian two years in prison and a fine of £1000. It was an ominous precedent for Cochrane.

CHAPTER 11

The Romantic

Cochrane's next target was an old obsession: prize money. As already noted he had long been infuriated by the system, for reasons of personal self-interest as well as altruism, by which Admiralty officials were able to claim most of the rewards obtained by men risking their lives at sea. He had made the valid point that as long as there was little to be obtained in the way of prize money, there was little incentive for money-strapped naval officers and their crews to attack enemy shipping. Even St Vincent had vigorously campaigned 'that the officers of His Majesty's Navy should be allowed a larger proportion of the seizure in order that they might have an inducement to be more alert in the execution of their duty'.

A commission of inquiry in 1804 had written that 'gross and abominable frauds were practised upon sailors with respect to their prize money'. The worst offender was the prize court in Malta, which on occasion had actually charged Cochrane more in fees than the prize was worth. On another, only 1900 crowns remained out of 8608 – all the rest having gone in fees. Sir Jahleel Brenton, his fellow captain, had been paid just £285 by the court for a prize worth £1025 after the court's fees had been deducted. Cochrane had infuriated the court by a clever trick:

> It was my own practice, when any money was captured in a prize, to divide it into two portions, first, the Admiral's share, and next our own. We then buried the money in a sand-bank, in order that it might not be in our possession; and, as opportunity occurred, it was afterwards taken up, the

Admiral's share being transmitted to him, our share was then distributed at the capstan, in the usual proportions. As I never made any secret of my own transactions, the Maltese officials regarded me with perfect hatred; they, no doubt, honestly believing that by appropriating our own captures to our own use, we were cheating them out of what they had more right to than ourselves! By their practices they appeared to entertain one idea only, viz that officers were appointed to ships of war for the sole purpose of enriching them!

With time on his hands at the beginning of 1811, Cochrane decided to see for himself how the system worked, and set aboard his yacht, the *Julie*, on his unlikeliest mission yet. Arriving in Valleta he asked for documentation of all the prizes he had won in his Mediterranean campaigns aboard the *Speedy* and the *Imperieuse*. The prize court was unable to provide him with any.

Turning up at the court one day he demanded of an official, the judge advocate, Mr Moncrieff, to see the table of fees, which by act of parliament should have been on public display. On being told that no such document existed, he prowled about trying to find it, the protesting Moncrieff in tow. Suddenly inconvenienced, he had to use the judge's lavatory, where he saw the table of fees pinned up behind the door. Taking it down, he brushed Moncrieff aside as he left the court, and hurried off to give it to a naval friend leaving for Sicily.

On learning what had happened, the session judge ordered Cochrane's arrest for insulting the court. The marshal who had to enforce this was called Mr Jackson, into whose hands was delivered any prize ship on arrival in Malta, and whose job was to deliver this into the custody of the proctor of the court. The two men each charged substantial fees for this nominal procedure (about £2000 in today's terms), which involved preparing legal documents for one another.

To Cochrane's astonishment, he discovered that Jackson was also the proctor, while the deputy martial was also the deputy proctor, as well as the deputy auctioneer. Thus these men were engaged in a large and elaborate scam, charging colossal fees for legal niceties – often from the same man to himself! By the time these huge exactions had been made, and the standard 5 per cent on prize money had been levied, there was often little left for the capturing crew.

Cochrane told Jackson that as his tenure of both offices was illegal, he had no authority to arrest him. He said the same to his deputy, a man called Chapman. The judge ordered another man to arrest Cochrane, who had kept the officers of the fleet in Malta fully informed about his antics. Eventually this official arrived at the naval commissioner's office which was full of officers. They watched with high amusement as Cochrane refused the parole he was offered and insisted on being taken to the town jail. When asked to come, Cochrane replied: 'No, I will be no party to an illegal imprisonment of myself. If you want me to go to gaol, you must carry me by force, for assuredly I will not walk.'

At length a group of Maltese soldiers arrived to carry Cochrane from his chair to a carriage. Being escorted to reasonably comfortable rooms on the top floor of the jail, the jailer asked him what he would like for dinner. He replied: 'I have been placed here on an illegal warrant, and I will not pay for so much as a crust; so that if I am starved to death, the Admiralty court will have to answer for it.'

It was decided to sidestep this by supplying him at the prize court's expense from a nearby inn. Cochrane immediately set up a dinner table to entertain his naval officer friends:

At what cost to the Admiralty court I never learned nor enquired; but from the character of our entertainment the bill when presented must have been almost as extensive as their own fees. All my friends in the squadron present at Malta were invited by turns, and assuredly had no wardroom fare. They appeared to enjoy themselves the more heartily as avenging their own wrongs at the expense of their plunderers.

Cochrane insisted on being tried in court, but once there

denounced the proceedings as illegal. All of Malta was agog by now at this remarkable public display. Ordinary seamen were getting restive, threatening to sack the jail to get their hero out. The officers of the fleet decided that matters were getting out of hand. Captain Rodney was dispatched to tell Cochrane: 'The seamen are getting savage, and if you are not out soon they will pull the gaol down, which will get the naval force into a scrape. Have you any objection to making your escape?'

Cochrane agreed, and over a three-day period the bars on his window were filed away.

> I worked the bars, the marks being concealed in the day-time by filling up the holes with a composition. When all was in readiness, my friends and I held our last symposium at the expense of the Admiralty Court. The gaoler was purposely made very tipsy, to which he was nothing loth; and about midnight, having first lowered my bedding into the streets, to be carried off by some seaman under the direction of my servant, I passed a double rope round an iron bar, let myself down from the three-storey window, pulled the rope after me, so that nothing might remain to excite suspicion, and bade adieu to the merriest prison in which a seaman was ever incarcerated.

Cochrane was taken to the port and rowed away aboard a gig to a packet ship waiting to depart for England. Arriving there, he delivered a sparkling parliamentary performance exposing the scandal, to uproarious merriment on both sides of the house:

> This proctor acts in the double capacity of proctor and marshal, and in the former capacity fees himself for consulting and instructing himself as counsel, jury and judge, which he himself represents in the character of marshal; so that all those fees are for himself in the one character, and paid to the same himself in the other.

He unrolled the bill of charges in a single case along the floor of the House of Commons, from the bar to the Speaker's table. Lord Eldon, the Lord Chancellor and persecutor of Cobbett, icily remarked that Cochrane's speech was 'a species of mummery never before witnessed within these walls, and altogether unbecoming the gravity of that branch of the legislature'. The establishment was not amused.

Was this whole performance no more than undignified, childish buffoonery and jolly japes, detracting from Cochrane's reputation as a great seaman and passionate parliamentarian, as his enemies suggested? It was certainly done in a spirit of fun and ridicule that incensed the hard old political figures of the time. But it was also an immensely serious matter – an exposure of outrageous practices: brave men were bring stripped of their just deserts by the practices of minor officials that were little short of criminal.

An even more serious injustice espoused by Cochrane was the pay and conditions of ordinary seamen. In this he could not be accused of self-interest. In another fine speech to the House he complained of the way men were denied their inadequate pay – which was given to them only on their return to England – and had to suffer years of absence abroad. He declared:

> I have in my hands a list of ships of war in the East Indies. The *Centurion* has been there eleven years, the *Rattlesnake* fourteen years, came home the other day with only one man of the first crew. Not one farthing of pay has been given all that period to all those men. I have made a calculation on the *Fox* frigate, and supposing only one hundred of the men returned, there would be due to the crew £25,000, not including the officers.
>
> What has become of these sums all the while? The interest ought to be accounted for to government or to the seamen themselves. The *Wilhelmina* has been ten years, the *Russell* seven years, the *Drake* six years – of which the men will be exiles from England for ever – and another vessel four years . . . The seamen from want of their pay, have no means

of getting many necessaries of the utmost consequence to their health and comfort.

He was one of the very first to fight for the conditions of the crew below decks: for a serving naval captain to do so was unprecedented and outrageous in the eyes of an Admiralty determined to preserve discipline and the status of an ordinary seaman as something beneath that of a normal human being. The First Lord of the Admiralty, Charles Yorke, responded with lofty disdain.

Cochrane soon found another cause utterly devoid of self-interest to him or anyone else, which caused him to lose support and votes among his fellow countrymen, but was a matter of simple humanity. He visited Dartmoor, where one of the eight British prisoner-of-war camps was located, but was prevented from entering and spent hours observing the conditions inside from the top of a nearby hill. He reported back to the House:

> The health of the prisoners has suffered by exposure to heavy rains whilst standing in an open space for several hours receiving provisions issued at a single door; the cooking-room being several hundred yards from the prison, which now contains six thousand prisoners divided into messes of six . . . Consequently one thousand are soaked through in the morning, attending to their breakfast, and one thousand more at dinner. Thus a third are consequently wet, many without change of clothes.

It was these speeches that must excite the greatest admiration of outsiders for the man's idealism. For the time, these were issues of the utmost unconcern not just for the government, but for the vast majority of Britons. He stood to gain nothing except enemies by raising them. None of these people had the vote; the plight of the common seaman was of rather less interest to most middle-class Englishmen than that of their own servants; the plight of foreigners who had recently been fighting Englishmen rather less so. Cochrane was one of Britain's great naval heroes.

The idea widely propounded by his enemies, that he was a self-interested buffoon, finds no echo in the selflessness with which he championed the unpopular causes of those years. No other great hero of British history fought for the interests of his own subordinates, and even his enemies, in the way Cochrane did.

Cochrane as a human being remained an elusive personality. The descriptions we have suggest that to meet he was a quiet and even gentle person, a dreamy intellectual in stark contrast with the professional reality of him as a man of action in battle or controversy in parliament. He was certainly outspoken in private company and impressed some as a fool. There was indeed a certain ingenuousness and naïvety in him as a personality; but it is impossible to conclude that a man of his resourcefulness and inventiveness was dull-witted. Rather he had something of the genius in him, and like many such men he did not wish to put down people of lesser intelligence or rush in with glib ideas.

One of the most notable aspects about the young Cochrane was the lack of sexual interest ascribed to him even by his enemies. While almost all of Cochrane's fellow officers saw it as a test of manhood to pursue girls or visit prostitutes without a second thought, there are no rumours or even accusations of sexual indulgence on the part of the Sea Wolf. As with alcohol, he was remarkably abstemious for a man who was now in his mid-thirties. This can be ascribed perhaps to his philosophical bent and natural high-mindedness – which had also led him to take up the cause of the oppressed. He was a Gambier without the hypocrisy of the tracts. He seemed almost above passion – another paradox. When he decided he was wealthy enough to get married and start a family, it was done with the sort of abruptness that characterised all his decision-making.

During that period, enjoying the fruits of his prize money, he divided his time between a house he had bought near Southampton and his Uncle Basil's sumptuous house in Portman Square, London. Cochrane had only come to know this uncle some five years previously, and the two instantly became friends.

Basil had made a fortune working for the East India Company in Madras, and on his return had come to the rescue of the young man's indebted father, as well as buying an estate for himself in Scotland.

Unlike his nephew, he was no sexual abstainer, fathering several children by different mothers in India and becoming the subject of an embarrassing blackmail attempt by a girl he had seduced who alleged that he had tried to have her baby aborted by inviting her into his exotic Turkish bath – one of the first of its kind – in Portman Square. The story came out, and the blackmailers were convicted.

Portman Square provided an ideal base for Cochrane, the parliamentarian, and Uncle Basil, as well as taking him in, hatched dynastic ambitions for the famous young man. Basil decided to restore the fortunes of the great but impoverished Dundonald earldom by settling a large part of his fortune on Cochrane. There was a condition attached. He must marry one of the richest young women in the land, becoming the mainstay of a wealthy and thriving family once again. Cochrane was heir to a great title, was Britain's greatest living naval hero, was young, still vigorous and, although he had put on weight, was tall, ginger-haired and good-looking, his striking Roman nose accentuated by the damage done at Fort Trinidad.

Basil, like some Middle Eastern potentate or grey-haired dowager, decided upon a suitable bride – the daughter of an official at the Admiralty court who had become hugely wealthy through the very practices that Cochrane had campaigned against for so many years. The two men had a blazing row, with Cochrane insisting that to marry such a girl would make him a national joke. Basil Cochrane remarked: 'Please yourself. Nevertheless my fortune and the money of the wife I have chosen for you would go far towards reinstating future earls of Dundonald in their ancient position as regards wealth.'

However embroidered Cochrane's later account of the matter, it showed that his celebrated drive for riches was subordinated to the romantic streak in his nature, particularly in the matter of love. Basil's choice was extraordinarily inappropriate –

for the thirty-five-year-old Cochrane to have had an arranged marriage of the kind common in the Indies, but which in early nineteenth-century Britain was a thing of the past, would indeed have made him look ridiculous.

Furthermore, Uncle Basil did not know that Cochrane had already secretly been smitten. Worse, the object of his attentions was an utterly unsuitable sixteen-year-old schoolgirl less than half Cochrane's age of comparatively humble origin, who almost certainly had been born out of wedlock. It was believed he had met her on a chance encounter in Hyde Park as she walked in a crocodile of schoolgirls. None of this mattered at all to Cochrane, with his customary disregard for the opinions of others.

She was small, slim and well-proportioned, with a pretty snub-nose, a pert, rosebud mouth and a diminutive but well-shaped chin. Her eyes were large, dark, pretty and vivacious. Her hair fell in fashionable curls. She exuded self-possession even at her tender age. She was, in short, a remarkable beauty.

It may be assumed that she was enormously flattered by the attentions of this distinguished, handsome, national hero, and did nothing to discourage them. To her he must have seemed a godsend; a passport to escape what until than had been a miserable life. Her name was Katherine Barnes, the daughter of a Midlands businessman and a Spanish dancer and she had been brought up as an orphan by a respectable man, John Simpson, of Portland Place. She was a deeply unhappy child. Later she wrote: 'How much more happy should I have been had I been brought up under the affectionate eyes of a fond mother, rather than by relations who only felt for me in the moment of childhood and left me to support in ignorance and poverty my growing years.' Cochrane had a gentle social charm that masked the fact that he was not entirely at ease with the opposite sex. Perhaps her very enthusiasm and youth made relations easy from the beginning. Without Basil's knowledge, the two courted in secret.

Like so much in Cochrane's life, the relationship was implausible and romantic. Cochrane was besotted with her, while she was to prove every bit his match in passion, strength of character, courage and devotion. The differences in their two characters were to emerge only a decade later, perhaps rendered inevitable by the age gap, which eventually created a vast change in their interests. For the moment their passion was one.

When Cochrane was ill Katherine would peek in at his Portman Square home, unobserved by the matronly Uncle Basil, to encourage his recovery. He dubbed her 'Mouse'. On 6 August the couple eloped to the Queensbury Arms in Annan, Scotland, for a civil wedding in the presence of two servants. Exhausted by the long journey, she asked him, surprised by the brief, legalistic form of the ceremony, 'Is this the way you marry in Scotland?' Alarmingly, Cochrane danced a sailor's hornpipe around her, proclaiming, 'Now you are mine, Mouse, mine for ever.'

He soon reverted to less romantic mode and told her he must leave at once for his Uncle Basil's wedding. The poor, exhausted, love-intoxicated schoolgirl thus spent her wedding night alone in a dingy inn room with no bath. Happiness, it seemed, was still a little way away for the bewildered orphan. When she returned to London in his wake, they kept the wedding secret at first and continued to live apart.

Cochrane's dash to his uncle had been in vain. When the latter found out, Cochrane was disinherited. Thomas had disappointed Basil's hopes of an illustrious and wealthy regeneration of the Cochrane family. Basil and the Earl of Dundonald, Cochrane's father, were so furious that they went to the Prime Minister, the Earl of Liverpool, to denounce the marriage between the heir of one of the greatest titles in Scotland and a penniless bastard waif. There was nothing to be done. Cochrane later recorded philosophically: 'I did not inherit a shilling of my uncle's wealth, for which loss however I had a rich equivalent in the acquisition of a wife whom no wealth could have purchased.'

Cochrane's romantic interlude and his intense political activities had not stopped him thinking about naval matters. He was now to display a genius, that some thought bordered on madness, for anticipating subsequent developments in military technology. The corpulent Prince Regent had been bemused to receive, earlier, in the year a 'Plan for the Destruction of the Naval Power of France' addressed to him by the famous captain. It contained two proposals.

First, to employ three or four old hulks and place iron embedded in clay in their bottom; the sides would be reinforced with timber. Above this would be a layer of 2000 barrels of gunpowder and, above that, wadding, supporting a huge layer of armaments; some 15,000 shells and 5000 incendiary shells and hundreds of grenades. These 'explosion ships' – his old idea on a vastly larger and more elaborate scale – or 'temporary mortars' would act as nothing less than a giant cannon barrel, with the reinforced bottom and sides directing the colossal explosive mix to rain massive bombardment upon the enemy.

They were to be brought to a position close to such enemy strongholds as Flushing and Cherbourg at night, tilted, through shifting their ballast, to the appropriate angle and fired. The idea was that in place of the ineffectual long-range bombardment of these ports from the sea, with short-range bombardment being hazardous and futile because ship's guns could not fire over the massive reinforced walls, the whole deadly rain of missiles could be fired over the top of the fortification.

His second idea was for what he graphically labelled after-wards 'stink vessels' or 'sulphur ships'. These would consist of ships whose bottoms were similarly reinforced with beds of clay. There would be gaps in these to allow air to circulate to aid combustion at a carefully predetermined rate. Above these would be laid a poisonous sulphur compound. Cochrane argued: 'All fortification, especially marine fortifications, can under cover of dense smoke be irresistibly subdued by fumes of sulphur kindled in masses to windward of their ramparts.' If the Spaniards had actually used such methods against Gibraltar, they would have won, he claimed: 'For the volumes of noxious effluvia, evolved from masses of sulphur and charcoal, burning close to the lines, and driven by the wind into the interior of the place, would have destroyed every animal function, until the walls would have been in ruins.'

Cochrane had invented poison gas warfare, nearly a hundred years before it was put to real use in the First World War.

Neither idea was dismissed by officialdom, in spite of its grudge against Cochrane. Instead a secret committee was set up to consider the proposals under the commander-in-chief, the Duke of York, and including Cochrane's old C-in-C, Admiral Keith, as well as William Congreve, who had tested his rockets at the Battle of Aix Roads. Congreve pronounced favourably on the ideas from a scientific viewpoint, while Keith was dubious because of the military dangers, in particular sudden shifts in winds and tides which could affect the tilt of the explosion vessels, and the direction of the poison gas. But he urged a trial run at Toulon. The British commander there, Lord Exmouth, was however doubtful and Cochrane vigorously opposed giving the secret away except in a major attack.

The main objection was raised by Sir Arthur Wellesley, who argued that the other side might retaliate in kind. There was also immense squeamishness about the use of such inhuman weapons in an age which still retained some notion of chivalry in battle. Cochrane was not so sentimental. In terms which still resonate in a nuclear age, he argued:

No conduct that brought to a speedy termination a war which might otherwise last for years, and be attended by terrible bloodshed in numerous battles, could be called inhuman . . . The most powerful means of averting all future war would be the introduction of a method of fighting which, rendering all vigorous defence impossible, would frighten every nation from running the risk of warfare at all.

After a few months his ideas were shelved. Cochrane was bitterly disappointed: but the episode shed further light on his extraordinary character. This defender of the rights of ordinary seamen and French prisoners appeared inhumanly to favour weapons of mass bombardment and poisonous gas. Yet to him the rationale was simple. It was more inhuman to prolong a war by not using them. Although a champion of humanity, he was businesslike and unsentimental about winning war as fast and decisively as possible.

At least, though, Cochrane was still being taken seriously by the Navy. Having turned down an offer to go and win prizes in the Mediterranean, which he regarded as insulting and an attempt to get him out of the country, he also applied his inventive mind to more peaceful projects such as trying to develop his father's idea for a new gas lamp in the streets, as well as seeking to revive his old ideas for convoy lamps.

Early in 1814 it seemed his naval career was to be rescued by a respectable offer from the Admiralty at last: to act as captain aboard the flagship of his uncle, Sir Alexander Cochrane, in North America, which was now at war with Britain. After nearly five years' absence Cochrane was to experience the heady rush of command of one of the greatest ships in the Royal Navy.

Sir Alexander decided to go on ahead to take up his command of the British fleet, while Thomas was to prepare the ship, the massive 80-gun *Tonnant* and take it across the Atlantic to join him. It was a magnificent prospect of action in a new theatre and showed that however many enemies Cochrane possessed in the Admiralty, there were still friends who looked on him with admiration as a great fighter. A successful tour could only foreshadow his appointment as admiral. Five years' exile from the sea had been deemed enough punishment for his behaviour after Aix Roads. Cochrane reckoned without the deep reserves of hatred towards him that still lingered in some sections of Horse Guards Parade, and among the governing political diehards he had so offended.

At a dinner to discuss preparations before Sir Alexander's departure, Cochrane was introduced to an officer of mixed German-French origins improbably called Captain Random de Berenger, apparently a baron deposed by the French Revolution. De Berenger enjoyed the patronage of one of the highest, if not most reputable, military dandies in the land, Lord Yarmouth, son of the Prince Regent's current mistress.

Sir Alexander was concerned that American naval tactics included the use of sharpshooters firing down from the masts and spars onto the enemy's decks, and was contemplating employing his own. De Berenger had applied to go as an instructor – he had been a former adjutant in Lord Yarmouth's regiment of sharpshooters.

De Berenger was a formidably ugly man, with a parrot's nose, indented mouth and protruding chin, and a manner that did not impress Cochrane, who replied to his later pleas with pointed lack of warmth, but he said he would consider taking him on board. He also met De Berenger for lunch at the home of his uncle Basil, with whom he was still living, in spite of their quarrel. Meanwhile Cochrane supplemented his preparations for the *Tonnant* and his work on his new inventions with a new experiment – a little tentative dabbling on the nascent London Stock Exchange.

Cochrane had been persuaded to do so by the pay clerk at Portsmouth, Richard Butt, an astute money-man whose brokerage had by February 1814 yielded Cochrane the comfortable, if hardly enormous, dividend of nearly £5000. This was undoubtedly pleasing to Cochrane, but his mind was occupied with many other things, in particular the news that Kitty – as she was nicknamed – was expecting a baby. Accordingly Cochrane had just taken a house at 13 Green Street, near Grosvenor Square, and proposed to move there from his uncle's house, where relations were still strained. It was a profoundly exciting moment in both his professional and personal life.

CHAPTER 12

The Stock Exchange Fraud

A little after midnight on Sunday, 20 February 1814, a man wearing a vivid scarlet jacket – the uniform of a senior officer of the general staff – covered by a grey coat, was found hammering at the door of an inn in Dover. He was welcomed into the one opposite, the Ship, and revealed that he was Lieutenant-Colonel du Bourg, aide-de-camp to the British ambassador in Russia, who had just been discreetly landed by a French cargo boat. He composed the following letter to the port admiral at Deal:

> Sir, – I have the honour to acquaint you that the *Aigle* from Calais, Pierre Duquin, Master, has this moment landed me near Dover to proceed to the capital with despatches of the happiest nature. My anxiety will not allow me to say more for your gratification than that the Allies obtained a final victory; that Bonaparte was overtaken by a party of Sachen's cossacks who immediately slayed him, and divided his body between them. General Platoff saved Paris from being reduced to ashes. The Allied sovereigns are there, and the white cockade is universal; an immediate peace is certain. In the utmost haste, I entreat your consideration and have the honour to be, Sir,
>
> Your most obedient humble Servant, R. du Bourg
> Lt-Colonel and Aide-de-Camp to Lord Cathcart

He had a boy take the message to Admiral Foley and then set off at speed in a chaise-and-four to London. Foley, awoken in the early hours, sought confirmation of this astonishing news.

Nevertheless he proposed to telegraph it to London, although a thick fog at daybreak prevented this.

It was momentous news. The war in Europe had been seesawing backwards and forwards. Napoleon had been forced back into eastern France, but had counter-attacked with extraordinary vigour. The Emperor had nearly been killed by a patrol of Cossacks on 29 January, and the general expectation was that the allies were close to victory. Now these hopes seemed confounded – until du Bourg had brought his startling news. The officer, meanwhile, on his arrival in London, had switched from a post-chaise to a common hackney carriage in Lambeth and drove to Grosvenor Square. Rumours were already spreading around the capital of a decisive victory over the French.

At midday a coach decorated with laurels containing three French loyalist officers wearing the white cockades of the House of Bourbon in their hats clattered over London Bridge into the heart of the City, down Lombard Street and back over Blackfriars Bridge, the officers tossing out papers inscribed, 'Vive le Roi! Vivent les Bourbons!'. It seemed that a great victory had indeed been achieved, although this was still subject to official confirmation from the Admiralty.

The City at the time was in the early stages of its development as a Stock Market. Among the most recent innovations was a technically illegal form of transaction which today would be called margin trading. A stock called Omnium was a principle vehicle for this. It was possible for speculators to buy this volatile stock and sell quickly enough to make a profit while not actually having had to put up the money for their purchase. Unsurprisingly, this was much favoured by those who lacked sufficient funds to buy large amounts of stock.

This was not the case for Cochrane, whose adviser Butt had urged him to buy Omnium. Cochrane had put up some £36,000 to buy stock valued at 28¼ of its normal value of £139,000, but Omnium stock had fallen to 26½ by the time the Stock Exchange opened that Monday morning. Cochrane had left a standing instruction with Butt to sell his stock when it rose by only 1 per cent over its price of purchase, which would have given him a modest profit of around £2000 – an understandable attitude for a cautious beginner.

Cochrane was anyway not that interested in the market. Among other things this would pay for the wine bill for the *Tonnant*, which would cost more than £1000 including nearly 1500 bottles of wine, 120 bottles of claret, 720 bottles of vidonia, 650 bottles of vintage port, 240 gallons of ordinary port and 218 gallons of Madeira. But Cochrane, that fateful Monday morning, seemed more likely to make a small loss than a profit on his investment.

Two other men he knew were in a much more exposed position. Butt, Cochrane's broker, had just purchased some £224,000 of Omnium stock and £168,000 work of consoles. Andrew Cochrane-Johnstone, eight years older than his nephew, had just bought a whopping £410,000 worth of Omnium and £100,000 worth of consoles. Neither man possessed the money for the purchase – they were buying on the margin, and the value of the stock had just gone down. They would be legally obliged to put up the entire sum on 23 February or sell at a loss which Cochrane-Johnstone at least, who stood to lose about £5000 on the price that Monday morning, could not afford to do.

Cochrane-Johnstone was the black sheep of the Cochrane family. Showing promise initially, he had joined the army, rising to the position of colonel in 1797. Appointed governor of Dominica, he quickly acquired a reputation for dishonesty and exploitation that became a byword in the West Indies. He also had lucrative interests in the slave trade, and built himself a harem of local girls. In 1803 his name had become so notorious that he was prosecuted for corruption by the government, but he had tried unsuccessfully to shift the blame to his immediate deputy. Even so he narrowly escaped censure and had returned under a cloud to Britain, where he quickly dissipated his fortune.

However, he enjoyed the friendship and admiration of his nephew, whom he had been instrumental in persuading to stand for his first parliamentary seat at Honiton. Cochrane-Johnstone was now in serious financial difficulties and had managed to stay out of the debtors' prison because he represented the rotten borough of Grampound. He had recently become a close friend of the same de Berenger whom Cochrane had met a couple of times at the houses of his uncles Alexander and Basil. De Berenger had something in common with this most roguish of the Cochranes: financial insolvency, which meant he had to reside on parole 'within the bounds of King's bench', lodging with a family which stood surety for him.

The rumours of Napoleon's defeat quickly permeated the City, which then as now was gullible and volatile to a fault. The price of Omnium started to climb as speculators moved in. By noon it had risen from 26½ to 30¼. It fell back slightly in the absence of official confirmation, but with the appearance of the coachload of French royalist officers it rose to 32. As the afternoon progressed, it became apparent that the rumours were false, and the stock fell back to the 26½ at which it had started. Both Cochrane-Johnstone and Butt managed to sell at just the right time. Butt, however, obeying the standing instruction from Cochrane, had sold his shares when they rose just 1 per cent over the original purchase value, netting him his modest £2000.

Cochrane himself was apparently unaware of the excitement that morning. He had breakfasted with Cochrane-Johnstone and Butt, then dropped them off at the Stock Exchange before going on to the factory where he was developing his two lamps at Cock Lane. After about three-quarters of an hour his footman, Thomas Dewman, arrived with a message. An army officer had arrived at Cochrane's new house in Green Street with urgent news. He believed this concerned one of his brothers, who was seriously ill on the Peninsular campaign.

Returning home Cochrane was annoyed to discover that the officer was de Berenger, whom he knew slightly and disliked, in a high state of agitation, asking to be taken aboard the *Tonnant* so as to flee creditors' demands for £8000. Cochrane replied that he could not take him on board without Admiralty permission – tantamount to a refusal, as this was unlikely to be given.

De Berenger altered his request: he asked to be allowed a change of clothing. He was wearing his green sharpshooter's uniform from Lord Yarmouth's regiment, for the purpose of absconding aboard ship, and if he was seen in it, he said, he would be suspected by his parole-keepers of trying to flee, his privileges would be withdrawn and he would be imprisoned. Cochrane took pity on him and gave him a long greatcoat to wear. Cochrane described the crucial meeting in his affidavit a fortnight later:

> I hastened back, and I found Captain Berenger, who, in great seeming uneasiness made many apologies for the freedom he had used, which nothing but the distressed state of his mind, arising from difficulties, could have induced him to do. All his prospects, he said, had failed, and his last hope had vanished of obtaining an appointment in America. He was unpleasantly circumstanced on account of a sum which he could not pay, and if he could, that others would fall upon him for the full £8000. He had no hope of benefiting his creditors in his present situation, or of assisting himself. That if I would take him with me he would immediately go on board and exercise the sharpshooters (which plan Sir Alexander Cochrane, I knew, had approved of). That he had left his lodgings and prepared himself in the best way his means allowed. He had brought the sword with him which had been his father's, and to that, and to Sir Alexander, he would trust for obtaining an honourable appointment.
>
> I felt very uneasy at the distress he was in, and knowing him to be a man of great talent and science, I told him I would do everything in my power to relieve him, but as to his going immediately to the *Tonnant*, with any comfort to himself, it was quite impossible. My cabin was without furniture; I had not even a servant on board. He said he would willingly mess anywhere. I told him that the wardroom was already crowded and besides I could not with propriety take him, he being a foreigner without leave from the Admiralty.
>
> He seemed greatly hurt at this, and recalled certificates

which he had formerly shown me from persons in official situations. Lord Yarmouth, General Jenkinson and Mr Reeves, I think, were amongst the number. I recommended him to use his endeavour to get them or any other friends, to exert their influence, for I had none, adding that when the *Tonnant* went to Portsmouth I should be happy to receive him. I knew from Sir Alexander Cochrane that he would be pleased if he accomplished that object.

Captain Berenger said that not anticipating any objection on my part from the conversation he had formerly had with me, he had come away with the intention to go on board and make himself useful in his military capacity; he could not go to Lord Yarmouth or any other of his friends in this dress, alluding to that which he had on, or return to his lodgings where it would excite suspicion (as he was at the time in the rules of the King's Bench), but that if I refused to let him join the ship now he would do so at Portsmouth. Under present circumstances, however, he must use a great liberty, and request the favour of me to lend him a hat to wear instead of his military cap.

I gave him one which was in a back room with some things that had not been packed up, and having tried it on, his uniform appeared under his greatcoat; I therefore offered him a black coat that was laying on a chair, and which I did not intend to take with me. He put up his uniform in a towel and shortly afterwards went away in great apparent uneasiness of mind; and having asked my leave he took the coach I came in and which I had forgotten to discharge in the haste I was in. I do further depose that the above conversation is the substance of all that passed with Capt. Berenger, which, from the circumstances attending it, was strongly impressed upon my mind, that no other person in uniform was seen by me at my house on Monday, the 21st of February, though possibly other officers may have called (as many have done since my appointment); of this, however, I cannot speak of my own knowledge, having been almost constantly from home arranging my private affairs.

Later the same day it became apparent that the City had been the object of a spectacular hoax. In some ways it was laughable, a prank of the highest daring. But innocent interests had been duped and the exiled King of France, Louis XVIII, had even celebrated with neighbours, inviting them to France and pouring out white wine. *The Times* thundered:

> Great exertions will, no doubt, be made by the frequenters of the Stock Exchange to detect the criminal ... If his person should be recognised he will probably be willing to save himself from the whipping-post by consigning his employers to the pillory, an exaltation which they richly merit . . .

As Cochrane later remarked:

> The wrong was not then, and still is not, on the statute-book. Such a case had never been tried before, nor has it since – and was termed a 'conspiracy'; or rather, by charging the several defendants – of most of whom I had never before heard – in one indictment, it was brought under the designation of a 'conspiracy'. The 'conspiracy' – such as it was – was nevertheless one, which, as competent persons inform me, has been the practice in all countries ever since stock-jobbing began, and is in the present day constantly practised, but I have never heard mention of the energy of the Stock Exchange even to detect the practice.

The Stock Exchange, now something of a laughing stock, decided to vindicate its reputation by setting up an inquiry. The exorbitant profits made by Cochrane-Johnstone and Butt soon came to light and, not unreasonably, the small profit made by Cochrane, the nephew of one and business associate of the other, was duly noted, as were the takings of two wine merchants, Holloway and Sandom, and one Alexander McRae.

As early as 4 March the committee had leaked to the press that the bogus du Bourg had taken the hackney carriage from Lambeth to 13 Green Street. They had also discovered that du

Bourg was none other than Random de Berenger. Astonishingly, it seemed that the bloody footprints led to Cochrane's door. With rumours buzzing round London, his friend William Cobbett, no doubt at Cochrane's prompting, sprang to his defence in the *Weekly Register* of 21 March:

> Under no wild democracy, under no military despotism, under no hypocritical or cunning oligarchy, under no hellish tyranny upheld by superstition, was there ever committed an act more unjust or more foul than that which has during the last three weeks been committed in the City of London, through the means of the press against these three gentlemen.

Cochrane had already travelled up to London on 10 March to swear his affidavit: he clearly understood the gravity of the allegations. His old enemy Croker had written to him to say that the Admiralty required further explanations of the events surrounding the Stock Exchange scandal and was appointing a temporary captain to the *Tonnant*. Cochrane was furious, rightly interpreting this as a virtual presumption of guilt. In reply Croker wrote silkily:

> Your lordship states that as the case now stands, their lordships have virtually given judgment on ex parte evidence and superseded you in the command of your ship. Now my lords had hoped that your lordship would have been sensible that so far from giving judgment and superseding you in the command of the *Tonnant*, my lords had treated your lordship with all possible attention and delicacy; your lordship had leave of absence granted to you on the application of a near relative, to enable your lordship to come, if you should choose to do so, to town for the purpose of taking such measures as you might think proper on the subject of the Stock Exchange report but as his Majesty's service could not be permitted to stand still on account of your lordship's absence from the ship, an acting captain was appointed to her, and the choice of the officer so to be appointed was left to your lordship.

Cochrane's enemies had spotted their chance: they were closing in.

He took affidavits from his servants on the vital matter of what de Berenger had been wearing when he came to Green Street. Although Cochrane, if innocent, could not have known about the arrival of du Bourg in the scarlet uniform of a staff officer in London that morning, if a humble sharpshooter like de Berenger had been wearing one, his suspicions should instantly have been aroused. Thomas Dewman, his footman, swore that, 'The officer who sent me to the city wore a grey regimental coat buttoned up; I saw a green collar underneath it; he had a black silk stock or handkerchief round his neck; he was of middle size and of rather a dark complexion.' A former black servant present in the kitchen called Davis stated that, 'he had on a grey great coat, buttoned, and a green collar under it. I knew him having seen him when his Lordship lived in Park Street.' Mary Turpin, another servant swore that, 'The said officer had on a great coat and a sword, and that his under-coat or his great coat had a green collar to it.'

This seems overwhelming evidence. But the prosecution was quick to point out that they all referred to the collar – which might have been of a different colour to the tunic itself. Dewman, who was subsequently examined by the defence on the matter at the trial, was not asked about the colour of the tunic. Davis, remarkably, found employment with the Navy and departed aboard ship before the trial began – which suggested that the Admiralty, or possibly one of Cochrane's naval colleagues, for opposite reasons, was keen to spirit him away.

It was later alleged that Cochrane had struck out a statement by Turpin saying that de Berenger had been wearing a red tunic under his coat – although this may have been a simple mistake by the defence lawyers. There is a real mystery about this, and it is possible that Cochrane, being the aloof and sometimes unworldly person he was, simply failed to notice, or give any importance to, what de Berenger was wearing, which a more narrow and punctilious officer immediately would have; then, realizing this was a potentially fatal flaw in his case, he may have covered up. The prosecution was able to cast doubt on the veracity of servants of long service and loyalty to the Cochranes.

Dramatic developments followed. On 24 March a bundle of clothes was dredged up in the Thames by Old Swan Steps, which were clearly the scarlet uniform worn by de Berenger, now cut into pieces. On 8 April de Berenger was arrested at Leith, waiting to take ship to Holland. He had been traced by banknotes he used, some of which originated in a payment Cochrane had made to Butt. The notes were of small denomination, although Cochrane had given Butt easily identifiable ones of £200 or more for a share transaction. It was alleged that this was an early form of money-laundering, to disguise the origin of the payments. It was remarkable, indeed suspicious, that de Berenger had stayed so long in the country and made no attempt to flee abroad sooner in the nearly seven weeks he had been on the run. On 27 April Cochrane was indicted, along with Cochrane-Johnstone, Butt, de Berenger, and the three who had dressed as French officers, as the conspirators behind the Stock Exchange fraud.

Cochrane's indictment had probably been inevitable from the beginning. There was too much circumstantial evidence against him. He had, most damningly, met de Berenger and provided him with a change of clothes on the morning of the fraud. He had breakfasted with his two alleged co-conspirators, Cochrane-Johnstone and Butt, the same day. All three had made money in Omnium stock as a result of the fraud. His money had found its way into de Berenger's pocket, albeit indirectly, via Butt.

Yet under closer scrutiny the case against him disintegrated. If Cochrane had been a party to the fraud, why had he not revised his long-standing instructions to Butt to sell his Omnium shares once they had risen only 1 per cent above their purchase price, when he stood to gain far more in the speculative frenzy after the news of Napoleon's death had reached London – as, in fact, Cochrane-Johnstone and Butt did?

Why did Cochrane need this relatively small amount of money when by all accounts he was reasonably off and had bought his stock not on the margin, as his business partners had, risking exposure and ruin, but legitimately with funds in his possession. Cochrane stood to lose little even in the event of a fall in price; the others stood to be ruined.

Why did Cochrane agree to return to meet de Berenger at his house when he must have known this would implicate him devastatingly in the plot? By what insane oversight had Cochrane allowed de Berenger to think of coming to his house in full view of witnesses in the first place? Surely if Cochrane had been implicated he would have arranged for de Berenger to meet him anywhere but there – even if it had been necessary for the two to meet at all on the day of the crime? The fact that Cochrane was not there to meet him suggests that this was no part of a prearranged plan.

Would Cochrane really have indulged in a hoax involving sending a famous admiral false news – news which could have lulled the Dover port authorities into a sense of false security – given Cochrane's astonishing record of commitment to his country, bravery and loyalty to the navy (if not to the Admiralty itself)? Moreover, Cochrane had been a tireless champion of honesty against naval corruption. Would he have stooped to such abject dishonesty, placing his entire reputation for probity at risk for the sake of a comparatively small amount of money? He had just spurned two fortunes – those of his uncle and the rich girl he was intended to marry – so as to wed the penniless orphan he loved. Would so high-minded and other-worldly a man stoop to crime to make a small amount of money which he did not need?

Cochrane had just been given the opportunity to resume the naval career he so relished in a highly distinguished post after nearly five years' frustration on land. To engage in a madcap scheme of this kind as he went about his preparations to depart for North America would suggest he was almost deranged. He was happily married, relatively prosperous, and about to take up his most challenging captaincy yet. Cochrane may have been headstrong, but he was certainly not insane, and he was always fiercely protective of his honesty and reputation. On motivation alone, his involvement in the Stock Exchange plot made no sense at all.

As for the evidence, it boiled down to four substantive points. First, he had been associated with the alleged principals – which was true, but this may have been deliberately engineered by them to try and shelter under his reputation and his acquaintance with de Berenger was slight, to say the least. Second, he had made money out of the Omnium transactions – but not much under an arrangement made long before which he would surely have altered had he been privy to the conspiracy in order to make more. Third, he had furnished the payment to de Berenger – but this had been a legal transaction with Butt, who had handed on payments in small denominations to de Berenger, and proved nothing. Fourth, and most damagingly, he had lent de Berenger a change of clothes on the morning of the crime.

In all the arguments about whether de Berenger was wearing green or red, one key point was overlooked. Why had Cochrane the temerity to lend him his own hat and coat, which he must have feared would be easily identifiable if de Berenger was apprehended, instead of merely sending him away? Surely because he genuinely believed de Berenger's hard-luck story and had no idea that he was involved in the incidents of that morning. Further, why had the latter gone to the house of the 'conspirator' he knew least well as a place of refuge, when he was on much closer terms with both Cochrane-Johnstone and Butt? Examined closely, it is much less plausible that Cochrane was part of the conspiracy than that he was a man in high places used as an innocent dupe by others.

Indeed, one can go further. It stretches credulity to believe that he was in on the plot in terms of his character, career prospects at the time, the huge respect he was held in for his integrity and fearlessness by a large part of public opinion, his devotion to the Navy (precisely the service that was to be duped under the plot) and the manner in which he behaved towards de Berenger when the latter turned up. The question remains: why did de Berenger go so obviously to Cochrane's house? The answer must await an account of the trial.

Cochrane was appalled by the Admiralty's decision not to let him sail with the *Tonnant*, which dealt a blow to the glorious revival of his naval career, but he seems to have underestimated the danger he was in and the enemies that now circled him, convinced that their prey was trapped at last. He devoted only a few meetings to preparations for the defence at his trial. He agreed to stay away from the proceedings on the advice of his defence, and, fatally, he agreed to pool his own defence with those of Cochrane-Johnstone and Butt, convinced as he was of their innocence, so that they would stand or fall together.

When it emerged that the others were indeed guilty, he was to be dragged down with them. Why he took this decision is not clear: either because he genuinely believed they were innocent or, more probably, and more in keeping with his vanity, out of misguided loyalty to his uncle. He could not conceive of the possibility that he, one of Britain's foremost national heroes and a popular parliamentarian, could be convicted, and therefore his business partners would be saved as well. It was hugely in their interests to link their fate with his, in the hope that his aura would protect them, too. It may have been their intention to make use of him in this way all along or, indeed de Berenger, in a panic because of the morning mist and the belief that he had been recognized, may simply have run to Cochrane's house that fateful morning in a desperate and misguided attempt to find refuge aboard his ship.

While Cochrane exuded the complacency of one for whom the charges were almost beneath contempt, the knives of his enemies, unsheathed for so long, were being sharpened. Croker had been the first. It was announced that Cochrane's own lawyer, who had advised him on the affair, Edward Gurney, had been appointed to lead the prosecution. The man in charge of the prosecution case was to be the official Admiralty solicitor, Germain Lavie, the very same who had acted against Cochrane on the Gambier court martial and had been responsible for producing the charts which Cochrane claimed were falsified.

The jury was selected from a panel of forty-eight city worthies selected by the Sheriff of London – not from among voters generally. Such a jury could be expected to seek to uphold the institutions of the City and, in particular, the Stock Market, whose reputation was so much at stake.

Finally, the trial judge was to be none other than Lord Ellenborough who had sent another prominent Radical, Leigh Hunt, to jail in 1812. This had been as much a *cause célèbre* as the Burdett and Cobbett imprisonments which preceded it. The offence Hunt had committed had been to write an article published by his brother John in the *Examiner* in which he had replied to a ludicrous panegyric in the *Morning Post* to the Prince Regent. For this the two brothers were sent to jail by Ellenborough for two years each and fined £500 apiece.

The establishment had unleashed its fiercest hound on Cochrane now that they believed they had him trapped. Ellenborough, as Edward Law, had made his reputation by successfully defending the ruthless if effective consolidator of British India, Warren Hastings, from impeachment. He had no time for men who challenged the settled order. As the clouds gathered over Cochrane, he had only one piece of good news. On 8 April, the eighteen-year-old Kitty gave birth to their first child, a son, called Thomas.

CHAPTER 13

The Trial

At 9 a.m. on 8 June the trial opened before the King's Bench at Guildhall. Cochrane was not present at all, on the advice of his lawyers, but also displaying a certain smugness about the outcome. Gurney launched into a vigorous presentation of the prosecution case. He argued that the three bogus royalist officers who had travelled through the centre of the City at midday were part of the same conspiracy – although the three men arrested for this crime vigorously denied any link. In fact, the prosecution had no evidence to connect the two. Gurney argued:

> That this part of the plot could have had no effect but for the foundation laid by the appearance of the pretended officer at Dover, and his journey to London, for a post-chaise coming through the City with white cockades and laurel branches, would have had no effect except to excite laughter and derision, but for preparation made by de Berenger in the character of du Bourg, and when you find for the purpose of producing the same effect, such a coincidence of plan, and such a coincidence of time, the one the basis, and the other the superstructure, although I shall not be able to prove all the parties meeting together, conferring together, consulting together, still it will be impossible to doubt that these are two parts of one whole; that this is, in short, not two conspiracies, but one and the same conspiracy.

Then he came to the tricky issue of why de Berenger should have gone without concealment to Cochrane's house, if the latter was part of the plot. Here he was on weak ground in arguing lamely that the conspirators must have slipped up:

> In settling their plan of operations, they had forgotten to provide where de Berenger should resort on his arrival in town, and on his way his heart failed him as to going to his own lodgings; he dared not enter into his own lodgings in a dress, which dress would lead to detection, and he therefore drove to Lord Cochrane's to get rid of his dress; and there he, by Lord Cochrane's assistance, did get rid of it: he procured a round hat and a black coat, and then went confidently and safely home to his lodgings . . .
>
> If Mr de Berenger was the hired agent of these persons for the purpose of committing this fraud, what would you expect? – why, that after they had used him they would pay him and send him away. I will prove to you, that they so paid him, and that they did send him away.

After questioning a number of witnesses, the prosecution's star was called, a youth called William Crane, who had driven the hackney carriage that had conveyed de Berenger to Green Street. Crane swore on oath that de Berenger had been wearing a red jacket when he arrived at Cochrane's house – in flat contradiction to the evidence of the latter and of his servants. At the time this evidence could not be contested.

After the trial, however, it emerged that a fortnight earlier Crane had been banned from driving a hackney carriage for viciously beating his horses, and two witnesses came forward to say that they had seen de Berenger enter Cochrane's house wearing green. Another witness claimed that Crane had told him, 'I will swear black is white, or anything else, if I am well paid for it' and that at one stage he claimed it was Cochrane himself whom he had carried in his cab, disguised as du Bourg. The Stock Exchange claimed to have paid just £17 towards Crane's expenses for testifying, yet shortly afterwards he had enough to pay for a new hackney cab. Some twelve years later he was sentenced to seven years' transportation for armed robbery, but he was pardoned after serving only three, which suggested he enjoyed a degree of official favour.

The word of such a man should have counted for little as a witness; but it was on the basis of his evidence that the prosecution rested its case. If indeed de Berenger had already changed his uniform, as Cochrane contended, it was almost certainly in the post-chaise coming up from Dover, whose curtains had been drawn, although just possibly in Crane's own hackney cab. Crucially, however, Crane revealed that du Bourg had been carrying a portmanteau large enough to carry two coats in it – which might comfortably have contained the scarlet uniform.

Gurney and his fellow prosecutors ploughed on with their case until ten o'clock the same night. All present assumed that the case would be adjourned until the following morning after thirteen solid hours, with only brief adjournments for refreshment. To general astonishment, Lord Ellenborough insisted that the defence begin its case because key witnesses would be absent next day. One of the defence lawyers immediately protested:

> The difficulty we feel, I am sure your Lordship will feel as strong as we do, is the fatigue owing to the length of our attendance here . . . I have undergone very great fatigue, which I am able to bear; but I would submit to your Lordship the hardships upon parties who are charged with so very serious an offence as this if their case is heard at this late hour; and then a fresh day is given to my learned friend to reply.

Ellenborough tersely replied:

> It will not be a fresh day when you will be here by nine o'clock, and the sun will be up almost before we adjourn; I will sit through it if you require it, rather than that.

In fact, the judge's excuse was bogus; most of the important witnesses had to attend just the same on the next day. But Sergeant Best for the defence did what he could, ploughing on into the night for another five hours until 3 a.m. while heads in the jury, which had been clear that morning for the prosecution's evidence, nodded off.

On one point at least Best made short work of the prosecution's case, the allegation that Cochrane had paid du Bourg. How much the jurors were taking in by this time in the small hours remain uncertain. Crucially however, Best, perhaps out of weariness, said 'Cochrane could have been mistaken as to the colours of the uniform', thus half-conceding the prosecution's key point. It is possible that Cochrane had simply not taken in the colour of the uniform or given it much importance, and the fact that his servants were not to testify openly in court as to the colour was made much of by the prosecution. Later, his defence team was to say that the refusal to let them testify was deliberate – although they were entirely convinced of Cochrane's innocence. This was certainly the weakest point in his case.

The court sat again after only seven hours' adjournment and defence witnesses were called, including the First Lord of the Admiralty, Lord Melville, to show that de Berenger's connection had been to Admiral Sir Alexander Cochrane, not to his nephew. The prosecution then had their final say. Gurney was at his most eloquent:

Gentlemen, that Lord Cochrane would have been incapable of deliberately engaging in anything so wicked some time ago, I am sure I as earnestly hope as I am desirous to believe; but you must see in what circumstances men are placed, when they do these things; Lord Cochrane had first found his way to the Stock Exchange; he had dealt largely in these speculations, which my learned friends have so liberally branded with the name of infamous; he had involved himself so deeply, that there was no way, but by this fraud, of getting out of them; he had got out of them in this way, and then he found, as guilty people always do, that he was involved still deeper; he found the great agent of the plot traced to his house, and traced into his house in the dress in which he had perpetrated this fraud; he was called upon for an explanation upon the subject.

Gentlemen, he was gone to perdition, if he did not do

something to extricate himself from his difficulty; then it was that he ventured upon the rash step of making this affidavit, and swearing to the extraordinary circumstances upon which, as I commented so much at length in the morning of yesterday, I will not trespass upon your attention by making comments now.

Lord Ellenborough summed up in one of the most loaded and devastating speeches ever uttered by a supposedly impartial trial judge, which was to become the subject of major controversy for the rest of the century. Of the uniform provided as evidence he said in a lofty tone of scorn, irony and contempt, 'You have before had the animal hunted home, and now you have his skin'. He went on

> De Berenger stripped himself at Lord Cochrane's. He pulled off his scarlet uniform there, and if the circumstance of its not being green did not excite Lord Cochrane's suspicion, what did he think of the star and medal? It became him, on discovering these, as an officer and a gentleman, to communicate his suspicions of these circumstances. Did he not ask de Berenger where he had been in this masquerade dress? ... This was not the dress of a sharpshooter, but of a mountebank. He came before Lord Cochrane fully blazoned in the costume of his crime.

Senior lawyers present were aghast. Scarlett, who later became a senior Tory minister (and thus was no political admirer of Cochrane) wrote afterwards:

> As one of Lord Cochrane's counsel and fully acquainted with all the facts of the case, I was satisfied of his innocence, and I believe it might have been established to the satisfaction of the jury if the judge had not arbitrarily hurried on the defence at a late hour.

Lord Campbell, another future Lord Chancellor, wrote afterwards:

The following day, in summing up, prompted no doubt by the conclusions of his own mind, he laid special emphasis on every circumstance which might raise a suspicion against Lord Cochrane, and elaborately explained away whatever at first sight might seem favourable to the gallant officer. In consequence the jury found a verdict of guilty against all the defendants.

Indeed, this happened after just three hours.

Cochrane, not present and stunned when the news was brought, immediately demanded a retrial. This was denied him by Ellenborough. On 14 June Cochrane himself appeared in court for the first time for sentencing, and was allowed to read a digni-fied rebuttal of the accusations against him under the cold eye of his inquisitor. He stated that he barely knew de Berenger, although he was of course intimate with his uncle.

> I must however be here distinctly understood to deny the accuracy of the opinion which Lord Ellenborough appears to have formed in this case, and deeply to lament the verdict of guilty which the jury returned after three hours' consultation and hesitation.

Of de Berenger he said:

> It has been said that there was a suspicious degree of famil-iarity in his treatment of me and my house. I can only observe that over his conduct I had no control . . . The circumstance of his obtaining a change of dress at my house could never have been known if I had not voluntarily disclosed it . . .
> My own fixed opinion is that he changed his dress in the coach because I believe that he dared not run the risk of appearing in my presence till he had so changed it.

He went on with unanswerable logic:

> The pretended du Bourg, if I had chosen him for my instru-

ment, instead of making me his convenience, should have terminated his expedition and found a change of dress elsewhere. He should not have come immediately and in open day to my house. I should not rashly have invited detection and its concomitant ruin . . . I look forward to justice being rendered my character sooner or later; it will come most speedily, as well as gratefully, if I shall receive it at your Lordship's hands. I am not unused to injury; of late I have know persecution; the indignity of compassion I am not yet able to bear . . . I cannot feel disgraced while I know that I am guiltless.

Cochrane was later to point out that if de Berenger had arrived in the incriminating tunic 'the winter's fire in my grate would in five minutes have destroyed the coat and its evidence together.' Gurney implacably sought the severest sentence.

For all this, what return has he made? He has engaged in a conspiracy to perpetrate a fraud, by producing an undue effect on the public funds of the country, of which funds he was an appointed guardian, and to perpetrate that fraud by falsehood. He attempted to palm that falsehood upon that very board of government under the orders of which he was then fitting out, on an important public service, and still more as if to dishonour the profession of which he was a member, he attempted to make a brother officer the organ of that falsehood.

The port officer, Admiral Foley, had fought at Cape St Vincent, had commanded Nelson's flagship at Copenhagen and had led the fleet into action at the Battle of the Nile. He was no deskbound Admiralty placeman, but one of the kind of officers Cochrane most admired – which made it all the more unlikely that he should have tried to play so shabby a trick on him.

Cochrane, along with his fellow defendants, was sentenced to a year in prison, a £1000 fine and an hour in the pillory opposite the Stock Exchange. By this time Cochrane-Johnstone had already fled the country, implying his guilt, never to return for fear of spending his life in a debtors' prison. An observer present said that 'when the sentence was passed he [Cochrane] stood without colour in his face, his eyes staring and without expression and it was with difficulty he left the court like a man stupified.'

Thus ended a trial almost without precedent in British legal history. On the evidence of a seventeen-year-old, with the judge, proceedings and jury all stacked against him in the most blatant manner possible, Britain's greatest living seaman had been convicted of a shabby if imaginative fraud against not only a distinguished admiral and the navy itself, but the Stock Exchange and his own country – to earn the sum of some £2000.

This at last was the revenge of the powerful men he had so frequently offended. Burdett, Cobbett, Leigh, now Cochrane: the price of real dissent against the system, of exposing the myriad injustices of the Royal Navy, of championing the ordinary seaman, of taking on Young, Gambier, Croker and the Wellesleys so fearlessly, was disgrace and prison. The system, in thus reacting viciously against the simmering discontent of the early nineteenth century, was to buy itself nearly another two decades in power before the Great Reform Bill lifted the lid off the boiling pot of popular discontent.

Yet while there can be little doubt of Cochrane's innocence, two huge question marks hung over the whole affair. The first was: why did Cochrane not defend himself more effectively, and choose to make common cause with Cochrane-Johnstone and Butt, who were almost certainly guilty? The second much larger mystery was: why had de Berenger gone to Cochrane's house that fateful Monday morning?.

The first can be disposed of fairly easily. Loyalty was one of Cochrane's most attractive traits. He had formed an attachment to the plausible but roguish Cochrane-Johnstone many years previously. He could not believe that the latter would involve himself in a criminal conspiracy, still less seek to implicate his own nephew in it. In a poignant letter just after he had been imprisoned to his uncle's daughter, his cousin Elizabeth, he expressed the depth and sincerity of his loyalty to her father:

> My dear Eliza – The feelings which you must have experienced, unused as you have been to the lamentable changes of this uncertain life, must have even exceeded that which I have suffered in mind from the unexpected and unmerited ruin in which I am unhappily involved. Shocked as I am, and distressed as I am, yet I feel confidence. God is my judge that the crime imputed to me I did not commit. Had I been accessory to the deception practised on the exchange I should not have protested my innocence in the manner I have done . . . The deception may have originated in thoughtless levity . . . indeed if such was its origin, an offence against the laws of justice and honour probably never occured to the mind of the contriver . . . I am distressed on your account more than on my own; for knowing my innocence, and unable to speak of the private acts of any other, I cannot bring myself to believe that I shall be disgraced and punished without a cause.

He was making plain, however, that he at last believed in her father's guilt. Nearly half a century later she, now the Dowager Lady Napier, showed not just that she forgave him but that she too was convinced of her father's guilt:

> O my dear cousin, let me say once more while you are still here, how ever since that miserable time I have felt that you suffered for my poor Father's fault – how agonising that conviction was – how thankful I am that tardy justice was done you . . . I always knew that it was for my sake that [you] would never throw the blame on my poor father, and I have often regretted that [you] remained silent.

Brougham, one of Cochrane's most distinguished defenders, was certain that concern for his uncle had been the reason for his own rather flaccid and tactically misplaced defence, at least initially:

I take upon me to assert that Lord Cochrane's conviction was mainly owing to the extreme repugnance which he felt to giving up his uncle, or taking those precautions for his own safety which would have operated against that near relation. Even when he, the real criminal, had confessed his guilt by taking to flight, and the other defendants were brought up for judgment, we the counsel could not persuade Lord Cochrane to shake himself loose from the contamination by giving him up.

Behind his brilliance, Cochrane possessed a strong streak of naïvety.

The second question is much more intriguing, and less easy to answer. If Cochrane was innocent, why did the principal of the hoax incriminate him in broad daylight by going directly to his house? There are three possible explanations: first, that the operation had been botched and de Berenger panicked, seeking immediate help to escape aboard the avenue that must have seemed most obvious to him, Cochrane's flagship, soon to sail. Alternatively, he and his co-conspirators may have wished to involve Cochrane inextricably in their affairs and trust to his good name to extract them from possible conviction. Or, third, de Berenger may have been deliberately seeking to implicate Cochrane in the crime for reasons of his own.

The first possibility cannot be dismissed. The mist in the early hours of Monday morning could not have been predicted, and prevented Admiral Foley from telegraphing news of Napoleon's 'defeat'; if this had arrived in time for the opening of the Stock Exchange, the effect on share prices might have been much more dramatic. Against that Foley was unconvinced by the story initially, which was without corroboration, as was the Admiralty. Even if he had signalled the news from Dover it would not have been released, certainly not with official authorisation, until there was some certainty about the matter. Cochrane, with his long experience of signalling and naval procedures, would surely have known this – although not Uncle Andrew, a soldier, and his friends. In any case, de Berenger left

Dover long before dawn, and before he had any idea that a mist would prevent his story being telegraphed from Dover, so that could not have given him reason to panic. Arriving in London, he would still not have known about the mist in Dover.

In his own version of events (which shall be returned to) he makes no mention of things going wrong. He claimed that he wished to avoid passing through towns where there were military depots, so as to avoid the risk of being questioned by officers who might force him to betray himself. Cochrane, according to de Berenger, told him to come to his house, but to change the hackney coach on his way and informed him of his change of address from Park Street to Green Street.

De Berenger said he did not change coach because someone he knew (a Mr Barwick) was in a coach behind and might have recognized him. He added that he had left his letter to Admiral Foley on the table of the inn on purpose to tempt the curiosity of the people there, with the result that two expresses sent from Dover with the good news reached London before him. In other words, there was no reason whatsoever for him to believe the plan had gone awry by the time he arrived at Cochrane's house. De Berenger never asserted, years afterwards, that it had. So the idea of a panic rush to Green Street can probably be discarded.

The second possibility – that he and his friends wanted to ride on the coat-tails of the famous Cochrane to extricate them from trouble should the crime be found out – is unverifiable. It is certainly possible. If so, it requires a degree of cynicism, in particular on the part of Cochrane-Johnstone, that is almost beyond belief from an uncle prepared to sully and destroy his good friend and nephew's reputation purely so that he would stand a better chance of escaping conviction should the plot be discovered. But Cochrane-Johnstone was certainly capable of this.

The third possibility is that de Berenger himself had a deliberate motive in implicating Cochrane. The latter believed that 'a higher authority than the Stock Exchange was at the bottom of my prosecution' and that de Berenger was a government agent. Here there seems a good deal more plausibility in the argument. For de Berenger was very far from simply being a rogue inexplicably wafted in off the streets, adopting Sir Alexander Cochrane as his patron and then moving in on his nephew. He had been the acting adjutant of the Earl of Yarmouth's regiment of sharpshooters and was, in spite of his financial problems, a man of some military standing, his aristocratic pretensions taken seriously. He inhabited a *demi-monde* that countless spies and perpetrators of dirty tricks have before and since. Given the hare-brained nature of the scheme, he could easily have been employed by a vicious, implacable government to bring disrepute upon one of its greatest enemies – a national hero who was also a Radical. How better than by implicating him in a crime?

Although de Berenger served his sentence and a little longer, on account of his debts, he was able to publish his own book, *The Noble Stock-Jobber*, just four years after the whole affair and by 1835 was a prosperous country gentleman, writing such enlightening tomes as *Helps and Hints how to protect life and property* and *Rifle and Pistol Shooting*. By all accounts it was de Berenger who first approached the villainous and financially desperate Cochrane-Johnstone with the whole incredible scheme. By some accounts he also approached Butt (who like Cochrane continued to protest his innocence throughout the whole affair, although he undoubtedly gave de Berenger the money he was found with on his arrest). Cochrane retained a favourable opinion of Butt well after the case.

The possibility that de Berenger was part of an elaborate plot to discredit Cochrane cannot be discounted. In fact, it is almost impossible to see de Berenger's action in going to Cochrane's house on arrival in London in any other light if, as has been argued, the latter was innocent. Even if he was guilty, it seems an extraordinary thing to have happened.

There remains a further remarkable twist to the case. De Berenger's patron was the commander of the sharpshooter regiment, the Earl of Yarmouth. This young man was no ordinary peer. He was the son of the Marchioness of Hertford, who at that time was the mistress of the Prince Regent, later George IV, who was already ruling in place of mad old King George III. Lady Hertford was both sanctimonious and snobbish, and had been installed into the home of the Prince's real, although bigamous wife, Mrs Fitzherbert (who could not become Queen because he was already married and because she was Catholic). The long-suffering Mrs Fitzherbert had put up with this for some time.

Yarmouth had become the Prince's favourite. When the Cochrane case came to court he was forced to testify as a defence witness that he knew and had protected de Berenger. This was highly inconvenient because the Prince Regent had appointed him to act as a personal aide to the Tsar of Russia who, along with the King of Prussia, was triumphantly visiting London on the occasion of Napoleon's defeat at the precise moment that the trial was taking place. Indeed, one of Ellenborough's reasons for keeping the trial going into the night of 8 June was that Yarmouth needed to get away to his official duty of escorting the Tsar the following day.

Henry Brougham, the lawyer and future Lord Chancellor, had written as early as 12 March that 'Yarmouth [was] at first much talked of in respect of the Stock Exchange fraud' – unsurprisingly so, because of the relationship between Yarmouth and de Berenger. (The aim of Yarmouth's attendance upon the Tsar, incidentally, was to ensure that the latter would show respect to his mother, then publicly accompanying the Prince Regent, which the Tsar pointedly refused to do.)

The Prince Regent had actually written to Yarmouth on the subject of the scandal, saying that the 'Bow Streeters are now after' Cochrane and that he and his associates 'might from pique, resentment and disappointment induce him or persuade him to invent against you'. It was obviously a major concern in the highest circles. Ellenborough's grandson, in a vigorous defence of his kinsman, had this to say of Yarmouth:

Lord Yarmouth had been subpoenaed for the defence, and was seated on the Bench, but no one in the court, except the prisoners' counsel and attorneys, could have any notion of the nature of the evidence which he would be called upon to give. We know now that he was only examined to confirm the statement of previous applications having been made on the part of de Berenger to obtain employment on board the *Tonnant*, and that he was asked questions as to the handwriting of the letter, and as to the uniform of his corps of sharpshooters.

But, for all that Lord Ellenborough knew, the defence might be going to call him to prove that de Berenger had actually visited him on that eventful morning in the disguise supplied by Lord Cochrane, and to question him as to what had taken place. Even if direct criminality was not imputed, the mere insinuation could not fail to draw him into the circle of those to whom guilty knowledge was attributed. If it could be shown that the pretended messenger had come to Lord Yarmouth from Lord Cochrane's house, there would be a strong suggestion that the one knew as much of the fraud as the other.

De Berenger himself had written a grovelling letter to Cochrane immediately after his apprehension:

> My Lord – I have the honour of acknowledging the receipt of your Lordship's favour, which has this moment been delivered.
>
> Rest assured, my Lord, that nothing could exceed the pain I felt when I perceived how cruelly, how unfair, my unfortunate visit of the 21st of February was interpreted (which, with its object, is so correctly detailed in your affidavit); but my agony is augmented, when I reflect that acts of generosity and goodness towards an unfortunate man have been, and continue to be, the accidental cause of much mortification to you: a fear of increasing the imaginary grounds of accusation caused me to refrain from addressing you.

De Berenger, writing after his release, said that Cochrane had suggested to him to fabricate a story that he was 'employed by Lord Yarmouth in this hoax; anything about him will go down'. Indeed, according to de Berenger, he was offered large bribes 'to induce his consent to fixing the whole transaction on Lord Yarmouth'. The key point is that Yarmouth, the son of the sovereign's mistress, was much closer to the rogue de Berenger than either Sir Alexander Cochrane or his nephew – who hardly knew him at all. By all accounts it was de Berenger who sold the whole daft scheme both to Cochrane-Johnstone and to Butt.

Was Cochrane set up? De Berenger's unnecessary arrival at his home on the morning of the crime suggests that he was. By whom? Possibly by those establishment enemies long awaiting their chance to get their revenge on Cochrane: the one-sided nature of the ensuing trial supports this. Or possibly by Yarmouth himself, as the real perpetrator of the fraud? Certainly de Berenger displayed an extraordinary sensitivity to the possibility that his patron might be accused. The Prince Regent, no less, was alive to the possibility of Yarmouth's being implicated.

In *The Noble Stock-Jobber*, de Berenger set out in detail how the plan was hatched with Cochrane as the criminal mastermind. As the third Lord Ellenborough summarised this:

> The writer points out the absurdities of Lord Cochrane's affidavit, in which it appeared that Lord Cochrane actually believed that De Berenger would go to Lord Yarmouth and other high officials, unshaven, with undressed hair though wearing powder, dressed in a coat that was a great deal too long for a man of his height, with a broad-brimmed, low-crowned hat, and in dirty boots that had been under a quantity of straw during a journey of seventy-two miles. None but a madman, so accoutred and so dirty, would have gone in such a costume to call on officials of the highest rank. He would have been the laughing-stock of their servants, who would have shut the door in his face, believing him to be either mad or drunk.

> De Berenger left Green Street in the hackney coach that had brought Lord Cochrane there. He tells us that on leaving

Lord Cochrane's he first went to a hatter's, as he could not face his servants in Lord Cochrane's queer 'Obadiah' hat, and that he paid off one coach and took another at the hatter's.

He says Lord Cochrane had never seen him at any time in his military dress as a sharpshooter, and that he dined at Basil Cochrane's in Portman Square on the evening of the fraud, and that Lord Cochrane came in afterwards. At this entertainment the fraud was the principal subject of conversation, as it probably was at every other evening party in London on that night. All looked pleased, and Lord Cochrane smiled sweetly at him.

Before Mrs Basil Cochrane's party broke up, Mr Johnstone asked him to dine next day, 'when the party consisted of Miss Cochrane-Johnstone, her father, Lord Cochrane, Mr Butt and myself. Instead of the cheering and glowing smiles of Monday, all was gloom and pensive distance. Few were the words at dinner – the room was scarcely to ourselves (the lady having left), than I was requested to state the whole of my proceedings. During the adventurous recital all were gay, animated, nay delighted; but scarcely had it been closed when the former gloom prevailed.'

The implausibility of these jolly meetings between the lordly sponsors and the ruffianly executors of the crime seems obvious. But the determination with which in 1818 de Berenger was used to hammer home Cochrane's guilt suggests he was being backed by powerful interests determined either to cover up a crime committed by the son of the sovereign's mistress – Yarmouth's involvement would have been a huge scandal at a time when the indiscretions of the later George IV were already under unprecedented attack – or to destroy the greatest contemporary scourge of the establishment, who also happened to be Britain's greatest seaman since Nelson, or both.

CHAPTER 14

The Shame and the Anger

The degradation and disgrace of Thomas Cochrane following the guilty verdict, were executed with speed and thoroughness. His chief persecutor was, astonishingly (but not perhaps in light of the Yarmouth connection), none other than the Prince Regent. According to several officers present at dinner with him at Portsmouth, he expounded

> his indignation at the conduct of Lord Cochrane, and went on to state in strong and impressive terms, his determination to order his degradation: 'I will never permit a service, hitherto of unblemished honour, to be disgraced by the continuance of Lord Cochrane as a member of it. I shall also strip him of the Order of the Bath.'

These remarks were calculated and premeditated. Cochrane was dismissed from the Navy he had served so courageously for so long within a week of the verdict. Then, at midnight his banner as Knight Commander of the Bath, along with his coat of arms, helmet and sword, conferred after the great victory at Aix Roads, were taken down from the stall at Henry VII's chapel at Westminster Abbey and kicked down the steps of the Abbey. His knight's spurs were severed from his boots with a meat cleaver, a man standing in them as proxy, in a further medieval touch. Meanwhile Cochrane wrote movingly to his wife:

> My lovely Kate. You know the inconveniences of this place, and how impossible it is for me to make a single room in a

prison comfortable to you. I would not willingly put you to inconvenience, and induce you to sacrifice anything to my satisfaction. No, not for the whole world. This is not a place favourable to morality. I wish you to remain, as you are, uncorrupted by the wickedness of this world; I wish to see you good, sensible in point of education, and in every respect blessed, Kate. Oh! my dear soul, you do not know how much I love you and my dear Tom. My conduct may not have shown it, distressed as my mind has been, but I have felt towards you as I ought to feel, my lovely Kate.

One of his worst anxieties was the financial future of his family. His main hope was the success of a patent for his new gas lamp, which was soon tried experimentally in Westminster:

I have nothing new to tell you, but I believe and anxiously hope that our lamps will answer. I have been writing an advertisement today for the papers. It will be a happy thing for us both if God blesses us with independence from such a source, after the punishment He has been pleased to inflict upon me.

He busied himself in prison working on the design. He appeared to be a broken man in his disgrace and humiliation. Mary Russell Mitford, his old friend and Radical supporter, reported: 'Did papa tell you that he had seen poor, poor Lord Cochrane, that victim to his uncle's villainy, almost every day? He wept like a child to papa.'

He was taken to his two-room prison on the upper storey of the King's Bench jail. He was briefly released to defend himself in the House of Commons, to oppose the order moved by the government for his expulsion. There, freshly out of jail, he threw away his carefully prepared speech, and the whole cup of his bitterness spilled over into such invective that Lord Castlereagh, that arch-apostle of the establishment, remarked that those who reported the speech would be liable for prosecution. We therefore have only the censored version:

Have I been tried by a jury of my country? Sir, I have been tried by twelve men. If there be any meaning in the word packed as applied to juries; to pack a jury means to select, by one of the parties, men, who, it is known will decide, as that party wishes them to decide. And was not that the case in the present instance? Was not the master of the Crown office [deleted] For what other purpose than that of securing [deleted] was the case removed from the Old Bailey to the Court of King's Bench? I ask for what other purpose? and I defy anyone to answer me, unless he add that it was also for the purpose of securing [deleted].

I shall satisfy myself as to this point, in having shown that the jury, whose verdict was produced in the House [deleted] and that it was as juries in such cases are [deleted].

I would rather stand, in my own name, in the pillory every day of my life than I would sit upon the Bench in the name of [deleted] . . . Never in the history of this country was a case of such gross and cruel injustice recorded.

He finished, loyal to his family to the last:

I solemnly declare before Almighty God that I am ignorant of the whole transaction and uniformly I have heard Mr Cochrane-Johnstone deny it also.

George Ponsonby, Leader of the Opposition, remarked sadly that Cochrane's worst enemy could not have done more harm to his case than he just had. However, no fewer than forty-four members voted against his expulsion, although nobody voted against that of Cochrane-Johnstone. The young Lord Ebrington moved that Cochrane's sentence in the pillory be suspended. Cochrane himself criticized this stand:

I had flattered myself from a recent note of your Lordship, that in your mind I stood wholly acquitted; and I did not expect to be treated by your Lordship as an object of mercy on the grounds of past services, or severity of sentence . . . If I am guilty, I richly merit the whole of the sentence which has been passed upon me. If innocent, one penalty cannot be inflicted with more justice than another. If your Lordship shall judge proper to persist in the motion of which you have given notice, I hope you will do me the justice to read this letter to the House.

Alone and wretched in the King's Bench jail, confined to two cold rooms poorly lit by small windows, he seemed broken. By the standards of prisons of the time, and even now, his confinement was luxurious. But for Britain's greatest living naval officer to be viewed as guilty of the basest act of dishonesty, baser even than the sleaze of which he had so often accused the Admiralty, was a bitter cup.

The evidence against him was so slender that he had never believed for a moment he would be convicted. He had failed to make allowance for the corruption both of the law and of politics. His trial had been one of the great political trials of British history. Stripped of his honours, expelled from parliament, cashiered from the Navy, everything he had ever lived for had gone. Not quite: dressed in plain clothes to avoid being recognized, his plucky young wife, caring for their infant son, nevertheless regularly made the journey to the drab prison building, taking out bundles of his clothing to be washed. His enemies implied that he was being visited by a prostitute.

To a man accustomed to free thinking and high living, the transformation from universal acclamation, a comfortable house with servants and celebrity as a naval hero to a prison cell must have been traumatic indeed – all the more so because his downfall had come so quickly and unexpectedly. In the space of a few weeks the captain destined to command the flagship of a great expedition to North America had become a common prisoner dependent on his jailers for his few privileges.

At last a little light began to seep into the cell, as he pondered his past triumphs and the bleak future ahead of him. A by-election was necessary to fill the Westminster seat from which he had been expelled. Cobbett vigorously campaigned on the absent MP's behalf, defying Lord Ellenborough to send him to prison a second time. The two favoured candidates were the veteran, drunk and endearing playwright, Richard Brinsley Sheridan, and the young lawyer, Henry Brougham. But Cobbett put Cochrane up as his candidate, and both the others stood down out of respect. Burdett, who had remarked that if he had sold his stock on the same day, he too would now be in prison, made a passionate speech for his friend, offering, in *The Times* report of the day, to stand in the pillory alongside him:

> It now remained for the electors of Westminster to vindicate the character of an illustrious person who had rendered great services to the country (loud applause): services which, even if he had been guilty of the meanness imputed to him, should, as he thought, have protected him from the degrading infamy which it was now intended to have inflicted upon him. (No! No! from many persons, as expressing the hope that the sentence would not be inflicted). He should hope that the malice of his enemies would not prevail; but even if he were to suffer that degrading punishment, he would confidently look for his acquittal to the unpacked and uncorrupted verdict of his constituents and his countrymen at large. He said, that if Lord Cochrane was to stand in the pillory, he should feel it his duty to attend also (loud shouts of applause which lasted for many minutes).

Cochrane's opponents resorted to intrigue. The *Sun* newspaper secured an interview with Cochrane's old father, who had finally been forced to sell Culross Abbey House on the death of his second wife, whose fortune had saved it years earlier. Now sixty-six and drinking heavily, the old Earl of Dundonald claimed that he had tried to warn Thomas against the influence of Cochrane-Johnstone, that he had thought up the strategy for Aix Roads and been given no credit for it by his son, and that he had been left in penury. Cochrane pointed out with dignity in rebuttal that he had contributed £8000 in ten years to his father's upkeep.

The smear backfired. Cochrane, in prison, was re-elected by acclamation at a meeting of 5000 voters – the largest and most representative election in the land at that time. The common people of Britain clearly believed their hero was innocent. The later Lord Chief Justice Campbell wrote:

> The award of this degrading and infamous punishment upon a young nobleman, a Member of the House of Commons, and a distinguished naval officer, raised universal sympathy in his favour. The judge was proportionately blamed, not only by the vulgar, but by men of education on both sides in politics, and he found on entering society and appearing in the House of Lords that he was looked upon coldly. Having now some misgivings himself as to the propriety of his conduct in this affair, he became very wretched.

The government, at last, showed a modicum of good sense following Cochrane's re-election. Fearing a riot or worse, Lord Castlereagh, the good-looking, cold apostle of reaction declared that the royal pardon would be extended to Cochrane and all those sentenced to stand in the pillory. This punishment was never again used in Britain.

Meanwhile Sir Alexander upheld the family honour in the tour of duty on which he should have fought side-by-side with his nephew. He captured Washington, burning down the White House and the Capitol and laying waste the whole of America's eastern coastline until he was blocked at the mouth of the Mississippi by Andrew Jackson. During the same month Lord Ebrington met Napoleon in exile in Elba. 'Such a man should not be made to suffer such a degrading punishment,' the former Emperor remarked of his former naval opponent.

The months of confinement moved slowly past. Cochrane's most frequent visitors, apart from Kitty, were Cobbett and Burdett. It was the former who mischievously put to him that he should do what he had in Malta – escape. It was a profoundly foolish idea: London was not Valletta, and the British authorities were far more formidable than the second-rate governor of the Maltese port. Yet the idea readily took root in so frustrated and restless a man as Cochrane. Had he not been re-elected to the House of Commons after his expulsion, and was it not illegal to imprison an MP?

What followed was to confirm the suspicions of many observers that he was temperamentally unstable. Yet this was no mere act of folly or desperate bid for freedom. Cochrane was nothing if not an accomplished showman, and he had a huge popular constituency at his feet. How better further to draw attention to the injustice of his conviction? He at least had from an early age understood the importance of public opinion, and the value of keeping a story running. In March, having survived the bleak cold of a London winter in his two rooms and with just three months of his sentence still to run, he made his decision.

When his warder entered his cell on the morning of 7 March 1815, he found it empty. Cochrane's servant (or possibly Kitty) had managed to smuggle in a rope, not a very good or a very long one. But to the experienced seaman who had once ascended the rigging to save a ship in a violent storm, this was all he needed.

At around midnight he climbed up to his window, which was unbarred because of the long and fatal drop to the ground outside, and skilfully looped a rope over one of the huge spikes on the outer wall of the jail some 15 feet away. He made the rope tight, then climbed hand over hand, foot over foot, along it; had he fallen he would have been killed. Reaching the wall, he hauled himself up, avoiding the sharp spikes, and from this precarious position lowered the rope down to the street below, which he could not see in the dark, before descending.

As he climbed down, he was unaware that the rope was fraying precariously on the edge of the ledge above and, when he was still some 20 feet up, it snapped. He fell on his back, unconscious but, remarkably, with none of his bones broken. When he awoke the street was still deserted, but he could hardly move. Painfully he crawled to the nearby house of his old nurse, as had been arranged, where she tended him before he was fit to travel, a couple of days later.

The British public was agog to hear that the hero had escaped. Officialdom was incensed. A considerable reward for the times and in view of the minor nature of the offence he had committed, 300 guineas, was put on his head. Wanted posters were put up all over London:

> Escaped from the King's Bench Prison, on Monday the 6th day of March, instant, Lord Cochrane. He is about five feet eleven inches in height, thin and narrow chested, with sandy hair and full eyes, red whiskers and eyebrows. Whoever will apprehend and secure Lord Cochrane in any of His Majesty's gaols in the kingdom shall have a reward of three hundred guineas from William Jones, Marshal of the King's Bench.

The newspapers gleefully took up the chase. He had fled to France, to the Channel Islands, to Hastings, he was still in the City, he had gone mad and was still in the prison building. In fact, he had travelled down to his house of Holly Hill in Hampshire, to stay with Kitty and tiny Thomas. None of his neighbours gave him away, while the authorities failed to look for him there.

As the frenzied search for the missing naval hero continued, in the early afternoon of 21 March 1815, in a sparsely attended House of Commons, messengers were astonished to see the familiar figure of the tall, gangling member for Westminster, in his customary grey pantaloons and frock coat walk calmly through the lobby, intending to take his seat. It was now clear beyond doubt that his escape had been a public relations stunt, rather than the crazed action of a desperate man, although he continued to insist, wrongly, that having been elected an MP it was illegal for him to be in prison.

The elderly and burly ex-servicemen who sat as messengers were completely flummoxed. They told him that he could not take his seat, as he had not sworn the oath of allegiance since his re-election. He went to the Clerk's office behind the Speaker's chair to do so, but was told that the writ for his re-election would have to be fetched. There he waited patiently for two hours (the accounts are conflicting; one suggests he actually took his seat, but he would have had to get past the messengers to do so) while arrangements were made to deal with the fugitive. Eventually Bow Street Runners and tipstaffs arrived at the House of Commons to arrest him. Cochrane protested that his arrest was illegal, and demanded by what authority they acted.

As in Malta he refused to budge. They had to seize him and carry him on their shoulders past the ranks of MPs who had flocked to witness the spectacle. In a nearby committee room they searched him for arms, and found only a box of snuff. 'If I had only thought of it before, you should have it in your eyes,' Cochrane remarked sarcastically. The newspapers instantly proclaimed that this dangerous criminal had threatened his captors with vitriol.

Back in prison he was placed in a punishment cell – a dark, windowless room below ground level; unlike in Malta, his persecutors were implacable. A parliamentary inquiry visiting the prison reported:

> I found Lord Cochrane confined in a strong room fourteen feet square, without windows, fireplace, table or bed. I do not think it can be necessary for the purpose of security to confine him in this manner. According to my own feelings it is a place unfit for the noble Lord, or for any other person whatsoever.

A doctor was sent for. He wrote:

> This is to certify that I have this day visited Lord Cochrane, who is affected with severe pain of the breast. His pulse is low, his hands cold, and he has many symptoms of a person about to have typhus or putrid fever. These symptoms are, in my opinion, produced by the stagnant air of the strong room in which he is now confined.

Cochrane was eventually taken to a better room and two months later, as news of the great victory at Waterloo began to reach London, he was released – on condition he paid his fine. For a fortnight he refused to do so, until Kitty, Basil and his Radical friends persuaded him. He wrote on the £1000 note:

> My health having suffered by long and close confinement, and my oppressors being resolved to deprive me of property or life, I submit to robbery to protect myself from murder, in the hope that I shall live to bring the delinquents to justice.

He was released.

Cochrane had a few months to return to normal life before the next parliamentary session began. He was bitter, self-centred and resentful during those months, as is hardly surprising in a man who had undergone the ordeal of the past year. When he returned to parliament it was not to champion the dispossessed or the cause of reform, but himself. He tabled a motion of censure against Lord Ellenborough, speaking for hours on the subject to an empty chamber. When the house divided, only he and Burdett as tellers represented the ayes. He had become considered a bore, pursuing his own grievances. He was squandering his support. He prosecuted one of the government witnesses in the trial for perjury, but failed to secure a conviction. Then at last he seemed to understand that his own reputation was being damaged.

Cochrane returned to the front line of the Radical movement during those strange, dangerous days for British politics, when the governing class seemed incapable of reacting to the resentments boiling up underneath except through obscurantist repression. Britain was probably as close to revolution after 1815 as at any time in its history. The grievances of the new working class in their 'dark satanic mills' were just beginning. Thousands of soldiers had returned from a glorious victory to face the stark realities of destitution and unemployment. In Scotland widespread agricultural clearances were under way, taking Highland crofters out of a way of life they had enjoyed for generations so that vast sheep pastures could be created to feed the textile mills further south. As far back as March riots had broken out, many of them against the introduction of machinery. Two men had been killed and five hanged by the authorities.

The response to this unrest was a determined exercise in paternalism. William Wilberforce, the tireless campaigner against slavery, was wheeled in to head the Association for the Relief of the Manufacturing and Labouring Poor. The essence of Wilberforce was that he was good-hearted, deeply religious and politically conservative. He had personally distrusted Cochrane since the latter's quarrel with Gambier, an epitome of Christian self-righteousness after Wilberforce's heart.

On 29 July Wilberforce presided over a remarkable gathering at the City of London Tavern, flanked by the great and the good of the British establishment: only the Prince Regent and his heir, the Duke of Clarence, were missing. Present were three other royal brothers – the Duke of York, commander of the British army, the Duke of Kent and the Duke of Cambridge – as well as the Archbishop of Canterbury, the Bishop of London and several senior members of the government, to suggest that philanthropy was the one way to help cope with the 'great local distress' sweeping the country.

Cochrane, who had arrived with many of his Westminster supporters, rose, amid cheering and jeering. The problem was not one of charity, he claimed, but greed. He went on

> I came here with the expectation of seeing the Duke of Rutland in the chair; and with some hopes, as he takes the lead on this occasion, that it is his intention to surrender that sinecure of £9000 a year which he is now in the habit of putting in his pocket. I still trust that all who are present and are also holders of sinecures have it in their intention to sacrifice them to their liberality and their justice; and that they do not come here to aid the distresses of their country by paying half-a-crown per cent out of the hundreds which they take

from it. If they do not, all I can say is, that to me their
pretended charity is little better than a fraud.

He demanded that the government be censured. As the meeting
descended into chaos, the Duke of York withdrew, quickly
followed by the Duke of Kent. Within two weeks the establishment struck back. Cochrane was formally charged with having
escaped the year before, a wholly unnecessary step and one
inspired by vindictiveness. The jury sensibly decided:

> We are of opinion that Lord Cochrane is guilty of escaping
> from prison, but we recommend mercy, because we think his
> subsequent punishment fully adequate to the offence of
> which he was guilty.

Cochrane was fined £100, which he refused to pay, his own
electors doing so by public subscription to avoid his reincarcera-
tion.

The autumn was turning ugly, with riots and revolution in
the wind. In November 1816 a large open-air meeting was held
at Spa Fields and the orator Henry Hunt was asked to carry a
petition to the Prince Regent which was disdainfully refused.
The following month rioting broke out after another mass
meeting. In January 1817 Cochrane took charge of petitions
with no fewer than 400,000 signatures calling for universal
suffrage. Samuel Bamford, his Radical supporter, records the
scene:

> A number of the delegates met Hunt at Charing Cross, and
> from thence went with him in procession to the residence of
> Lord Cochrane in Palace Yard, where a large petition from
> Bristol and most of those from the north of England were
> placed in his Lordship's hands. There had been a tumult in the
> morning; the Prince Regent had been insulted on his way to
> the House. We were crowded around and accompanied by a
> great multitude, which at intervals rent the air with shouts.
> Now it was that I beheld Hunt in his element. He unrolled

the petition, which was many yards in length, and it was carried on the heads of the crowd, perfectly unharmed. When questions were asked: 'Who is he? What are they about?' and the reply was 'Hunt, Hunt, huzza!', his gratification was expressed by a stern smile.

On arriving at Palace Yard we were shown into a room below stairs, and whilst Lord Cochrane and Hunt conversed above, a slight and elegant young lady, dressed in white and very interesting, served us with wine. She is, if I am not misinformed, now Lady Dundonald. At length his Lordship came to us. He was a tall young man, cordial and unaffected in his manner. His face was rather oval; fair naturally, but now tanned and sun-freckled. He took charge of our petitions, and being seated in an armchair, we lifted him up and bore him on our shoulders across Palace Yard to the door of Westminster Hall; the old rafters of which rang with the shouts of the vast multitude outside.

While Hunt addressed the crowds outside, Cochrane spoke in parliament:

The petitioners have a full and immovable conviction – a conviction which they believe to be universal throughout the kingdom – that the House does not, in any constitutional or rational sense, represent the nation; that, when the people have ceased to be represented, the constitution is subverted; that taxation without representation is a state of slavery.

The petitions were rejected. When the Prince Regent arrived to open parliament, the window of his coach was shattered by a stone or a bullet from the mob.

The government reacted in the only way it knew how – Habeas Corpus was suspended. The press was to be controlled. No fewer than eighteen prosecutions for seditious libel were brought – juries acquitting the defendants in all but four cases. Cobbett, fearing another spell in prison, fled to the United States: his exile was a bitter disappointment to Cochrane.

Burdett withdrew from public advocacy of the Radical cause, a fatal loss of nerve.

But the two members for Westminster decided to table a motion for reform of parliament and the introduction of universal suffrage – the first time this had ever been debated in the chamber. To his credit, Cochrane publicly foreswore the cause of revolution for the more sensible one of seeking to ally the popular protest outside with the reformists in the Whig party:

> I have resolved to steer another political course, seeing that the only means of avoiding military despotism for the country is to unite the people and the Whigs, so far as they can be induced to co-operate, which they must do if they wish to preserve the remainder of the constitution.

He thus espoused peaceful reform, and helped to defuse the pressure for a violent uprising. There were those in government who believed he intended to set himself up as a kind of revolutionary fighter, a new Cromwell: he was much too patriotic and disinterested for that.

But the government had ways of applying pressure. Cochrane's finances were distinctly rocky. His revolutionary oil lamp had been superseded by the advent of gas lighting, and he had been formally disinherited by Uncle Basil. The authorities dug up an old forgotten bill – for the entertainment of the electors of Honiton after his election there, a trick sprung upon him after his own disgraceful conduct during the course of that election.

He refused to pay the £1200 owing. He placed bags of charcoal by the windows and doors of his home to resemble gunpowder before the Sheriff of Hampshire and twenty-five of his officers arrived to lay siege. He sent a letter through the lines to his secretary, which was naturally opened and read by the authorities: 'Though the castle has several times been threatened in great force . . . explosion-bags are set in the lower embrasures, and all the garrison is under arms.' This induced terror among the besiegers, as was the intention, and for six weeks they hesitated to break in. Finally one lone policeman entered through a window and found Cochrane sitting down to breakfast, where the officer was congratulated for his courage. Cochrane at last grudgingly paid the bill.

At about this time the Spanish government asked him to take command of the great naval expedition being planned to crush the rebellions sporadically breaking out throughout Latin America. Cochrane refused, because he did not want to help a reactionary government in a cause he did not believe to be right. But he was under intense financial pressure as well as political persecution, and it seemed the Radical cause in Britain was truly lost. Apart from Cobbett, the poet Percy Bysshe Shelley was in exile in Italy, relentlessly criticizing the British government.

Cochrane had also made the decision to leave in principle. He had let it be known that his skills as a sailor were for hire. This made sense because he had no prospect whatsoever of being readmitted to the Navy, still less given a command. The Napoleonic Wars were over and he was making himself available as a soldier of fortune or, in modern terms, a mercenary. There was little to detain him in Britain. His father had left for France, to escape his creditors, after marrying a third time and incurring the wrath of his domineering younger brother Basil, who had previously supported him. The third Countess of Dundonald, Anna Maria, had soon died. Now the old man, nearly eighty years old, lived in Paris with a mistress. Of his uncles, one, Andrew, had fled abroad after ruining Cochrane's career; another, Basil, had disinherited him; and a third, Sir Alexander, could do no more for him.

On 2 June he addressed parliament in a speech which astonished the few members present. It was well crafted and, for him, eloquently delivered:

> As it is probably the last time I shall ever have the honour of addressing the House on any subject, I am anxious to tell its members what I think of their conduct. It is now nearly

eleven years since I have had the honour of a seat in this House, and since then there have been very few measures in which I could agree with the opinions of the majority.

I will say, as has been said before by the great Chatham, the father of Mr Pitt, that if the House does not reform itself from within, it will be reformed with a vengeance from without. The people will take up the subject and a reform will take place which will make many members regret their apathy in now refusing that reform which might be rendered efficient and permanent . . . The gentlemen who now sit on the benches opposite with such triumphant feelings will one day repent their conduct. The commotions to which that conduct will inevitably give rise will shake not only this House, but the whole framework of government and society to its foundations. I have been actuated by the wish to prevent this, and I have had no other intention.

He had shown moderation, foresight and humility. Revolution in Britain was to be averted because the ruling classes acted on exactly that advice and reformed themselves before revolution became inevitable − although it would be too much to claim that Cochrane's speech made any difference. But he showed himself to be a visionary, once again a man of his time, while others dragged behind. It was to be the last occasion on which he was to address the House of Commons.

For Cochrane had been bought: and the buyer was José Alvarez, the London emissary of the newly independent republic of Chile, which desperately needed a superb seaman to defeat the Spanish Navy's domination of the long coastline of the country. It was exactly the kind of quixotic liberal cause that most appealed to the romantic in Cochrane − to take on the toughest empire in the world (whose beard he had so frequently singed in the Mediterranean). Alvarez reacted with delight to Cochrane's acceptance:

I have extreme satisfaction in informing you that Lord Cochrane, one of the most eminent and valiant seamen of

Great Britain, has undertaken to proceed to Chile to direct our navy. He is a person highly commendable, not only on account of the liberal principles with which he has always upheld the cause of the English people in their Parliament, but also because he bears a character altogether superior to ambitious self-seeking.

Cochrane believed he was departing Britain's shores forever. He sold his house, temporarily rented a cottage in Tunbridge Wells where Kitty bore their second son, William Horatio (after Nelson) Bernardo (after Chile's liberator, Bernardo O'Higgins), and arranged for his remaining money to be transferred to the distant land that beckoned him. He also married Kitty a second time, in church, to make sure that she would be acceptable in Chilean society.

Cochrane also engaged in another of those extraordinary ventures that mark him out as an impractical man of genius. He had long decided that the future of sea-travel was steam, not sail – at a time when barely any steamships existed. With the few remaining funds at his disposal, he decided to build one of the world's first armed steamships, confident that the Chilean government would pay for it when he brought it across. Most of the £20,000 necessary was in fact raised by his brother William, who himself put up £12,000. But the 500-ton *Rising Star* was unready by the time the Chileans insisted that Cochrane embark. Captain Bissell, a comrade from the Battle of Aix Roads described it as having:

oars to be worked by steam in calm weather, for which purpose he has put 200 chaldrons of coal in her. The oars do not appear at the side of the vessel but pass through the bottom, and for security iron plates are laid over the lower part of the ship. When the oars are worked the consumption of coals will be four chaldrons in twenty-four hours.

In the event, although it made a historic first steam journey across the South Atlantic and into the Pacific, it played no part in the war of independence. The ship had two 45hp engines and a retracting paddle but was also fully equipped with sail, fortunately, as her engines worked for only 19 hours on the journey across the Atlantic. Thus the last romantic figure from the age of sail was also the man who first understood the full potential of steam – to Admiralty scoffing he predicted that steam would sweep sail away from the oceans. Again, he had anticipated a revolution.

The government had a last sting in its tail. It introduced a bill prohibiting British subjects from fighting for a foreign power. But by the time this passed Parliament, Cochrane had already sailed. He was now again a criminal in British eyes – but beyond the reach of the law.

It was worse than that. For Cochrane, the sea-fighter who had tormented Napoleon, in fact reciprocated the former's admiration. He had concocted a fantastic plan to pick up the deposed Emperor *en route* to South America from his island exile of St Helena and place him on the throne of a great confederation of South American states to balance the United States in the north. Napoleon himself had floated such an idea before Waterloo and it must be supposed that the message had reached Cochrane, possibly as a result of Lord Ebrington's visit while Cochrane was still in jail. He was 'determined at all hazards to outwit the [British] Government, whose ministers were full of suspicion against him, believing that he had a plot in view for the rescue of the Royal Exile'. The scheme was based on the reputation Napoleon still enjoyed as a great liberal figure; but it was nevertheless hare-brained. The South American revolutions had been ignited in opposition to Napoleon's invasion of the Iberian Peninsula; and the Liberator, Simon Bolivar, for one had consciously regarded Napoleon as a despot not to be imitated. There was no possibility of Cochrane's scheme ever being realized – even if Napoleon could be prised off St Helena.

With a typically melodramatic flourish, on learning that the government was seeking to stop him leaving, Cochrane left the picturesque little harbour of Rye in a small fishing boat bound for Boulogne. At the age of forty-two, he had reached another turning point. He was a man who had already lived more lives than the majority of his fellow men. The upward path of his reputation had been checked by official obstruction after the Gambier trial, and then the ferocious backlash which followed with the Stock Exchange trial had destroyed his naval career, although not his personal popularity. As a Radical leader he had bravely taken on the system, and been crushed by it.

He had not been to sea for more than nine years, so there could be no certainty that he would regain his old skills. As the little boat carried him, Kitty and their two small children across to Boulogne, only he, with his wild plans for placing Napoleon on the throne of South America, could have had much cause for optimism about the future. His career in the Royal Navy had been marginalized; he had almost run out of money; his parliamentary life had been cut short by a vindictive government determined to stamp out opposition; and he was more or less an outlaw. He could little suspect that his exploits in South America were to eclipse anything he had achieved so far, both in audacity and effect.

PART THREE

Sailor of Fortune

Lord of the sea come to us
We are as water and sand oppressed,
We are a people mute and beseiged
Lord of the sea, we call you, singing, to battle
Spanish chains deny us the seas.
Our hopes wither in the Spanish night.
Lord of the sea, grief and rage await you in harbour.
Southern seas are calling you, Lord of the sea . . .

The seaman has arrived! Southern tides welcome the
    man who fled the fog
Chile stretches out dark hands to him, not hiding the
    danger.
When the warrior's ship receives the four gifts,
The starred cross of the southern sky, the clover with
    four diamonds,
He looks down at my poor country, ragged and
    bloodstained,
And understands without arrogance, that here he
    must found
Another star of the sea which will defend
With iron-wrought rays the cradle of the afflicted . . .

And now I ask the void, the shadowed past, Who
  was
This unquiet champion of liberty and the waves?
Is this the man whose enemies clothe him in dark
  colours?
Is this the man who deviously hides a bag of gold in
  London?
Was this the sword expelled from the abbey?
Is this the man whom the tireless enemy still abuse in
  their texts?
Admiral, your eyes open each day as you come from
  the sea.
The narrow hemisphere is lit with your unconquer-
  able splendour!
At night your eyes close on the high mountains of
  Chile.

Pablo Neruda, extracts from *Cochrane de Chile* (1970).
Reproduced by kind permission of Douglas Cochrane.

CHAPTER 15

Admiral Cochrane

Cochrane decided to wait in Boulogne no longer for his tardy steamship and on 15 August left aboard the *Rose* for the Azores and the journey across to South America. The long voyage provided ample time for reflection. The dullness and occasional drama of a long, uneventful sea journey is a powerful sedative for a man of irrepressible activity. As the ship approached St Helena, news reached him from another ship that the Spanish had struck back against Chile, landing an army at the port of Valdivia. Cochrane was ordered to proceed as fast as possible to his new command. He could not stop at St Helena and embark his mutual admirer (yet how he proposed to get Napoleon off the island, and what the reaction of the Chileans would have been if he had, were not obvious). Yet he did not abandon his project. He fully intended to return to pick up the Emperor after he had sorted out the opposition in the Pacific.

The *Rose* sailed southwards and downwards past the barren Patagonian coast towards Cape Horn. The seas grew rougher and the jagged mountains of the promontory came into view. As they turned the Cape a violent westerly gale blew, bringing freezing rain and snow in the early spring of the southern hemisphere. It took three days to round the Horn and, in easier seas, they sailed up past the astonishingly beautiful fiords of southern Chile, where virgin forests extended to the water from the coccyx of the Andean spine of South America. Even for a man of Cochrane's experience this was a spectacular and unknown territory.

They sailed several weeks along that staggering coastline

which gave way to open plain before the shimmering grandeur of the high Andes behind, before reaching the Chilean port of Valparaiso in the magnificent splendour of its bay on 28 November 1818. Cochrane, Chile's admiral, rose to his new appointment at once. He was received with the usual warmth of welcome and emotion of Latin Americans. The government of Valparaiso promptly held a large ball in honour of the exhausted sailors and the Liberator of Chile, Bernardo O'Higgins, travelled the 100 miles or so from the capital, Santiago, to greet him. Cochrane, not to be outdone, invited his new Chilean friends to a dance on St Andrew's night and attended in the full costume of a Highland chief, wearing Royal Stuart tartan. According to one of those present:

> Extraordinary good cheer was followed by toasts drank with uncommon enthusiasm in extraordinary good wine. No one escaped its enlivening influence. St Andrew was voted the patron saint of champagne, and many curious adventures of that night have furnished the subject of some still remembered anecdotes.

At this entertainment, Cochrane had the opportunity to survey both his new colleagues and the enormity of the task he had taken on. There were four principal leaders on the Chilean side. The first was O'Higgins himself – a far from impressive figure at first sight. Small, ugly and paunchy, with a squashed, piggy face framed by prominent sideboards, he yet had a steely eye and directness of expression which immediately impressed Cochrane.

O'Higgins was the illegitimate son of the former Viceroy of Peru, an Irishman who had worked his way up from obscurity to the pinnacle of power in Spanish America. This bastard son had been treated with appalling emotional cruelty by his father, and his private life had been stunted as a result. He never married or found an emotional attachment other than to his adored mother and sister. He had won his reputation through a series of remarkable military actions in southern Chile, culminating in one of the most terrible battles and breakouts in history, at Rancagua. Cochrane warmed to the honesty, straightforward-ness, naïvety and courage that were his hallmarks – and also his defects as a national leader. Although the squat O'Higgins could hardly have been more of a physical opposite to the tall, gangling Cochrane, they were temperamentally similar.

The second and more powerful figure Cochrane encountered was an altogether different personality: José de San Martín was tall – although not as tall as Cochrane – withdrawn and calcu-lating. Although capable of animated and articulate conversa-tion, he was often taciturn and militaristic with a secretive side that trusted few men – a 'cold fish' in the English term. Statuesque, good-looking with a fine profile, a prominent nose and a long face, he was self-contained and highly intelligent. Although an Argentine, he had been the real author of the liber-ation of Chile, leading an army across the Andes with minimal loss of men to surprise and rout the Spaniards.

San Martín was the real power in Chile, but he had wider ambitions: to conquer and take the jewel in the Spanish crown, Peru. The general, who worked through the secret quasi-Masonic Lautaran lodge and was a superb spymaster, was such an enigmatic figure that it was impossible for Cochrane to compre-hend him or to get on well with him. Soon their acquaintance was to turn into intense dislike – a tragedy because San Martín was much more honest and straightforward in his aim of liber-ating South America than his guarded and secretive personality suggested, and Cochrane was much less arrogant than he affected. The two men, from the first, distrusted each other – which is often the case when two supremely self-confident egotists fight for territory.

There were two minor figures present. Blanco Encalada, the twenty-eight-year-old Chilean naval commander being replaced by Cochrane, was young and vigorous, and had only just returned from a remarkable coup for an inexperienced commander: he had captured a 48-gun Spanish frigate from under the guns of Spanish batteries. He had also performed well at an action off the Chilean port of Valparaiso which had been blockaded by the royalist flagship, the *Esmeralda*, and the brigantine, the *Pezuela*. The *Lautaro* (formerly the 800-ton East Indiaman the *Wyndham* with 34 guns) under a former British naval officer, William O'Brien, and the dashing but inexperienced Blanco Encalada, had attacked and briefly boarded the much bigger ship. O'Brien had been killed when the much bigger crew of the *Esmeralda* beat off the boarders. But both Spanish ships fled to Talcahuano, ending the blockade. With some grumbling, but on the whole extraordinary good grace, he agreed to serve under Cochrane. The Chilean navy minister, José Ignacio Zenteno, an able if devious figure who welcomed the country's new naval deliverer with a certain amount of apprehension, was also there.

There were British personalities present. The foremost was Major William Miller, just twenty-three years old, tall, utterly fearless, highly intelligent and destined to become one of the influential participants in Latin America's wars of independence. For someone so similar in character to Cochrane, and a possible rival, it was astonishing that the two from the first became close friends. Miller's admiration for Cochrane was without reservation. He went on to feats as astonishing on the appalling terrain of the Andes as Cochrane was to achieve at sea, and was to suffer terribly in the process. Undoubtedly the difference in age was a help: Cochrane treated the much younger man with encouragement and admiration.

The other two senior Englishmen present were of a very different calibre. Captain Martin Guise was a fine seaman of very little intelligence while Captain Spry was a rough-minded minor sailor who had persuaded him to sail an 18-gun brig into Valparaiso and sell it to the Chileans. Both had entertained hopes of commanding the Chilean navy until Cochrane's appointment.

Besides this mix of friends and rivals, Cochrane's eyes alighted on the extraordinary beauty of Chilean girls, their hair 'adorned with jasmine and other flowers', according to Miller. The jasmine buds 'in the course of an hour will open and present the appearance of a bushy, powdered wig'. But Kitty Cochrane and

Señora Encalada dominated the entertainments, 'both young, fascinating and highly gifted'. O'Higgins invited Cochrane to a lavish entertainment in the government palace of Santiago, a round of picnics, and a performance of *Othello*.

He and his crew, after the long, dreary journey, indulged in the simple pleasure of playing cricket with the substantial body of Englishmen present in this remote corner of the earth. There were two Royal Navy ships in port, the *Blossom* and the *Andromache*, and many expatriates. In the gentle, temperate climate of mid-Chile, it must have been wonderfully relaxing.

Within a few days, Cochrane began to size up the 'navy' he had been appointed to command as 'admiral'. After the formidable efficiency of a Royal Navy crew, and the sleek line of the British ships he had commanded, the shambles that presented themselves to his experienced eye must have come as a shock. The squadron consisted of the ship just captured by Encalada, the impressive 48-gun Spanish frigate now predictably renamed the *O'Higgins*, as well as two large converted East Indiamen, the *San Martin* and *Lautaro* which had 34 guns each. There were four smaller ships – the *Galvarino* – the boat sold to the Chileans by Guise and Spry – the *Pueyrredon*, the *Chacabuco* and the *Araucano*.

With this little force he was supposed to take on the might of the Spanish Pacific fleet headed by the 44-gun *Esmeralda*, a frigate, and thirteen more of its size, as well as twenty-eight gunboats. The Chilean fleet was outnumbered more than four to one. The crews were inexperienced, untrained and spoke little English. Fortunately, to his mind, they were largely officered by seasoned Englishmen and Americans. The latter were amongst the best sailors in the world, reared on the east coast, constantly protecting the waters of their hemisphere, and now briskly being trained to form the backbone of the American Navy.

Cochrane made his preparations for only seven weeks before he decided to set sail from Valparaiso. Although he had relished the feel of a ship under him for the past few months, he had not been its captain. Now he was in charge of a fleet, albeit of a fairly rudimentary kind, for the first time in his life, and after nearly ten years' absence from command. He had no doubt of his ability to subdue the enemy: had he not captured Spanish ships time after time in the past? His destination was 1500 miles to the north along the long Pacific coast, the port of Callao serving Lima, the very heart of Spain's Latin American empire.

After 300 years, with revolutionary ferment underway in Spain, following Napoleon's invasion, the empire itself was beginning to crumble, but the mother country's fightback was vicious, cruel and determined. In the north the Liberator, Simon Bolivar, had four times tried to liberate his native Venezuela, and four times been driven off amid scenes of grotesque carnage: now he commanded a guerrilla camp in the remote Orinoco basin. In southern South America, Argentina had secured a precarious independence, and through San Martin's heroic crossing of the Andes with an army had come to Chile's aid in securing hers.

Now, in a breathtaking display of strategic genius, San Martin had decided to liberate Peru from the sea, rather than across the punishing uplands of the altiplano of what is now modern Bolivia. To do this he needed to wrest control of the Pacific from the Spaniards. Thomas Cochrane was the necessary instrument for this – in spite of the fact that from the moment they had met the two men could not stand each other.

He arrived after a long voyage off Callao, a beautifully sited port along the strip of arid land that lies between the Pacific and the Andes. Callao was the key to Lima, because it supplied all the food and luxuries for the city, as well as exporting Peru's huge mineral treasures back to the mainland. Lima was dependent on Callao, deriving little sustenance from the barren earth or the mountains further inland. The key to Lima's wealth was the gold and silver to be found in the mountains of the interior, which had financed the creation of what to this day is probably the most architecturally distinguished city on the continent.

Cochrane, on his long journey from Valparaiso to Callao, had one unexpected consolation. As he embarked, his four-year-old son had managed to persuade a seaman to carry him to the water's edge to wave his daddy goodbye. His mother, Kitty, suddenly spotted little Thomas on the shore. She ran desperately down among the crowd assembled there to find that the child had managed to scramble aboard one of the departing boats and was being rowed to the flagship.

With the entire fleet preparing to sail, Cochrane was not the kind of man to delay departure for his son to return to shore (Bolivar, at about this time, had excited odium for delaying an invasion of Venezuela so that his mistress could come aboard). So the tough sailors amused themselves by sewing a tiny midshipman's uniform for little Thomas, and he became the ship's mascot, trundling about to their salutes, an object of affection and good cheer.

As already noted, Cochrane's ships were not manned by disciplined British crews, but by a mixture of some British, some American, some Chilean and many other nationalities. Quite quickly he realized that despite his natural authority, their loyalty could not be assured, except aboard his own flagship where his personality made itself felt. After hearing that the crew of the *Chacabuco* was in a state of mutiny and refusing to raise anchor, Cochrane threatened to blow it out of the water unless the ringleaders were put aboard a boat. They were then sentenced to jail and handed over to the civilian authorities. Such draconian measures were essential: one of the first things Cochrane had to do was to impress discipline upon his dishevelled crew, and this had presented him with the perfect opportunity.

It was much less easy to impose victory upon the enemy. It must be remembered that Cochrane was a supremely confident man: in spite of his sufferings at the hands of the Admiralty and of the courts, he had performed with flawless skill as a seaman and captain against the two greatest naval rivals to Britain, France and Spain, only losing one of dozens of battles. The tottering Spanish Empire in South America must have seemed an easy target. It proved not to be so at all, least of all for his ropy little fleet of three medium-sized frigates and four gunboats. Soon his Chilean allies were wondering whether he had lost his touch during his many years ashore and whether Encalada after all would make a better admiral.

He failed to capture a Spanish bullion ship off the Peruvian coast before arriving at Callao; and his subsequent attack on the port – for the first time in his career – was a total fiasco, proving that even he was merely mortal. Cochrane picked his moment to attack in the middle of a carnival. The Viceroy had come down to the port to inspect the fortifications for the event. Cochrane, not knowing this, decided to send in his flagship and another ship, both flying the flags of the United States. As they sailed in, a series of explosions rang out, and Cochrane fired back, blowing his cover. In fact it had been a celebratory salute to the Viceroy. The batteries in the Spanish fortifications started to fire back at the 'American' ships in earnest.

Cochrane was overwhelmingly outgunned. There were 350 guns ashore at Callao and 160 guns on board ships in the port. With mounting horror he realized he had sailed straight into a hornet's nest. Worse was to follow: the fogs that pervade that gloomy coastline suddenly descended as he moved to attack a small Spanish gunboat, preventing the enemy gunners seeing him but also immobilizing him. When the fog lifted, the wind had dropped, and he was becalmed under the enemy guns, which resumed firing.

As he tried to use what little wind there was to sail out, another alarming incident concerning tiny Tom took place. On Cochrane's account:

> When the firing commenced I had placed the boy in my after-cabin, locking the door upon him; but not liking the restriction, he contrived to get through the quarter gallery window, and joined me on deck, refusing to go down again. As I could not attend to him, he was permitted to remain and, in a miniature midshipman's uniform which the seamen had made for him, was busying himself in handing powder to the gunners. Whilst thus employed, a round-shot took off the head of a marine close to him, scattering the unlucky man's brains in his face. Instantly recovering his self-possession, to my great relief – for, believing him to be killed I was spellbound with agony – he ran up to me exclaiming, 'I am not

hurt, Papa. The shot did not touch me. Jack says the ball is not made that can kill Mama's boy.'

Cochrane ordered him to go below but his sailors frustrated this. 'Put your head in the hole the shot made, and sit there. No shot will come through the same breach again,' the little boy was told by a seaman.

With some difficulty the two ships made off and rejoined the flotilla. They decided to occupy the little island of San Lorenzo some 3 miles off shore. There a small and sleepy Spanish garrison was surprised and Cochrane liberated a contingent of Chilean prisoners who had spent eight years in wretched confinement. Cochrane observed:

> The unhappy men had ever since been forced to work in chains under the supervision of a military guard – now prisoners in turn; their sleeping place during the whole week of this period being a filthy shed, in which they were every night chained by one leg to an iron bar. The joy of the poor fellows at their deliverance, after all hope had fled, can scarcely be conceived.

The Viceroy sent a pompous message:

> The regulating principles of the proceedings of the Viceroy shall always be those of such gentleness and condescension as shall not derogate from the dignity of his official situation; and he will not now comment on the occupation of a nobleman of Great Britain, a country in alliance with the Spanish people, employing himself in command the naval forces of a government hitherto unacknowledged by any nation on the globe.

Cochrane was preparing for his next assault on Callao. The opportunity presented itself to do what he had dreamed of ever since Aix Roads: to send in an explosion ship to Callao, followed by his small fleet. The enterprise was dogged by bad luck from the first.

A laboratory was formed upon San Lorenzo, under the super-
intendence of Major Miller. On the 19th of March, an acci-
dental explosion took place, which scorched the major and
ten men in a dreadful manner. The former lost the nails from
both hands, and the injury was so severe that his face was
swelled to twice its natural dimensions . . . He was blind and
delirious for some days, and was confined to his cabin for six
weeks.

At last Cochrane sent in his explosion vessel, but it was seized by
gunboats from Callao before it could go off. It was a lesson in
humility.

He tried to make up for it by raiding Spanish shipping coming
up the coast, including one ship at Pativilca with 70,000 dollars
aboard, and nearly as much aboard the *Gazelle*, and soon re-
established his old reputation as a buccaneer. He became known
as El Diablo – the Devil – in spite of his failures. In May he
returned to Valparaiso and young Tom was returned to his
anxious mother. O'Higgins put on the bravest face possible,
welcoming the little fleet but refusing to fund any more naval
operations.

Meanwhile the Spaniards were said to be massing an army of
20,000 men to recapture the colonies, landing first in the Plate
region, then Chile. San Martin argued that the fleet should sail
round Cape Horn to intercept the Spaniards. Cochrane refused,
partly because his men were unprepared to face the rigours of
such a voyage, partly because Chile would be left at the mercy of
the Spanish Pacific squadron. O'Higgins agreed. Soon it
emerged that the Spanish invasion force had been decimated by
the plague and would not sail.

Cochrane resolved to sail back to Callao. But José Zenteno,
the Chilean navy minister, insisted that he pledge not to come
within range of the shore guns. San Martin observed nevertheless:

Cochrane assures me that on the twenty-fourth of this month,
shortly after eight in the evening, the shipping in Callao will

all be ablaze and that by the 15th October I shall have received his despatch. I am sure that Cochrane will be as good as his word.

This seemingly impossible feat was to be achieved by 1000 rockets, fired at night, prepared by one of Congreve's assistants, Mr Goldsack. But these turned out to be disastrous duds.

Not more than one rocket in six went off properly. Some burst from the badness of the cylinders; some took a wrong direction, in consequence of the sticks being made of knotty wood; and most of them fell short. The shells sunk a gunboat, and did some execution in the forts and amongst the shipping; but the lashings of the mortar-bed gave way, and it was with difficulty that the logs of which the raft was composed were kept together. A great deal of time was lost in repairing the defective state of the fastenings. Daylight began to appear, and the rockets having completely failed, the rafts were ordered to retire, and were towed off ...

Spanish prisoners . . . as was found on examination, had embraced every opportunity of inserting handfuls of sand, sawdust, and even manure, at intervals in the tubes, thus impeding the process of combustion, whilst in the majority of instances they had so thoroughly mixed the neutralising matter with the ingredients supplied, that the charge would not ignite at all, the result being complete failure in the object of the expedition . . .

Cochrane tried to goad the Spanish fleet out to do battle, but to no avail. Worse, a boom had been constructed across the harbour entrance to prevent him breaking in.

Next day Cochrane sent in his latest 'explosion vessel', which became becalmed just short of the boom protecting Callao. The shore batteries opened up and spectacularly blew up the ship. Cochrane had now twice tried to seize the Spanish fleet at Callao with the same tactics and self-confidence with which he had attacked the French ships at Aix Roads and twice failed; it

seems that his touch had left him in middle age – or, more char-
itably, that commanding a fleet of mixed nationalities was an
entirely different business from commanding a well-disciplined
British ship. By this stage, he knew, the Chilean government
which had employed him was getting restless. Although he had
delivered some prizes, he had twice failed against the Spanish
fleet and had not yet secured a single significant victory. He
decided, as in the past, on a stroke of pure boldness.

CHAPTER 16

Valdivia and the *Esmeralda*

Forbidden to enter Callao, he sought another target. After returning to Valparaiso, Cochrane turned his thoughts to the port of Valdivia in southern Chile, known as Chile's Gibraltar for its impregnability, and a continuing Trojan horse for a possible Spanish landing behind Chilean lines. Ironically the fortifications had been constructed by O'Higgins's own father. The scene was now set for the first of the two greatest battles in the Pacific war.

Valdivia consisted of a finger of sea leading to the river Valdes, enclosed by land on almost all sides, approached by a single, narrow 1200-yard channel. The almost landlocked anchorage was covered on one side of the channel by no fewer than four forts, and by one significant fort and four smaller ones on the other side. In the middle of the channel was the fortified island of Manzanera. It would be suicidal for any ship to attack down the narrow channel under the guns of the forts, which made the harbour virtually unassailable.

Cochrane, on arriving off the coast, made a reconnaissance. Hearing that three Spanish ships were expected in Valdivia – one of which he knew had been delayed, another sunk off Cape Horn, and a third in hiding – he hoisted a Spanish flag, coolly dropped anchor off the port, and requested a pilot from the Spaniards. As soon as the pilot's party arrived, they were made prisoner, and the pilot compelled to lead Cochrane into the entrance of the channel, where he was able to ascertain the positions and strengths of the forts before sailing out again, to the astonishment of the Spaniards on shore. From the same pilot,

Cochrane learnt that another ship was approaching the estuary, and this he captured, together with the 20,000 dollars aboard. Cochrane sailed north to Concepcion, where he picked up 250 soldiers from the local Chilean garrison before returning, at the end of January 1820, opposite Valdivia.

On the night of 29 January, at the full height of the Chilean summer, while Cochrane was sleeping and only a midshipman was in charge, the *O'Higgins* ran aground in a wind. Cochrane vividly described the near-disaster:

> On the night of the 29th we were off the island of Quiriquina in a dead calm. From excessive fatigue in the execution of subordinate duties I had laid down to rest, leaving the ship in charge of the lieutenant, who took advantage of my absence to retire also, surrendering the watch to the care of a midshipman, who fell asleep. Knowing our dangerous position, I had left strict orders to be called the moment a breeze sprang up; but these orders were neglected, and a sudden wind taking the ship unawares, the midshipman, in attempting to bring her round, ran her upon the sharp edge of a rock where she lay beating, suspended as it were upon her keel; and had the swell increased she must inevitably have gone to pieces. The 600 men aboard attempted to abandon ship, although the boats would hold only 150. But the first sounding gave five feet of water in the hold, and the pumps were entirely out of order. Our carpenter, who was only one by name, was incompetent to repair them; but having myself some skill in carpentry, I took off my coat and by midnight got them into working order, the water meanwhile gaining on us though the whole crew were engaged in bailing it out with buckets.
>
> To our delight, the leak did not increase, upon which I got out the stream anchor and commenced heaving off the ship, the officers clamouring to ascertain first the extent of the leak. This I expressly forbade as calculated to damp the energy of the men, whilst as we now gained on the leak, there was no doubt the ship would swim as far as Valdivia, which was the chief point to be regarded; the capture of the fortress being

my object, after which the ship might be repaired at leisure. [Most of his ammunition had been destroyed.] About this I cared little as it involved the necessity of using the bayonet in our anticipated attack and to facing this weapon the Spaniards had, in every case, evinced a rooted aversion.

Miller confirmed the story, citing Cochrane's 'indefatigable activity and skill' and 'serenity and firmness'. Cochrane decided that the impossible expedition to Valdivia must proceed:

Cool calculation would make it appear that the attempt to take Valdivia is madness. This is one reason why the Spaniards will hardly believe us in earnest, even when we commence. And you will see that a bold onset, and a little perseverance afterwards, will give a complete triumph.

He transferred his men from the crippled flagship, which he feared would have been recognized in Valdivia, to two small companion ships, the brig *Intrepido* and the schooner *Montezuma*. He made for a surf-strewn beach just outside the entrance to the harbour, the Aguada del Ingles, behind Fort Ingles, determining not to attack from the sea but from the land, immobilizing the forts that made it so dangerous to enter the landlocked stronghold by sea. But his ships would have to come within range of Fort Ingles itself.

Once again raising the Spanish flag, his two small ships arrived off the beach. A Spanish-born officer told the commander ashore that they were escorts for a Spanish convoy which had been detached from the main fleet, and that they had lost their boats and so could not land. In fact, the boats were in the water on the seaward side of the ships, in preparation for a landing. One, however, drifted free, and the suspicious Spaniards saw that the officer was lying.

The alarm was given, and Fort Ingles opened fire at point-blank range. Cochrane immediately decided to attack, sending Miller in charge of forty-four marines. The boats set out for the beach, their oars snagged by a huge quantity of seaweed. The

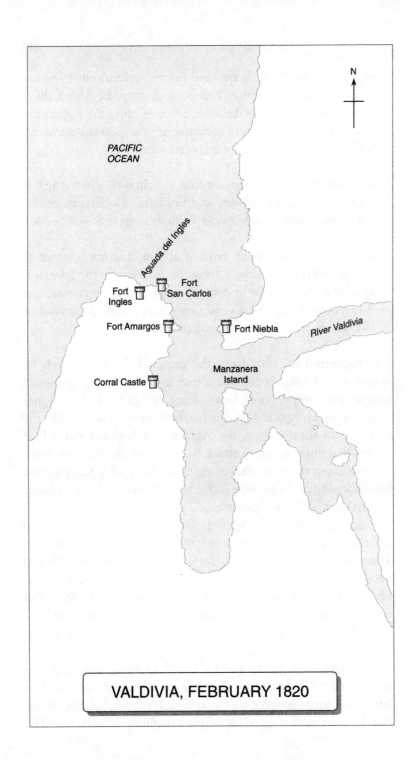

PACIFIC
OCEAN

Aguada del Ingles

Fort
San Carlos

Fort
Ingles

Fort Amargos

Fort Niebla

River Valdivia

Corral Castle

Manzanera
Island

N

VALDIVIA, FEBRUARY 1820

boats were peppered with musket shot from a force of seventy-five Spaniards ashore. But Miller led an ordered bayonet charge which soon dispersed the defenders on the beach. The 250 Chilean troops behind the advance guard were landed safely.

When darkness fell, Cochrane decided to stage the attack on Fort Ingles. He divided his men into two forces, one in front and one creeping around the back of the fort. Those in front attacked, firing into the air and creating the maximum disturbance. The larger second party, under Ensign Vidal, crossed the ditch surrounding the fort across an improvised bridge in silence and climbed the ramparts behind the Spaniards, who were concentrated to face the first assault.

The rear party attacked, with the furious cries of the savage Araucanian Indians of southern Chile. The garrison fled, and in so doing panicked the 300 Spanish troops sent to reinforce the fort when news of the Chilean landing had reached the other Spanish positions. With frenzied bayonet charges, the Chileans turned a retreat into a rout, pursuing them to Fort Carlos, where the defenders were unable to close the gates before the Chilean attackers broke in.

The disorderly retreat, now swollen by the occupants of the second fort, continued to Fort Amargos, and once again the Chileans were so hard on the Spaniards' heels that they broke into the garrison, routing the Spaniards. The ever-growing horde of fleeing Spaniards reached Corral Castle, where they at last succeeded in keeping out the Chileans. This buttress was much better defended, and could have withstood a prolonged siege.

As the exhausted but elated Cochrane surveyed the night's work, he had succeeded in taking three out of the four forts commanding the western approaches to the Channel. But the Spanish fleet was still protected from Corral Castle and Fort Niebla on the eastern shore, and Manzanera Island in the middle, which between them could inflict a withering crossfire on any ship attempting to make the passage. Cochrane could be satisfied, though, that he had captured part of the Spanish artillery on Fort Chorocomayo overlooking Corral Castle, and could bombard it at daylight.

He did not expect the Spaniards simply to give up. Yet they had lost 100 killed and 100 prisoners, and there were only about 300 left, facing about the same number of Chileans. Colonel Hayas, the commander of Corral Castle, was sinking into an alcoholic stupor, realizing the position was hopeless. Before daylight he ordered half of his men onto the boats below the castle to cross the harbour, and himself surrendered with the rest to Miller. Cochrane had secured the whole western bank of the 'impregnable' harbour at Valdivia at a cost of just seven dead and nineteen wounded, through the simple expedient of attacking from the land, not from the sea.

The following morning his two small ships, the *Intrepido* and the *Montezuma*, sailed into the channel under the fire of the smaller eastern forts, and anchored off Fort Corral to ferry Chilean troops across for an attack on the other side of the harbour. A moment later, on Cochrane's orders, the *O'Higgins* appeared and, assuming that the large ship was bringing a wave of fresh troops, Spanish morale finally collapsed. Fort Niebla and the other eastern defences were abandoned as the Spanish troops evacuated upriver to Valdivia. In fact, the *O'Higgins* had no troops aboard, not even enough to man the guns, only a skeleton crew and was steadily sinking; it only just made it to the beach. But Cochrane had guessed accurately that it would inspire terror in the demoralized Spaniards.

He wasted no time. Two days later he sent the *Intrepido* and the *Montezuma* upriver towards the town of Valdivia. The former ran aground. But when he reached the town he found that the Spanish garrison and the army had fled, and the local notables were suing for peace. Cochrane had captured the 'Gibraltar' of Spanish power, along with 10,000 cannon shot, 170,000 cartridges, 128 pieces of artillery, 50 tons of gunpowder and a ship – at a cost of seven dead.

Emboldened, Cochrane sent a force to Chiloe in the far south, but this failed, and Miller, leading the attack, was injured in the thigh and his right foot was crushed by a cannonball. The Chileans performed magnificently:

The marines who, with affectionate fidelity, had borne off Major Miller had been careful to protect him from fire, though two out of the three who carried him were wounded in the act; and when, on arrival at the beach, they were invited by him to enter the boat, one of them, a gallant fellow named Roxas of whom I had spoken highly in my despatches from Valdivia on account of his distinguished bravery, refused saying, 'No sir, I was the first to land and I mean to be the last to go on board'. He kept his word; for on his commander being placed in safety he hastened back to the little band, now nearly cut up, and took his share in the retreat, being the last to get into the boats. Such were the Chilenos.

Three weeks later, Cochrane returned to Valparaiso in triumph. But considering himself cheated of his prize money in England, and determined to make his fortune, he refused to hand over the booty he had seized at Valdivia. Chilean gratitude turned to anger, and the Scottish admiral was threatened with prosecution. Cochrane promptly threatened to resign, along with twenty-three of his officers, and had his chief rival, Captain Guise, arrested for insubordination. The Chilean navy minister, José Zenteno, begged him to stay:

> [Your] resignation would involve the future operations of the arms of liberty in the New World in certain ruin; and ultimately replace in Chile, your adopted home, that tyranny which your Lordship abhors, and to the annihilation of which your heroism has so greatly contributed.

O'Higgins and San Martin made the same plea. Cochrane, mollified, now felt emboldened to further his own private designs. He sent off an officer, Lieutenant-Colonel Charles, on the long journey around Cape Horn to St Helena, to summon the brooding potential liberator of South America. But by the time Charles had arrived, Napoleon's health had deteriorated badly and he was in no condition to come. Cochrane's most quixotic dream was over.

Back in the real world San Martin's large expeditionary force departed on 21 August 1820 aboard Cochrane's fleet. O'Higgins declared 'Four small ships once gave Spain the dominion of America; these will wrest it from her.' He wrote to the Peruvians: 'Liberty, the daughter of heaven, is about to descend on your lands.' The next great chapter in the vast enterprise of Latin America's liberation was now under way. It was not to prove quite so easy.

Cochrane bitterly resented San Martin's role as overall commander of the expedition, and relations between the two proud men were fraught from the beginning. San Martin decided to disembark at Pisco, 150 miles to the south of Lima, where he sent a force inland to begin the campaign against the largest and most entrenched Spanish army in the Americas.

The belligerent Cochrane fumed with impatience at these cautious tactics. He insisted that an attack be made on Lima immediately. At length San Martin re-embarked and sailed past Lima to land at Ancon. Cochrane had now decided to attack from the sea, whatever San Martin's plans, which he regarded as cowardly and dilatory. On 3 November, he sailed the *O'Higgins* down to Callao on a reconnaissance mission, daringly passing down the natural Boqueron Channel between the island of San Lorenzo and the port.

Two of the biggest Spanish warships, the *Prueba* and the *Venganza*, were absent from the port. But the 44-gun frigate *Esmeralda* was at anchor. It was the flagship of the Spanish fleet, which included 27 gunboats and several blockships. The shore battery had 300 guns, and the harbour was protected by an anchored boom.

There followed the most swashbuckling episode in Cochrane's career. Commanding just 160 seamen and eighty marines, he resolved not only to singe the King of Spain's beard, but to pull it off: he was aiming to hijack, or 'cut out', the Spanish flagship from the rest of the fleet at dead of night. William Stevenson, his able secretary, kept his orders for this astonishing escapade:

The boats will proceed, towing the launches in two lines parallel to each other, which lines are to be at the distance of three boats' lengths asunder. The second line will be under the charge of Captain Guise, the first under that of Captain Crosbie. Each boat will be under the charge of a commissioned officer, and the whole under the immediate command of the admiral. The officers and men are all to be dressed in white jackets, frocks and shirts, and are to be armed with pistols, sabres, knives, tomahawks or pikes.

Two boatkeepers are to be appointed to each boat who, under no pretence whatever, shall quit their respective boats, but are to remain with them therein and take care the boats do not get adrift. Each boat is to be provided with one or more axes, which are to be slung to the girdles of the boat-keepers. The frigate *Esmeralda* being the chief object of the expedition, the whole force is first to attack that ship which, when carried, is not to be cut adrift, but to remain in possession of the patriot seamen to ensure the capture of the rest.

At 10 p.m. the little force of fourteen small boats set out from the *O'Higgins*, which was anchored just out of sight of the harbour, rowing through a small gap in the boom which Cochrane had noticed two days before. Just past the boom, the small and silent armada was challenged by a gunboat. Cochrane brought his boat alongside, saying he would surrender. The Spanish commander was suddenly faced by a boatload of armed men and surrounded by others. He yielded quietly.

The little flotilla now rowed past the bulk of a United States warship, the *Macedonian*. As one of Cochrane's officers noted, 'many of her officers hung over the bulwarks, cheered us in whispers, wishing us success, and wishing also that they themselves could join us'.

However the sentries aboard a British ship, the *Hyperion*, loudly challenged Cochrane's boats, making him fear that the Spanish had been alerted. All remained silent elsewhere. Within a few moments, Cochrane's boat was alongside the *Esmeralda*, and he and his men were climbing the main chains from all sides.

The hyperbole of the Chilean historian Simon Camacho was justified:

> It was like a march of ghosts through the night shadows. The illusion was magnified by the white suits they all wore so as to recognise each other in the dark. Had it not been for the terrible and bloody image presented it would have had a poetic beauty.
>
> The Spanish, who with the withdrawal of the warships that had surrounded them were sleeping confidently, awoke startled and with the innate bravery of their race, which had made them so successful in the New World, hurried to defend their vessel. The patriots' daring, which for a moment paralysed the royalists, was comparable to the bravery of those splendid leaders born to fight and knowing no fear. The deck was too narrow for so many heroes. The night needed the midday sun to light up such prowess. Yet for those brave ones who fell shouting 'Long Live Spain', and hurling abuse at the 'pirates', it was in vain. The maintops were full of the admiral's sailors who, from their height, were able to shoot straight at their victims while their swords destroyed the brave Spaniards.

Cochrane himself was one of the first to reach the deck. But the sentries had heard the rattle of the chains and a blow from a musket butt sent him crashing back into his boat, severely injuring his back as the thole-pin, behind the oar, penetrated him near the spine. In agony, he climbed up again to shoot the sentry. Another sentry fired at him, although he succeeded in pushing his assailant overboard.

Cochrane's men streamed aboard, grappling with sentries and shooting at them from all sides. But they had lost the element of surprise, although most of the crew remained below deck. The Spanish admiral sounded the alert and gathered his marines on the forecastle, from which they rained a fusillade of shots down on the deck. Cochrane, along with Captain Guise, led an attack from the deck, but he was shot in the leg, and forced to pull back, directing the assault sitting on a gun. He had now been twice wounded, but was unbowed.

After a fierce firefight with British sailors climbing up the rigging American-style to fire on the Spaniards below, the tide turned against the latter and many dived into the sea, while Admiral Coig of the *Esmeralda* surrendered to Cochrane, but was himself injured by a stray shot shortly afterwards. Simply through staging a surprise attack at the very heart of Spanish strength, Cochrane had succeeded in capturing the flagship.

The difficult part was about to begin: getting it out of the harbour. As soon as he came aboard he had ordered men up the rigging to prepare for sailing. In charge of the ship with the loss of eleven dead and thirty wounded in just 17 minutes of intense fighting, he gave the order to prepare the sails – but not to move. He still wanted to capture two brigs which were nearby, and set other ships adrift:

> The two brigs of war are to be fired on by the musketry from the *Esmeralda*, and are to be taken possession of by Lieutenants Esmond and Morgell in the boats they command; which being done, they are to cut adrift, run out, and anchor in the offing as quickly as possible. The boats of the *Independencia* are to turn adrift all the outward Spanish merchant ships; and the boats of the *O'Higgins* and *Lautaro*, under Lieutenants Bell and Robertson, are to set fire to one or more of the headmost hulks; but these are not to be cut adrift, so as to fall down upon the rest.

Some 300 yards away the main shore batteries and gunboats were blazing blindly away in the dark. It seemed only a matter of time before the ship was hit and became an incandescent target. Cochrane coldly assessed the nearby British and American ships which were leaving the harbour to get away from the fighting. He ordered the same signal lights as they were showing to be hoisted aboard the *Esmeralda*. He judged that the Spaniards would be terrified of sinking a neutral ship. He was right: the guns suddenly fell silent.

Cochrane, having given his orders and been immobilized by his wounded leg and the pain in his back, left for his flagship to have his bleeding staunched. He was furious later to discover that Captain Guise, who he had left in charge, had given the order to sail *Esmeralda* to sail at full speed out of the harbour before, as Cochrane wanted, every vessel there was 'either captured or burned'. Guise claimed that the Chileans were plundering the ship and the English crewmen had broken into the liquor store and were drunk, and that anyway it was more important that the pride of the Spanish navy be attached to the rebel fleet than that it be exposed to further danger. Given the gallant conduct of the crews during the fighting, both stories seemed unlikely. When the Spanish guns opened up again the *Esmeralda* was safely away, along with two captured gunboats. A boat from the American ship, the *Macedonian*, which had cheered Cochrane on, went ashore at Callao the following day for provisions. Its crew were lynched for suspected collaboration in the raid. It had certainly been one of the boldest and most daring raids in naval history.

The significance of the capture of the *Esmeralda*, coming after the loss of the Spanish stronghold of Valdivia, was enormous. Just as San Martin's crossing of the Andes had provided the key to the consolidation of the independence of Argentina and Chile, or Bolivar's crossing of the northern Andes had at last flanked the Spaniards in the north, so Cochrane's mastery of seapower in the Pacific was the turning point in the destruction of the last great redoubt of Spanish power on the continent, Peru. As Captain Basil Hall put it, the capture of the *Esmeralda*

> was a death-blow to the Spanish naval force in that quarter of the world; for, although there were still two Spanish frigates and some small vessels in the Pacific, they never afterwards ventured to show themselves, but left Lord Cochrane undisputed master of the coast.

With Cochrane in undisputed control of the sea the remainder of the Spanish fleet did not dare to stir out of Callao, which was blockaded by the Chileans, and food became increasingly scarce in Lima. Some 650 Spaniards belonging to the crack Numancia battalion deserted to the Chileans in the aftermath of the capture of the *Esmeralda*. News also reached them that the 1500-strong garrison at the port of Guayaquil further up the coast had revolted against the Spaniards.

Control of the sea had allowed the Spaniards to dominate the western side of the continent. With its loss they were defenceless, particularly as Lima, surrounded by an inhospitable desert, was supplied from the sea. Without Cochrane's feats, it would have been impossible safely to transport and supply San Martin's expeditionary force to Peru. San Martin, for once, was generous in his praise:

It is impossible for me to eulogise in proper language the daring enterprise of the 5th of November by which Lord Cochrane has decided the superiority of our naval forces, augmented the splendour and power of Chile, and secured the success of this campaign. I doubt not that His Excellency the Supreme Director will render the justice due to the worthy chief, his officers and other individuals who have had a share in that successful action.

Francisco Encina, Chile's renowned historian, embraces Cochrane thus:

This attack had not the slightest possibility of success in rational terms, but what filled the most courageous sailor with dread was a stimulant to Cochrane. We often said that the impossible attracted him with a certain fascination . . . His career would certainly have lasted only a short time without the trait that constituted the essence of his genius: his incredible resourcefulness in the face of the unexpected and the catastrophic. Most of his attacks were doomed to failure before they began, but in the uproar of the fight, while others become blinded or confused, his eagle eye discovers the enemy's weakness or vacillation and, bewildered by his own reaction, takes advantage of the unexpected to creep out or escape where nobody, except he, could have managed. Because of this one feels tempted to believe that he wills men to succeed and can dominate the forces of nature.

Cochrane was for once modest about his achievement:

I had never seen a greater display of bravery than that of my comrades. The best crew of a British boat would not have improved the perfect way in which orders were carried out.

Cochrane urged San Martin to go in for the kill but the latter, well satisfied with his policy of blockade and slow strangulation of the Spanish capital, refused. Cochrane suspected there was a more sinister motive:

It now became evident to me that the army had been kept inert for the purpose of preserving it entire to further the ambitious views of the general, and that, with the whole force now at Lima, the inhabitants were completely at the mercy of their pretended liberator, but in reality their conqueror.

Cochrane's brilliance as a captain, his skilful and shameless use of deception and his phenomenal skill in using boldness to wrong-foot his enemies was not reflected in either his command of several ships, nor in his political skills. He was a loner, and cussedly awkward. He was soon involved in a furious row with his own crew, which objected to renaming the *Esmeralda* the *Valdivia* – one of Cochrane's triumphs, but also the name of the hated Pedro de Valdivia, *conquistador* of Chile.

Instead of bowing to the understandable feeling of his men, he court-martialled the rebellious officers. Captain Guise thereupon resigned his own command in sympathy, followed by Captain Spry, captain of the *Galvarino*, whom Cochrane court-martialled in retaliation. The two captains went to join San Martin's staff on shore. Cochrane by now had an obsessive hatred of the 'cowardly' commander-in-chief, and vented his frustration at the latter's refusal to attack Lima by continuing to blockade Callao.

On 14 July 1821, he ordered another daring raid, sending Commander Crosbie from his flagship, the *O'Higgins*, to break through another gap in the boom with eight boats: as firing erupted from the batteries in the fortress, Crosbie and his men boarded three small gunboats – *Resolucion*, *San Fernando* and *Mingo* – with 34 guns between them and 'cut out' all three, adding another valuable squadron to the Chilean fleet.

This triumph was followed by depressing news for Cochrane personally: on 5 May 1821 Napoleon, whom he had intended to place in power on the 'throne' of South America, had died aged fifty-one at St Helena. The madcap scheme whereby Cochrane had intended to install his own country's oldest enemy and the scourge of Europe as dictator of a whole continent was now unaccomplishable.

CHAPTER 17

Thomas, Kitty and Maria

Cochrane's disappointment was leavened by the arrival of Kitty aboard HMS *Andromaque* in January 1821. At the age of twenty-five she had established herself as a forceful figure in her own right. Having already endured the humiliation of her husband's imprisonment, once in Chile she had been the object of a knife-point attack by a man, demanding to see Cochrane's secret orders, who had broken into her country home at Quillota. She seized the only document on the table and was slashed with a stiletto. The man was sentenced to death, but after his wife had begged for his life to be spared, Kitty successfully urged that the sentence be commuted to exile.

She had also crossed the Andes in October, through the last of the winter snows to San Martin's old hometown of Mendoza and slept on a dead bullock's hide at the Puente del Inca, which San Martin had crossed so momentously three years before. On the way down a stray Spanish soldier had attacked her and very nearly pushed her to the edge of a precipice, before being driven off by Chileans accompanying her.

Now on arrival off Callao, Kitty arranged for the wife of the deposed viceroy of Peru, Doña Angela Pezuela, to be given safe passage to Europe. Doña Angela met Cochrane and told him he was 'a polite rational being, and not the ferocious brute she had been taught to consider him' – which amused the admiral.

Miller described the effect of the vivacious, spirited, pretty Kitty on his troops in the town of Huacho:

The sudden appearance of youth and beauty, on a fiery horse, managed with skill and elegance, absolutely electrified the men, who had never before seen an English lady: *que hermosa! Que graciosa! Que linda! Que guapa! Que airosa! Es un angel del cielo!* were exclamations that escaped from one end of the line to the other . . . Her ladyship turned her sparkling eyes towards the line, and bowed graciously. The troops could no longer confine their expressions of admiration to half-suppressed interjections; loud *viva*s burst from officers as well as men. Lady Cochrane smiled her acknowledgements and cantered off the ground with the grace of a fairy.

On an intrepid visit to the interior of Peru word reached Kitty that Spanish horsemen were galloping to seize her and her small daughter. She and her party had hastily to mount their horses and, with the Spaniards in hot pursuit, to cross a primitive bridge made up of strips of hide across a river gorge on her hands and knees, as it swayed and vibrated alarmingly and threatened to break. Paralysed by vertigo in the middle, she was unable to continue, and had to be rescued by a soldier, who crawled along to help and once they had got to safety cut the bridge behind them.

Soon afterwards she was aboard the *O'Higgins* when the vessel attacked a Spanish ship laden with treasure escaping Callao. When a sailor standing by her hesitated, in her presence, to light the fuse of a cannon, she directed his hand to it and fainted when it exploded. After the action the ship's company sang the national anthem in her honour. But she was by now desperately homesick and determined to return to Britain with her children, which she did in the early summer of 1821.

Lima fell at last on 9 July and Cochrane himself entered a week later to a hero's welcome. His main concern was now to ensure that his men, who had been promised their pay when victory was achieved, were rewarded and that he received his own share of the prize money. San Martin prevaricated. He had come under the influence of the sinister Bernardo Monteagudo, an Argentine-born mulatto, who combined a penchant for vindictiveness, conspiracy and extreme cruelty with a ferociously sensual nature. Monteagudo detested Cochrane and planned to get the Chilean fleet from under Cochrane's command and turn it into Peru's.

San Martin, increasingly befuddled by opium and drink, went along with this, to Cochrane's fury. On 4 August, the two men had a blazing row in the presidential palace. San Martin distrusted Cochrane as a hothead and the latter considered him a coward, a drunk and opium addict, and a potential despot. In fact San Martin was none of those things: his patience had secured the fall of Lima without a fight, and although his deteriorating health had required him to use drink and opium medicinally, he was in command of himself. He was to reveal a character that was anything but despotic in his decision to abandon Peru a few weeks later.

But he was short of money and acutely aware that his political power depended on the troops he had borrowed from Chile. He now sought to equip himself with a navy, offering to 'buy' Chile's fleet for Peru in exchange for the arrears of pay owing. Cochrane greeted the offer with such scorn that San Martin indignantly stood on his dignity and told him to remember he was addressing the 'Protector of Peru'. Cochrane replied, 'It now becomes me as the senior officer of Chile, and consequently the representative of the nation, to request the fulfilment of all the promises made to Chile, and the squadron, but first, and principally, the squadron.'

San Martin retorted angrily, 'Chile! Chile! I will never pay a single real to Chile! And as to the squadron you may take it where you please, and go when you choose: a couple of schooners are quite enough for me.' Then, recovering himself, he asked Cochrane to 'forget my lord what is past.'

'I will when I can,' replied Cochrane, turning on his heels. San Martin followed, offering him command of the new Peruvian fleet – which Cochrane described as a 'dishonourable proposition'. San Martin, turning angry again, told him that he would not pay the sailors.

San Martin, a man who had captured the viceroyalty of Peru almost without an army of his own – even Argentina had refused to send him more than a few men – had tried to 'buy' that of Chile. When this failed, he was to conclude that there was no further role for him in Peru. But Cochrane, who would not stoop to dishonour, was no stranger to drastic action. San Martin's treasure ship, the *Sacramento*, had just departed from Callao to Ancon, further up the coast.

With breathtaking nerve and simplicity, discovering that 'my own view coincided with' those of his crews, Cochrane set off in pursuit, boarded the *Sacramento* and helped himself to a 'yacht-load' of silver and seven sacks of gold. He took 285,000 dollars' worth to pay his men and gave 40,000 to the army – although, to his credit, he took none for himself. The furious San Martin ordered Cochrane to return to Lima, but he set off in pursuit of the two elusive Spanish frigates that had so far escaped him, the *Venganza* and the *Prueba*.

By January 1822 he had reached Acapulco in Mexico without sighting them, only to learn that they had taken refuge in Guayaquil, 1500 miles further south. Before he could reach them, they had surrendered to representatives of San Martin. Angry at being denied his prey and possibly in danger of arrest and execution, Cochrane wisely avoided landing at Callao and sailed south to Valparaiso where, after a splendid reception, he issued dire warnings about San Martin's treachery and attempt to cheat Chile by seizing its navy.

In this bitter dispute between allies, Cochrane was justified in suggesting that San Martin's refusal to pay the navy was indefensible. But Cochrane had acted illegally, like a pirate, in seizing the *Sacramento*, even in the conditions of blurred legality that characterized the wars of liberation. This was mitigated only by his decision to distribute the proceeds to his crews. San Martin was equally at fault in attempting to hijack the Chilean navy as he had hijacked an Argentinian army years earlier (without which, however, Chile would probably have never been liberated). San Martin was soon afterwards outmanoeuvred by Simon Bolivar, liberator of the north, at a famous meeting in Guayaquil and, broken in spirit, decided to hand over the task of liberating the rest of Peru to his rival. Cochrane was to do himself no credit when he attempted to get San Martin arrested in Chile on his sad way into exile a month later.

O'Higgins, meanwhile, had taken both sides. To Cochrane he wrote:

> I would have done the same, had I been in your place, so I repeat that everything has my approbation, and I give you and the worthy officers under your orders my warmest thanks for your loyalty and heroism in the cause of Chile . . . You have no reason to receive orders from Lima, either direct or indirect, since from the moment of the declaration of the independence of that country under the protectorship of San Martin, the provisional power entrusted to him over the fleet ceased . . . We must by no means declare him a pirate, as he might then turn the blockade against us or make common cause with some other country.

Cochrane saw that O'Higgins himself was increasingly being manipulated by another sinister adviser, Rodriguez Aldea. As Cochrane put it of O'Higgins, whom he admired:

> Being himself above meanness, he was led to rely on the honesty of others from the uprightness of his own motives. Though in every way disposed to believe, with Burke, that 'what is morally wrong can never be politically right', he was led to believe that a crooked policy was a necessary evil of government; and as such a policy was adverse to his own nature, he was the more easily induced to surrender the administration to others who were free from his conscientious principles.

Cochrane tried to warn the Chilean leader to his face:

> I wish to give Your Excellency one more proof of my attachment by imploring you to open your eyes to the general discontent prevailing amongst all classes regarding both the declared and the secret measures of Minister Rodriguez, who

has fallen in the public esteem, though he does not realise it, lower than Monteagudo himself, when the populace demanded his resignation and then his punishment. Should Your Excellency then attempt to continue your protection of him, you will yourself be involved in the most serious harm, possibly leading to the destruction of your work and of your personal endeavours for the welfare of the state.

San Martin was soon to depart back across the Andes for ever. Cochrane, living in Valparaiso, after securing full payment for his men, could not extract the payment of the further prize money he felt he was owed.

Cochrane's return to Chile in June 1822 marked the beginning of an extraordinary personal adventure for this most abstemious and seemingly temptation-proof of men. He had been married for just under ten years, the earliest of which had been romantic and fraught, with his family's opposition to the match being followed by Cochrane's imprisonment and his controversial political career. But Thomas and Kitty had at least been together in London. After they had travelled to South America he had seen her infrequently over the previous three years, as he journeyed on his adventures up and down the Pacific coast.

Separated for so long, she had resolved to join him in Peru; she had been unhappy in Chile, although it is not clear why. She wrote to him:

If I go to England I am resolved to live in Tunbridge Wells in the identical cottage that I lived in before we left England. Pray my dearest Cochrane write often and let me hear your sorrows but God forbid you should have any more. You as well as myself have had our share of vexation of the world . . . My dearest husband from whom I have so frequently parted upon former occasions without ever witnessing the least tendency to that despair which is now so strongly depicted in your letters . . . is it possible my dearest Cochrane that you who have left me a woman in this land of strangers and amongst villains as they have now turned out, and of the lowest stamp too, at a moment when I really want consolation can you have lost that strength of mind which it was your pride to know you taught me?

In spite of her escapades there, she seemed no happier in embattled Peru, and decided to return to England with the children. Cochrane must have felt somewhat abandoned by her desire to return to the comforts of civilization – specifically, Tunbridge Wells. When he sailed back to Chile a year later, he was alone.

The Midas touch of romanticism that characterized Cochrane had also been bestowed upon his love life. Kitty Cochrane emerges from her South American adventures as having developed from being a penniless orphan waif into an extraordinary woman: both beautiful and passionate, she had courted danger and adventure in her crossing of the Andes and her exploration of Peru, as well as remarkable fearlessness in fighting off two attackers and engaging in a naval action. She appeared to be every bit Cochrane's equal, and can hardly be faulted for momentarily leaving him and yearning for the comforts of civilization after following him through great perils half-way across the world. She clearly sometimes wilted under the snobbish personal attacks of Cochrane's family and others at her humble upbringing. But she was to be a fearless champion of his reputation in the very highest circles of the land.

She was also conscious of his failings as only a devoted and intelligent wife can be: she was alert to his cavalier assumptions that she must follow him whatever he chose to do, the financial recklessness in spending on his cherished inventions that so curiously was the other side of the coin to his acquisitiveness, his stubbornness, arrogance, self-righteousness and self-absorption; and when these defects became overwhelming, she was to detach herself. Already there were inner tensions within the relationship. Equally, it seemed inevitable that when this brave, spirited and beautiful young woman came to understand her hero's defects and temporarily absented herself from his side, he should himself be tempted to go astray.

In marrying Kitty, Cochrane had behaved with a truly reckless defiance of convention. For the heir to an ancient Scottish earldom to select a pretty, penniless orphan as his wife was almost unheard of in the stratified society of the early nineteenth century, and shocked not just his family, but society in general. Kitty, moreover, not only lacked social standing but, as Cochrane was soon to discover, her courage and zest for life were also accompanied by a passion for some of life's ordinary pleasures: pretty dresses, parties, jewels and ornaments. These the somewhat austere Cochrane, a repressed intellectual beneath the glamour of martial valour, affected to despise. He was not really interested in worldly ostentation – as only so successful a man could afford to be. One with so many advantages and admirers for his great feats could scarcely comprehend why his wife worked to secure the more mundane satisfactions of social success – particularly when she felt she was looked down upon by Cochrane's grand relations and high society in general. Kitty, moreover, was beautiful and – as her letters make clear – sensitive and intelligent; but she was no intellectual.

It was inevitable that someone should step into the vacuum – an equally remarkable woman of an entirely different kind. Maria Graham, unlike the low-born Kitty, came from a Scottish aristocratic background, moving in the same circles as Cochrane himself. She was undoubtedly extremely gifted – as a conversationalist, painter and, above all, as a writer. After resigning herself to mundane marriage but engaging in compulsive travel, she was every bit as unusual as Cochrane and Kitty – a restless, roaming, intellectually curious soul. To Cochrane, at a period in his life when relations with Kitty for the first time became strained, the appearance of this clever, good-looking and gifted intellectual proved irresistible – particularly because she plainly made a dead set at him, abandoning her customary literary objectivity for an embarrassingly doe-eyed hero worship.

To outward appearance, Mrs Graham was no more than the impoverished widow of a humble navy captain. She had arrived at Valparaiso in tragic circumstances. Captain Thomas Graham had fallen ill on the long journey from Rio down round Cape

Horn and on 9 April had died just before they reached the remote coastline which was their destination. Maria, daughter of Admiral Sir George Dundas, had met Cochrane as a girl, while Graham had served briefly under him as a midshipman. She had already travelled to South Africa, India, Italy and Brazil before this latest voyage.

In the tiny provincial society of newly independent Chile, and the even tinier circle of British expatriates there, she had shone with a glow of intellect, talent, personality and good looks that made her stand out among all. With Kitty absent, there was nothing in the way of Maria's characteristically indiscreet outpouring of public admiration for the Admiral, nor his own attentions.

She was lodged in a tiny house in a poorish quarter of Valparaiso, where she replied, to those concerned about her safety, 'I feel very safe, because I believe no one robs or kills without temptation or provocation; and as I have nothing to tempt thieves, so I am determined not to provoke murders.' She had the consolation of joining in the social whirl of the British officers visiting the port.

She had striking, albeit unusual, good looks: her close-cropped dark curly hair and strong chin made her slightly tomboyish in appearance, an impression enhanced by her forth-rightness. But her full lips, classical Greek nose and huge, lustrous brown eyes, together with fine cheekbones and a beautiful soft complexion and graceful neck combined with a flirtatious and mischievous expression to give her an overwhelming feminine allure and, together with her natural intelligence and ready wit, she was quickly established as a star in this provincial society.

The company of these gallant, rough-hewn naval officers was not enough for someone of her formidable talent and intelligence. Her first recorded meeting with Cochrane was when he invited her, along with other prominent members of the local community, including the Governor of Valparaiso, Zenteno, aboard his steam vessel, the *Rising Star*, which his brother

William had at last brought, too late to influence the outcome of the war, to Chile (nor could Cochrane get the Chileans to pay for it, so he was left considerably out of pocket).

The occasion was highly comic. All aboard were deeply impressed at a vessel that could move irrespective of the wind, at least until the engines stopped. As the ship fell victim to the swell, food and furnishings fell about, as did many Chileans who had drunk champagne, believing it to be white beer. Sails were hastily unfurled, but were holed by the engine's funnels. Eventually they drifted back to Valparaiso after an anxious night at sea.

Soon afterwards Maria was invited overland to Cochrane's estate at Quintero. Her hero-worship of him was extreme from the first:

> Lord Cochrane had now been two years and a half at the head of the naval force of Chile; he had taken, destroyed or forced to surrender every Spanish vessel in the Pacific; he had cleared the western coast of South America of pirates. He had reduced the most important fortresses of the common enemy of the patriots, either by storm or by blockade; he had protected the commerce, both of the native and neutral powers; and he had added lustre even to the cause of independence by exploits worthy of his own great name, and a firmness and humanity which had as yet been wanting in the noble struggle for freedom.

She also wrote that he had

> a singular gentle and courteous manner which veiled, while it adorned the determination of his character . . . If I had less cause for gratitude towards Lord Cochrane, I should probably do more justice to him, but to speak of him as he should be spoken of, would require not only an abler pen, but feelings more free from that sensitiveness that makes a friend modest in speaking of a friend, as though he were a part of himself.

Of San Martin, Cochrane's bugbear, she wrote that he was

> so odious as to gain full credit to the idea that he was the insti-
> gator of two attempts to assassinate the Admiral about this
> time, made by persons who contrived to get on board the ship
> by stealth.

San Martin nevertheless paid a visit to her little house on his
return from Peru, where he aroused her amusement by holding
forth for several hours on many subjects, concluding with the
boast that he had brought back the flag of Pizarro. 'Its possession
has always been considered the mark of power and authority. I
have it now!' Presumably he was interested in the personality of
Cochrane's reputed paramour.

Cochrane himself paid repeated visits to her home in mid-
afternoon; they took tea together – once they had to wait for a
cow to be lassoed to provide the milk. The rule of these visits
was that they never talked politics, a relief for Cochrane. It is not
recorded whether others were present; and although no scandal
was reported in Chile's discreet society, it seems obvious that at
the very least a serious platonic relationship was soon developing
between the unusual-looking and sparkling young conversationalist and the dashing middle-aged admiral.

It was obvious that this brilliant and beautiful woman of
thirty-seven had enormous appeal for Cochrane: he found the
female companionship he yearned for in Kitty's absence also
allied to an intellect and talent that his own wife never aspired
to; and to Maria, as to every woman in Chile, the tall, good-
looking naval hero of forty-seven was by far the most interesting
person in the country.

On 14 November she was invited again, in the company of
others, to Cochrane's estate at Quintero, where his own magnificent villa was nearly finished. They conversed, among other
subjects, on earthquakes. Cochrane departed a day later for his
ship, the O'Higgins.

Maria was at Quintero on the 20th when the tremor struck.

Maria's vivid eyewitness accounts remain one of the best descriptions of an earthquake:

> Nov. 20. Yesterday after dinner, Glennie [a seriously ill cousin] having fallen sound asleep in his armchair by the fireside, Mr Bennett and I, attracted by the fineness of the evening, took our seats in the veranda overlooking the bay; and, for the first time since my arrival in Chile, I saw it lighten. The lightning continued to play uninterruptedly over the Andes until after dark, when a delightful and calm moonlight night followed a quiet and moderately warm day.
>
> We returned reluctantly to the house on account of the invalid, and were sitting conversing when, at a quarter past ten, the house received a violent shock, with a noise like the explosion of a mine; and Mr Bennett starting up, ran out exclaiming 'An earthquake! For God's sake follow me!' I, feeling more for Glennie than anything, and fearing the night air for him, sat still; he, looking at me to see what I would do, did the same; until, the vibration still increasing, the chimneys fell, and I saw the walls of the house open. Mr Bennett again cried from without: 'For God's sake come away from the house!'
>
> So we rose, and went to the verandah, meaning of course, to go by the steps; but the vibration increased with such violence, that hearing the fall of a wall behind us, we jumped down from the little platform to the ground; and were scarcely there, when the motion of the earth changed from a quick vibration to a rolling like that of a ship at sea, so that it was with great difficulty that Mr Bennett and I supported Glennie. The shock lasted three minutes, and by the time it was over, everybody in and about the house had collected on the lawn, excepting two persons; one the wife of a mason, who was shut up in a small room which she could not open; the other Carillo, who, in escaping from his room by the wall which fell, was buried in the ruins, but happily preserved by the lintel falling across him . . .
>
> It was some time ere our spirits recovered so as to ask each other what was to be done; but we placed Glennie, who had

had a severe haemorrhage from the lungs instantly, under a tree in an arm-chair. I stood by him till Mr Bennett entered the house, and procured spirit, and water, of which we all took a little: a tent was then pitched for the sick man, and we fetched out a sofa and blankets for him.

Then I got a man to hold a light, and venture with me to the inner rooms to fetch medicine. A second and a third shock had by this time taken place, but so much less violent than the first, that we had reasonable hopes that the worst was over . . .

Having made Glennie lie down in the tent, I put my mattress on the ground by him. Mr Bennett and the overseer and the workmen lay down with such bedding as they could get, round the tent. It was now twelve o'clock: the earth was still at unrest; and shocks, accompanied by noises like the explosion of gunpowder, or rather like those accompanying the jets of fire from a volcano, returned every two minutes. I lay with my watch in my hand counting them for forty-five minutes; and then, wearied out, I fell asleep: but a little before two o'clock a loud explosion and a tremendous shock roused everyone; and a horse and a pig broke loose, and came to take refuge among us. At four o'clock there was another violent shock; and the interval had been filled with a constant trembling, with now and then a sort of cross motion, the general direction of the undulations being north and south. At a quarter past six o'clock there was another shock, which at another time would have been felt severely.

Since that hour, though there has been a continued series of agitations, such as to shake and even spill water from a glass, and though the ground is still trembling under me, there has been nothing to alarm us . . . As daylight came, people from several quarters arrived to enquire after our fate, or communicate their own . . .'

On the 24th she made a perilous journey across ruined roads to Valparaiso, where she found her little house relatively untouched. Cochrane had been aboard ship when the earthquake struck, and had immediately gone towards shore to give assistance in the ship's boat – but this was carried by a tidal wave far up and stranded on dry land, mercifully injuring no one. He ferried victims across to his ships, which seemed safer than on dry land. She went aboard the *O'Higgins*. One day

after dinner, leaning over the taffel-rail of the frigate, musing on all the discomforts of my situation, and the dreariness of my prospects, especially if the rains should come before Glennie was able to move to some warm dry house, I felt a heaviness of heart that few occurrences of my life – and many a painful one I have abided – had occasioned. I saw no prospect of comfort; and suddenly, it came from a quarter where I had not expected, indeed where I should not have dared to expect it.

Lord Cochrane came up to me where I stood and, gently calling my attention, said, that as he was going to sail soon from this country, I should take a great uneasiness from his mind if I would go with him. He could not bear, he said, to leave the unprotected widow of a British officer thus on the beach, and cast away, as it were, in a ruined town, and a country full of civil war! I replied I could not leave my sick relation – I had promised his mother to watch him. 'Nor do I ask you to do so,' answered Lord Cochrane. 'No, he must go too, and surely he will be as well taken care of with us as you could do it alone.'

Cochrane, whose new home had been demolished by the earthquake, and frustrated by the interminable quarrelling of Chileans, had decided to leave. After the destruction of Valparaiso by the earthquake, the Chilean treasury had been depleted. There seemed no more hope for Cochrane of obtaining the money he felt he was owed. Meanwhile Ramon Freire, Governor of Concepcion in the south, asked Cochrane to take part in a coup attempt against O'Higgins. Cochrane declined to do so against his friend, but the coup was staged anyway, successfully.

Cochrane had been approached with an astonishing request to embark on a new adventure: to help to secure the independence of Brazil. He left behind a brief statement:

You know that independence is purchased at the point of the bayonet. Know also that liberty is founded on good faith, and on the laws of honour, and that those who infringe upon these are your only enemies, amongst whom you will never find Lord Cochrane.

It was a curiously wise and moving testimonial for a man usually considered to lack any political sense. He was later bitterly to complain that, when sued by the owners of the neutral ships during the blockade of Callao, he had had to sell his Regent's Park House for £25,000. The Chileans were later to pay him only £6000 in settlement of what they owed him. Once again, Cochrane had failed to restore the fortunes of his illustrious forebears. But he had earned eternal fame, as one of Spanish America's liberators and the hero of Valdivia and the *Esmeralda*.

The day before they departed, Maria Graham reported:

This morning I walked with Lord Cochrane to the tops of most of the hills immediately between the house of the Herradura and the sea; perhaps it may be the last time he will ever tread these grounds for which he was doing so much. We gathered many seeds and roots, which I hope to see springing up in my own land . . . Everybody slept on board last night; and this morning was spent in getting in food and water.

At six o'clock Captain Crosbie went on board the *Montezuma* to haul down Lord Cochrane's flag, and thus formally to give up the naval command in Chile. One gun was fired, and the flag was brought on board the *Colonel Allen* to his Lordship, who was standing on the poop; he received it without apparent emotion, but desired it to be taken care of. Some of those around him appeared more touched than he was. Under that flag he had often led them to victory and always to honour.

That night they had supper on the spectacular promontory of the Herradura, and watched the sun go down, the snow-capped Andes reflecting its last rays.

On 18 January, Thomas and Maria began the long sea journey around the Cape to Rio, which they reached on 13 March. There Cochrane was swept up into a fulsome official welcome, while Maria was left, as she wrote:

> . . . alone and supperless – but thank God, not helpless. I have learned so much in my wanderings as not to be dependent; and, after a time, I had, from the huckster's shop in the neighbourhood, a tolerable tea to give my invalid, and got him to bed in pretty good spirits; and took time afterwards to be pretty miserable myself.

Soon the admiral had departed in his flagship for the north. Maria experienced some of the same feelings of withdrawal as Kitty had in Chile. She amused herself by indulging her interest in travelling outside Rio itself, and her insatiable intellectual curiosity allied to her passionate politics. Of the slave market she wrote:

> I went and stood near them, and though certainly more disposed to weep, I forced myself to smile to them and look cheerfully, and kissed my hand to them, with all of which they seemed delighted, and jumped about and danced, as if returning my civilities.

She also frequented the salons of the Brazilian aristocracy:

> I spent the day with Madame de Rio Seco. Her house is really a magnificent one; it has its ballroom and its music room, its grotto and fountains, besides extremely handsome apartments of every kind, both for family and public use, with rather

more china and French clocks than we should think of
displaying.

She was cutting, however, about her fellow British expatriates:

> However, they are all very civil to me; and why should I see
> faults, or be hurt at the absurd stories they tell of me, because
> they don't know me? Besides 'tis no great affront to be called
> wiser than one is . . .

Almost certainly the 'absurd stories' concerned her relationship
with Cochrane; gossipy Rio was very different from discreet
Chile; and contemporaries were later blandly to assert that she
had been Cochrane's mistress. She was received by the Empress
Leopoldina – plump, plain, scatty but charming, a Habsburg
princess and, like Maria, fascinated by plants and science.

In June 1823, a complication arose: Lady Cochrane arrived in
Rio with her daughter Elizabeth. The motives for Kitty's visit
were uncertain: she may have heard the rumours concerning
Maria from officers returning from Chile and Brazil, or she may
merely have felt she had been gone from her husband for too
long; it is known that 'puritan ladies' in the Cochrane family had
chided her in England, possibly on account of her supposed
desertion, and may have made life intolerable.

It was to Maria that Cochrane, not knowing of Kitty's arrival,
wrote on 2 July, bringing the first news of victory:

> My dear Madam, I have been grieved to learn of your indis-
> position; but you must recover now that I tell you we have
> starved the enemy out of Bahia. The forts were abandoned
> this morning; and the men of war, 13 in number, with about
> 32 sail of transports and merchant vessels, are under sail. We
> shall follow [the *Maria da Gloria* and *Pedro Primeiro*] to the
> world's end. I say again expect good news. Ever believe me,
> your sincere and respectful friend, Cochrane.

Kitty called on Maria for the first time when she fell ill. The two frequently encountered each other thereafter at social gatherings. But it is clear from Maria's journal that they did not get on. She refers to Kitty only in passing, once to suggest that Brazilian woman were as beautiful as she (Kitty was a notable beauty), and to remark about a ball:

> There were only two English-women besides Lady Cochrane and myself, and these were the wives of the consul and the commissioner for the slave business. A foreign gentleman remarked that though we were but four we hardly conversed together. This was perfectly true: I like, when I am in foreign society, to talk to foreigners.

Maria, intelligent, well-read, a spirited conversationalist from an aristocratic family, evidently looked down upon Cochrane's beautiful but unsophisticated wife from a modest background. Kitty, now Marchioness of Maranhao, was appointed a lady-in-waiting to the Empress; but Maria, to her astonishment, was asked to become governess to the Emperor's daughter, Maria de Gloria, later Queen of Portugal. It was a tribute from the bookish Empress to Maria's education. She accepted, obtaining permission from the Empress to visit England before taking up her duties, particularly because Cochrane was still absent up north:

> I saw the Empress, who is pleased to allow me to sail for England in the packet the day after tomorrow. I confess I am sorry to go before Lord Cochrane's return. I had set my heart on seeing my best friend in this country after his exertions and triumph.

With her rival gone, Kitty must have been mightily relieved. But she was soon bored by life in Rio, and fell ill, as had young Elizabeth. By 1824 Cochrane was writing:

> Lady Cochrane embarks this day 16th February for England for the recovery of her health, she having been ill ever since her arrival in this cursed hot place; and the little girl has only

been saved by the utmost attention and great skill of a Dr Williams who is now going home with Lady Cochrane.

Maria, meanwhile, had been staying with her friends the Earl and Countess of Spencer at Althorp, while preparing her journal for publication. She departed in July 1824 to take up her duties at the Brazilian court, and to see Cochrane again. She had her wish. She wrote to her London publisher, John Murray, from the palace in Rio:

> . . . I had a very good passage of only 33 days to Pernambuco, where I found Lord Cochrane blockading the place. He appeared in high health and spirits . . . It is a difficult place to do much with, on account of the very heavy seas that roll in on the shore. Yet what man can do, he will do. The rest of the empire is very quiet. I have a fourth little princess of 6 weeks old, and all things seem to be increasing as well as the imperial family.
>
> The Emperor and Empress received me most kindly. I have a charming apartment of seven little rooms immediately over her Imperial Majesty. The young Princess and I are already the best friends imaginable, and she has made a bargain that I shall not give her very long lessons . . . I am sorry to find that with all my care, there are some expressions in my Brazil that have offended some of the English here, and I found a regular mutiny against me when I came. However, they are beginning to be ashamed of themselves, and are dropping in one by one.

Again, the gossip almost certainly concerned Cochrane.

But the admiral never returned to Rio, sailing for Britain in May 1825. Soon afterwards Maria also left Brazil, after only a year in her royal duties, although no reason for her departure is known. It is not recorded whether she saw Cochrane on her return. She married the distinguished if unimaginative painter Augustus Calcott on 20 February 1827. When he was knighted she became Lady Calcott.

Sadly, her health broke four years later at the age of just forty-six, and although she pursued a vigorous literary career – apart from publishing her journals, writing a two-volume history of Spain and translating a French volume on Turkish history for John Murray – she was confined to her comfortable house in Kensington at the centre of a circle of friends for most of the next ten years.

In 1834 she conceived her idea of writing *Little Arthur's History of England* – a book that was to go through seventy editions and sell a million copies in a hundred years – one of the greatest early bestsellers. She died at the age of fifty-seven in November 1842. Cochrane's third son, Arthur, was just eleven when she finished *Little Arthur*, and she made it clear that the little boy of the title really existed, preparing a first copy for him. In spite of contemporary certainties, there is little direct evidence of any improper relationship with Cochrane; but it is clear that something powerful flared between them in Valparaiso that continued on the long journey to Rio, yet may have fizzled out in Brazil under the twin pressures of propriety and duty.

CHAPTER 18

The Master Deceiver

Cochrane's role in Brazil's war of independence was to prove no less decisive, and his conduct no less idiosyncratically brilliant than it had been in the Pacific – even if he was to stage no truly heroic action. Brazil had declared independence from Portugal in 1822 under the heir to the Portuguese throne, Dom Pedro de Braganza, in defiance of his father King Joao. While Rio de Janeiro and the south had flocked enthusiastically to his cause, the north remained loyal to Portugal: the unvanquished Portuguese fleet was based there. Cochrane had been approached in November 1822, by Antonio Correa, Brazil's consul in Buenos Aires. The admiral's initial response had been cool:

> The war in the Pacific having been happily terminated by the total destruction of the Spanish naval force, I am, of course, free for the crusade of liberty in any other quarter of the globe ... I confess, however, that I had not hitherto directed my attention to the Brazils; considering that the struggle for the liberties of Greece – the most oppressed of modern states – afforded the fairest opportunity for enterprise and exertion.

But as Rio de Janeiro was on his way back to Europe, he had not objected to calling in.

There he was offered 8000 dollars a year – a large sum for the times – to enter the service of the young Emperor of Brazil, Dom Pedro de Braganza. When Cochrane first met the young monarch, the two took an immediate liking to one another.

Only twenty-four years old, the dashing and impulsive young Emperor appealed to the paternal instincts in the forty-six-year-old Cochrane and the flamboyant, difficult and impetuous older man was genuinely admired by Pedro.

Cochrane found Rio a complete contrast to Santiago, both as a place and politically. With its huge black slave population, its sultry climate, the dense vegetation and the spectacular natural harbour, it bore little resemblance to the provincial, starchy, European-descended society of the temperate Chilean capital. He gazed with amusement on the liveried black slaves in bare feet, the huge mixed-race population and the women with their enormous wigs. Run by a young Emperor pitting himself against constant local intrigues, insurrections and the hostility of his father's Portuguese navy, it was a hotbed of tropical plotting. Although Cochrane seemed at first to warm to it, he soon found that the calibre of his crews was very far beneath that of the Chilenos. Fortunately, for him, the calibre of the Portuguese officers was also far beneath those in the Spanish navy on the other side of the continent.

The Emperor accompanied Cochrane on his first tour of the fleet: compared even with his flotilla in Chile, it made a sorry spectacle – just eight ships, two of them unseaworthy and two of them only of use as fireships. A fifth, the *Maria de Gloria*, was 'little calculated to do substantial service'. Only his flagship, the 74-gun *Pedro Primeiro*, and the frigate *Piranga* were impressive, while the *Liberal* was just adequate. The Portuguese fleet, by contrast, was known to consist of thirteen good ships, including a battleship, five frigates, five corvettes, a schooner and a brig.

Cochrane's first skirmish with the Portuguese suggested that at last he had taken on too much. The 160-strong crew of the *Pedro Primeiro*, under his command, consisted of some British and American sailors, freed slaves and the 'vagabondage' of Rio de Janeiro. It led the three other seaworthy ships proudly into battle, sailing through a gap in the Portuguese lines and cutting four ships off from the main fleet. When Cochrane ordered his ship into battle the three others kept their distance, and the *Pedro Primeiro* found itself on its own.

He soon noticed that only a few of his guns were firing sporadically. The two sailors directing the guns were trying to save on powder. Humiliated, the *Pedro Primeiro* had to retreat. In a fury, Cochrane, on returning to port, stripped the three ships of their British and American seamen and brought them all aboard the *Pedro Primeiro*. As with most occasions in his naval career, he was happiest commanding a single ship against far greater odds.

His next target was the Portuguese-occupied port of Bahia, 600 miles up the coast towards the Equator. He resolved to reconnoitre in typically bold fashion. In June 1823, he sailed at night into the huge Bay of Bahia, mapping the anchorage of the Portuguese fleet. When hailed by a nearby warship, he claimed to be a British merchant vessel. However, on that moonless night, the wind suddenly dropped and he was becalmed right under the guns of the Portuguese fleet and the shore batteries. Keeping his nerve, he allowed the ship to drift with the ebb tide downriver, skilfully using anchors to keep it clear of the rocks. Once again, luck had seemed against him on his Brazilian campaign.

But appearances were deceptive: the Portuguese, fearing that he was preparing fireships, were terrified of a repetition of the Battle of Aix Roads. Cochrane's reputation from both France and Chile had preceded him. When the Portuguese commander at Bahia, General Ignacio Madeira, learned that the mysterious interloper had been Cochrane's flagship, he was gripped with terror that the fleet, trapped in its anchorage, would be easy prey for fireships and explosion vessels:

> The crisis in which we find ourselves is perilous, because the means of subsistence fail us, and we cannot secure the entrance of any provisions. My duty as a soldier and as governor is to make any sacrifice in order to save the city; but it is equally my duty to prevent, in an extreme case, the sacrifice of the troops I command – of the squadron – and of yourselves . . .

Cochrane bombarded Madeira with psychological warfare,

urging him to surrender, for fear that civilians might be killed. The garrison at Bahia was running short of supplies, as Cochrane's ships blockaded the port. It seemed astonishing that so large a Portuguese fleet should be so terrified of so small a flotilla. But on 2 July Madeira decided to evacuate the entire garrison and most of the civilian population in an attempt to escape the trap.

The thirteen Portuguese warships were to accompany some thirty-two transport ships to the safer anchorage of Maranhao, 1000 miles to the north. Cochrane's four ships worked like predators and began to pick off the transports one by one. The Portuguese warships preferred to keep their distance while even the armed troopships put up little resistance. Cochrane's men simply boarded one boat after another and, lacking the men to man them, had them dismasted so that they could travel no further and drifted back to the Bay of Bahia.

After thus disabling a large number of boats, Cochrane's small fleet sailed off in pursuit of the rest of the large, unwieldy convoy. When the *Pedro Primeiro* boarded the *Gran Para* along with several troopships, several thousand soldiers were immobilized. Cochrane was hoping to lure the Portuguese warships into attacking him, and then pull them away from the rest of the convoy in a futile chase into mid-ocean. But the Portuguese warships steered clear. The chase extended from 13 degrees South to 5 degrees North.

With around half the Portuguese transport fleet disabled, he attempted to launch a night attack on 16 July upon the warships themselves. But the mainmast of the *Pedro Primeiro* split into two and his ship was crippled. Because of the dark, the Portuguese did not realize this, and Cochrane was able safely to break off the engagement. Having captured half of the Portuguese garrison at Bahia, he was deeply frustrated at seeing the other half – and in particular the warships – sailing off into the hazy mists of the Equator.

He now staged one of the greatest hoaxes in naval history, eclipsing even his previous escapades of deception and masquerade. Taking advantage of the much greater speed of the *Pedro Primeiro* once its mainmast was repaired, and leaving his three smaller ships behind, he decided that, while he had lost the Portuguese fleet, he knew where it was headed from captured despatches, and could overtake it. In ten days Cochrane's ships sped northwards towards Maranhao, arriving there on 26 July, well ahead of the sluggish Portuguese fleet.

He hoisted Portuguese colours, and awaited a brig sent out from shore to greet him. The Governor, Dom Agostinho Antonio de Fama, believed this to be the advance guard of the Portuguese evacuation force from Bahia. On boarding the *Pedro Primeiro*, the welcoming party were seized, and the captain dispatched ashore with a message from Cochrane to the governor. This asserted that the Portuguese fleet had been completely destroyed, and that the *Pedro Primeiro* was the advance guard of a huge Brazilian convoy. Cochrane's message declared:

> I am anxious not to let loose the Imperial troops of Bahia upon Maranhao, exasperated as they are at the injuries and cruelties exercised towards themselves and their countrymen, as well as by the plunder of the people and churches of Bahia.

Cochrane's own ship was supposedly filled with such blood-thirsty men. However, the admiral said he was prepared to grant generous terms, which included the repatriation of the Portuguese troops in Maranhao to Portugal, giving them safe passage aboard merchant ships. In fact, Cochrane was desperate to get them out before the remainder of the Portuguese fleet should arrive to expose his bluff. He had only a single ship's crew to pit against the several thousand men stationed at Maranhao, the well-defended shore batteries, and the truncated, but still formidable force being brought in by Madeira.

To Cochrane's own astonishment, Dom Agostinho agreed to his terms without further ado. Cochrane's meagre force occu-pied the defences of Maranhao while the Portuguese garrison was evacuated and fled the port before the arrival of the rest of the Portuguese fleet.

When Madeira's fleet reached Maranhao they found, to their surprise and horror, that the place was under Cochrane's control, and desperately turned north towards the final Portuguese stronghold of Para. But Cochrane had already dispatched Captain Pascoe Grenfell, another former British officer, with a captured ship to repeat the trick. There the authorities refused to be deceived; but they knew that without the assistance of the two main Portuguese armies, one of which had left for Portugal, the other still on its way, they could not hold out long. On 12 August Para surrendered.

After only three months under the Portuguese flag, Cochrane had delivered the whole of northern Brazil to the young Emperor. Of all Cochrane's escapades this, while by no means the most dangerous, was the most audacious deception of his entire career. Cochrane returned to Rio to a tumultuous popular welcome and the embrace of the Emperor.

With almost cyclical inevitability, Cochrane's triumph soon turned to personal ashes. José de Bonifacio Andrade, the brilliant, ruthless chief minister who had hired Cochrane in a moment of inspiration, was eclipsed by the 'Portuguese faction' – that is, that part of the traditional ruling class who had first supported Portugal and now swore their allegiance to the triumphant Emperor. Bonifacio's methods had been autocratic and high-handed; but along with the Emperor he had been the chief strategist of Brazilian independence.

Dismayed, Cochrane made no friends among the newly ascendant class by suggesting that they should be deported and that the Emperor should adopt the British constitution 'in its most perfect practical form'. This was considered far too liberal by many of his supporters, and the limited powers of the British monarch were not in fact to Pedro's taste, although he remained an instinctive admirer of the romantic admiral.

As usual an argument broke out over Cochrane's share of the prize money, put at a staggering £122,000 of the astounding £1m seized in Maranhao. Most outrageously, Grenfell was denied any share of the spoils at all and put on trial, although he was acquitted. Cochrane himself was awarded a fifth of what he sought, some £14,000. His life at Rio was agreeable, but he was again furious at being cheated of his just deserts.

As the months passed it became apparent that Cochrane's outspoken views were deeply disagreeable to the new authorities in Rio and by June 1824 it seemed that an attempt would be made to bring him to trial. While he was attending a royal review of the fleet, his ship would be seized and the £220,000 aboard – which he refused to surrender while the argument about prize money still raged – would be seized.

He was alerted to the impending coup by Madame Bonpland, the wife of the famous French naturalist, who also warned that his house had been surrounded by troops. After her departure, Cochrane climbed out of the window of his villa, mounted a horse and, without being seen by the soldiers, rode furiously to the Emperor's country villa at San Cristoval. There he pushed past protesting courtiers and told the half-asleep Emperor, still in his bed, about what he had learnt. Pedro told him he knew nothing of the plot.

The Emperor agreed to pretend to be ill and cancel the naval review. The ministers who had planned the coup would then be obliged to attend on the ailing Emperor while Cochrane and his men would slip aboard his ship and resist any attempt to board it by Rio's 'anti-Brazilian administration' who 'would certainly be regarded as pirates and treated as such'. The plan worked perfectly, and Cochrane himself called in on the Emperor the following day to pay his respects at the 'sickbed'.

Within weeks, the government of Brazil had need again of the man it had attempted to destroy. In Maranhao, civil war was raging between rival factions. In Pernambuco, an insurrection by republicans and radicals had broken out against the Emperor himself. But Cochrane's sailors had not been paid, and the admiral was deeply reluctant to co-operate. Pedro himself had to offer to pay Cochrane his salary as First Admiral of Brazil for as long as he wished, and half-pay for the rest of his life. In addition, the sum of £100,000 was to be awarded to the crews.

This proved acceptable, and 1200 troops were embarked to

control the rebellion. The expedition sailed up to Pernambuco, which it reached in mid-August. There Cochrane, so infuriated by the behaviour of the Brazilian government, showed some ambivalence towards the rebels. They argued that Dom Pedro would soon incorporate Brazil into the Portuguese Empire again and that it was necessary to secure a 'Confederation of the Equator, a kind of republican United States of Northern South America'. Cochrane got on well with the leader of the rebellion, Manuel de Carvalho, but refused to join him. Carvalho refused to accept Cochrane's offer of mediation.

Reluctantly, Cochrane sent in a force to bombard the rebels: the schooner *Leopoldina* was sent in, being the smallest available, to negotiate the shallow waters of the bay. The ship had to withdraw because of the damage the rebel bombardment was doing to her. But the governor of Pernambuco had been sufficiently demoralized by now to surrender to the troops that Cochrane put ashore. Carvalho escaped on board a raft and was later picked up by a British ship, HMS *Tweed*.

Cochrane went on to Maranhao, where he quickly worked out that the main instigator of the fighting was Miguel Bruce, 'president' of the local government, accompanied by an army of bloodthirsty freed slaves. While not taking the side of any of the other rival forces, he had Bruce's army rounded up and confined to ships in the harbour, and then set himself up as president. Fighting raged on between the rival factions.

In the fetid equatorial climate, Cochrane and many of his men began to fall ill. The Scotsman, now fed up with the politics of Brazil and certain he would get no further money from the provisional government in Rio, suddenly decided to sail in search of 'cooler climates' – something he may have planned all along since leaving Rio. He had already sent the *Pedro Primeiro* back to Rio, and moved onto a smaller ship, the *Piranga*.

This set off in May, and less than a month later had 'drifted' as far as the Azores. Cochrane insisted that he planned to return to Rio, once his men had recovered from the heat. But mysterious new problems arose. The timbers of the ships were found to be rotten and gales were said to have badly affected the masts and the rigging.

He found he could not go back across the Atlantic, and the *Piranga* arrived in Spithead a fortnight later. He had left the service of the Brazilian Emperor by a characteristically unusual means – hijacking one of his ships and sailing back home, arguing that the ship was 'unfit to sail back to Brazil.' The Brazilians were understandably incensed.

How crucial a role had Cochrane played in Brazil's independence struggle? Some local historians (for example, Sergio Correa da Costa, the excellent biographer of Dom Pedro), fail to mention him at all. Yet their reluctance is understandable. Cochrane, with his Gilbert-and-Sullivan approach to conflict, made victory appear almost ridiculously easy. He won through trickery, as well as effortless seamanship and a complete disregard for danger which contrasted sharply with the cowardice of local commanders. He had triumphed through nerve, effrontery and boldness. No great feat of arms had been required, as in Peru; the Portuguese opposition collapsed before his frontal attacks and his sheer ability to hoax.

Brazilians could boast of no heroic feat of liberation in hiring this foreign admiral to show how easily their opponents could be routed; and the local people were always in two minds about the depth of their rebellion – they derived much less pleasure from overcoming the relatively benevolent rule of the Portuguese than their partners in Spanish America had after centuries of oppression.

But without Cochrane's intervention, the revolt against Portugal would have been confined to the south: he secured the northern strongholds for the Emperor and sent the large Portuguese forces in Bahia and Maranhao packing at the cost of extraordinarily little blood spilt. His employment had been a remarkably good investment for the Brazilians – even if it ended, as usual, with a blazing row about money. Cochrane's effortless control of the eastern seaboard of South America with – in effect – one major ship consolidated Brazilian independence.

CHAPTER 19

For Greece and Freedom

Cochrane returned to Britain with mixed feelings. On the one hand, he had lost two fortunes in Chile and Brazil; news had reached him that his estates in Chile had been repossessed; and the Brazilian legation in London, furious at the hijack of the *Piranga*, presented Cochrane with a bill for £25,000 which it was unable to recover. On the other hand, he had helped to liberate the oppressed people of two empires and was a popular hero again, his career had been narrated in three volumes by William Stevenson, his achievements in the two volumes of Maria Graham's journals published by her friend John Murray.

When his ship anchored off Spithead he was unsure whether his status as First Admiral of Brazil would be respected by the British. To his joy his salute was returned, marking a double achievement: British recognition of the Brazilian flag, and British acceptance of his status as admiral. He was still technically an outlaw, who had broken the act prohibiting British citizens from enlisting under a foreign flag. But the government did not dare to act against this legend. Lord Ellenborough was dead, but Lord Liverpool was still Prime Minister and George IV still on the throne. Both Croker and the Duke of Wellington still held office.

Thomas Cochrane had been away for more than six years and was now nearly fifty, but he was still an impressive looking man: 'tall and bony-framed, strong and slim, though slightly corpulent: hair reddish, expression gentle though serious, pleasant and cultivated in his conversation'.

Cochrane had decided entirely to foreswear politics: Britain seemed as firmly in the hands of a diehard reactionary clique as ever. Besides he still needed to make money, his hopes of making a fortune in South America having been disappointed. He travelled about the country, taking Kitty to Scotland. There he was greeted at the theatre in Edinburgh by an enthusiastic demonstration as an authentically Scottish hero. So moving was the scene that Sir Walter Scott wrote an instant poem in honour of Kitty, who had fainted at this unexpected acclamation:

> I knew the Lady by that glorious eye,
> By that pure brow and those dark locks of thine,
> I knew thee for a soldier's bride and high
> My full heart bounded. For the golden mine
> Of Heavenly thought kindled at sight of thee
> Radiant with all the stars of memory.
>
> Thy name ask Brazil, for she knows it well,
> It is a name a Hero gave to thee.
> In every letter lurks there not a spell,
> The mighty spell of immortality?
> Ye sail together down time's glittering stream;
> Around your heads two kindred haloes gleam.
>
> Even now, as through the air the plaudits ring,
> I marked the smiles that in her features came.
> She caught the word that fell from every tongue
> And her eye brightened at her Cochrane's name,
> And brighter yet became the dark eyes' blaze –
> It was his Country and she felt the praise.
>
> May the Gods guard thee, Lady, wheresoe'er
> Thou wanderest in thy love and loveliness.
> For thee may every scene and sky be fair
> Each hour instinct with more than happiness.
> May all thou valuest be good and great,
> And be thy wishes thy own future state.

Cochrane, now variously described as the Lafayette of Latin America and the greatest seaman afloat, had long been wooed by the exiled government of Greece as a possible commander of its navy. The cause was dear to Cochrane's Radical friends. Sir Francis Burdett argued enthusiastically:

> Lord Cochrane is looking well after eight years of harassing and ungrateful service and, I trust, will be the liberator of Greece. What a glorious title!

Byron had died there, his most famous verse enduring as his epitaph:

> The mountains look on Marathon,
>   And Marathon looks on the sea:
> And musing there an hour alone,
>   I dream'd that Greece might still be free;
> For, standing on the Persian's grave,
> I could not deem myself a slave.

Cochrane decided to take on this dubious cause. In fact the Greeks were splintered into warring factions, were wholly undisciplined and mutinous both as soldiers and sailors, and were just as assiduous in perpetrating vicious atrocities as their opponents, the Turks. The cause was very far from being the romantic one of the cradle of democracy and European civilisation coming under attack by the barbaric Turks, as it was portrayed in Britain. In espousing it, Cochrane showed all his restlessness, political naivete and chronic hunger for money. Yet he had succeeded with what seemed like laughable ease in securing both Chile's and Brazil's coastlines. There was no reason to believe he could not repeat his triumphs in Greece.

The money was irresistible to a man who once again lacked any significant capital. This time he was offered a lump sum of £37,000 in advance of his arrival and £20,000 on the achievement of Greek independence. He also speculated in Greek loan stock. The Greeks had managed to raise a huge amount of money in London largely through the wave of sympathy that swept Britain after Byron's death. These rewards were not excessive: the Duke of Wellington, for example, had enjoyed lump sum payments of some £700,000 after his victories. At last, it seemed the wanderer might enjoy financial security; certainly his anxious family deserved it.

Cochrane specified that six steamships must be built in Britain and the United States to make up the Greek fleet. Before this could happen he was warned that he faced prosecution once again under the Foreign Enlistment Act – as a way of preventing him going off to fight for Greece, which would surely undermine the tortuous British diplomatic efforts in the region. Britain was seeking to mediate a compromise under which the Russians and the Turks, the principal powers in the area, would offer Greece a measure of self-government; Cochrane's help for the Greeks threatened to compromise British neutrality.

Once again Cochrane and Kitty slipped across to Boulogne to avoid arrest. Soon after he arrived he learnt he was to be prosecuted by the French for intercepting one of their merchant ships off the coast of Chile. The real reason was that the French were in league with Turkey. He fled again, this time to Brussels where his old enemy, San Martin, was also in exile, although they certainly did not meet. The Duke of Wellington passed through on his way to mediate with Russia at St Petersburg. He grandly left a message at Cochrane's hotel reception that he would receive nobody 'except Cochrane' – but refused to call on the fugitive seaman himself. He regarded it as the height of his official favour to be prepared personally to try and argue Cochrane out of his latest crazed enterprise.

Cochrane either never received the message or ignored it. Meanwhile none of the vessels he had ordered was ready. The contractor, Alexander Galloway, who had proved so slow in building a steamship for Chile, was also simultaneously building a steamship for the King of Egypt, Mehmet Pasha, who in league with the Turks had occupied most of the Peloponnese. Cochrane, in Brussels, was in no position to press Galloway to finish the work. When at last the first vessel, the *Karteria*, was ready, its maiden voyage, watched by curious spectators from the shore, proved disastrous: her paddles were too high out of the water, her boilers burst and her guns had not arrived from the United States.

These endless delays prevented Cochrane from reaching Greece until a year later, and then with only a brig and two yachts, leaving the *Karteria* behind. But at least his American frigate, the *Hellas*, was waiting for him: she had swallowed up the entire budget for both frigates, and he made her his flagship. The *Karteria* arrived soon afterwards, and thus Cochrane had the rudiments of a fleet. His belated appearance had a sobering effect: the Turks were deeply aware of his reputation and would not venture out of port.

His first task was to get the quarrelsome and murderous Greek factions to join together. He threatened not to take up his command until they united at a congress at Aegina. They did so, electing a comparatively neutral figure, Count John Capo d'Istria, for a seven-year term (remarkably he served for four, increasingly despotically, until he was assassinated in 1831). He turned to the next task, relieving a French force which had blundered its way into being besieged at the Acropolis. He wrote, with that misty-eyed British idealism which was shared by neither Greeks nor Turks:

Alas! What a change! What melancholy recollections crowd on the mind. There was the seat of science, of literature, and the arts. At this instant the barbarian Turk is actually demol-ishing by the shells that now are flying through the air, the scanty remains of the once magnificent temples of the Acropolis.

In fact, the Greeks had proved as barbarous as the Turks. At Tripolitza in 1821 they had slaughtered 8000 Turks, including women and children. At Chios in 1822 the Turks had retaliated by massacring 25,000 at Messalonghi. When Byron had died, the army of Mehmet Pasha, with a fine insensitivity to British feelings, slaughtered the islanders, dispatching ten barrels of ears as a present to the Sultan of Turkey, chopping off some 3000 heads as souvenirs, and taking 4000 women and children as slaves.

Even so, the Greek commander in Athens had been a man of such cruelty that the Turks had been greeted as saviours when they appeared. Now only the Parthenon held out, with a trapped force of around 600 Frenchmen, who had come merely to deliver supplies. These were the men Cochrane proposed to relieve. Yet the progress of the Greek army was blocked, on both sides of the Piraeus, by the formidable stronghold of the convent of Saint Spiridion, which was held by the Turks. Cochrane at first wanted to seize this, and he successfully captured the Turkish ships supplying it in an attempt to starve it out.

The French commander in the Parthenon sent desperate messages that his supplies were running out, which was not the truth. This compelled Cochrane to take more precipitate action. He decided to bypass the convent and land troops behind it at night. After this was successfully accomplished, the Turks sent down a force of some 300 men to attack Cochrane's bridgehead. To their astonishment, the admiral himself, carrying nothing more lethal than a telescope, led a Greek charge against the assailants. The Greeks rarely having reacted this way before to an attack, it was the Turks who turned and ran, sixty of them being killed to around of eight of Cochrane's men. He captured nine enemy redoubts.

The convent was left with only 300 Turks as its defenders against a Greek besieging force of 10,000 men. But it remained in a commanding and powerful position, and the Turks beat off three successive Greek attacks under General Karaiskakes. Cochrane ordered the *Hellas* to bombard the building. After a couple of days it was left 'a mass of ruins', and the 270 or so remaining Turks surrendered, being granted safe conduct through Greek lines to rejoin their main army.

As they watched from the ship, one of the officers alongside Cochrane told him, 'All those men will be murdered.' Cochrane was shocked but indeed, after a scuffle, the Greeks opened fire on the Turks, leaving 200 dead and only seventy survivors. He told Karaiskakes:

> I was no party to the capitulation this day. Fearing that some outrage might be committed, I sent you an order to retire, and I glory in the consciousness that I have saved you as well as myself from being inculpated in the most horrid scene I ever beheld – a scene which freezes my blood, and which cannot be palliated by any barbarities which the Turks have committed on you.

Karaiskakes, who had tried to prevent the massacre, was soon afterwards mortally wounded but on his deathbed urged Cochrane to land troops close to Athens for an assault on Cape Colias.

Cochrane organized a two-pronged attack on the Turkish position, one intended as a diversion, the other to go to the relief of the Parthenon, and landed an advance guard of 200 by moonlight on 6 May. However, the supporting troops of 3000 refused to follow, simply digging in lightly in an exposed position on the beach, while the diversionary attack did not take place at all. The 200 were soon cut off by the Turks and killed, while in the early hours of the morning the Turks descended in force onto the beach, massacring some 700 and taking 250 prisoners. Cochrane himself escaped by running into the sea and was rescued by a boat with water up to his neck. Some 2000 survivors were taken off. It was by far the biggest loss of troops Cochrane had ever witnessed – although he was not in charge of the land forces – and an unmitigated disaster. Cochrane had never before experienced such a defeat, and it shook him profoundly.

Soon afterwards, through French mediation, the troops in the Parthenon surrendered and were allowed to return through enemy lines. A massacre had been averted, but Cochrane was tasting the unfamiliar taste of military failure for the first time. He sought solace in a sea expedition to relieve Castle Tornese on the coast of the Peloponnese. When he got there he found it had fallen. He gave chase to two warships nearby, but his sailors

were incompetent and confused and either disobeyed or deliberately ignored his orders; he found it almost impossible to enforce
discipline. He was so distrustful of his men he carried a loaded
pistol at all times.

The following day he captured a merchant ship which was
filled with the women and children of Castle Tornese, destined
for the slave markets. Indignantly, he sent this cargo off to the
British base at Corfu. A day later he intercepted an armed brig
and found aboard it part of the Turkish Sultan's harem, which
he put respectfully ashore, none of these girls apparently wanting
to be liberated from their condition. Further humiliation soon
befell him.

He sailed to Poros to review his fleet and take it to sea. Instead
he was disobeyed, and a boat rowed over to demand a month's
pay in advance. He said he could spare only a fortnight's wages.
Thereupon, according to a British witness:

> The afternoon was calm, the sun was descending to the
> mountains of Argolis, and the shadows of the rocks of
> Methana already darkened the waters, when brig after brig
> passed in succession under the stern of the *Hellas*, from whose
> lofty mast the flag of the High Admiral of Greece floated,
> unconscious of the disgraceful stain it was receiving, and in
> whose cabin sat the noble admiral steadily watching the scene.

Cochrane resolved to regain his honour in the only way he
knew: another daring raid of the kind he had so often executed
throughout his career, taking the fight directly to the enemy –
an attack on Alexandria itself, where Mehmet Ali was preparing
another fleet. On 11 June he assembled a small fleet of loyal
ships: his own *Hellas*, the *Sauveur*, a French ship, fourteen
gunboats and eight fireships. He sailed on the 15th, declaring
ringingly:

> The port of Alexandria, the centre of all the evil that has
> befallen you, now contains within its narrow bounds
> numerous ships of war and a multitude of vessels laden with

provisions, stores and troops intended to effect your total ruin. The wind is fair for us, and our enterprise is unsuspected. Brave fireship crews resolve by one moment of active exertion to annihilate the power of the Satrap. Then shall the siege of Athens be raised in Egypt.

He soon discovered that the Greeks were less than enthusiastic in volunteering to man the fireships, and he could send in only two on the evening of the 16th, accompanying his own *Hellas* and *Sauveur*, with the intention of sailing right into the Egyptian port and scattering their ships. As he sailed in, his crews refused to continue in the face of such a concentration of enemy ships.

Eventually, Cochrane managed to send in one of the fireships, bravely manned under Captain Kanares, which grappled with an Egyptian warship, soon set alight. The rest of the Egyptian fleet, panicking, decided to escape the close confines of the port, assuming that explosion ships would be sent in next. The civilian population, fearing bombardment from the sea, also took to the roads out of the city.

As the Egyptian craft sailed pell-mell past his two ships, the remains of Cochrane's small fleet, further out, assumed that they were attacking in force and fled. Cochrane went off in pursuit of the huge Egyptian force. After sailing all night and all of the next day, he failed to catch them, and busied himself with rounding up his own scattered force. He had failed again, but not for want of boldness or imagination; he simply lacked the necessary raw material he had enjoyed aboard British and even South American ships: courageous crews which would obey orders. He sailed cheekily to the Turkish coast where he wrote an insulting letter to the Egyptian King from his ally's territory.

While Cochrane fumed with frustration, the Great Powers pursued a settlement for Greece. British, French and Russian envoys met in London to formalize the St Petersburg Accord drawn up by the Duke of Wellington under which Greece would enjoy virtual self-government under nominal Turkish sovereignty. This would be backed up by the threat of force if the two sides did not stop fighting. As the Turks and their civilian allies had nearly captured the whole country, this was not in their interests, and they made a grab for as much territory as possible before expiry of the Great Power deadline.

Cochrane meanwhile had patched together his flotilla as best he could and sailed off to Navarino where the huge Turkish fleet had been joined by the Egyptian fleet, swelling it to as many as 100 ships. It was a fine anchorage, four miles by three and protected by the island of Sphacteria. Spotting his depleted navy, a corvette and four other ships set out to attack him. For 24 hours he outmanoeuvred them as they pursued his force, certain of victory. On 1 August, after a brilliant display of seamanship, he suddenly closed with his pursuers and raked the corvette with broadsides. Cochrane's gunnery was precise and devastating in these calm waters. His opponents were slow to reload and surrendered after an hour. He found the corvette contained the usual cargo of slaves, which he set free. It had been a model action of its kind. Cochrane little knew it, but it was to be the last prize of his career, and the last time he was to be engaged in armed action after a career as a fighting captain spanning thirty-five years, at the age of fifty-two.

His able second-in-command, Captain Frank Hastings, at last proved the value of the armed steamship in which Cochrane had placed so much faith. Firing red-hot shot and manoeuvring without effort to run rings around the wind-driven Turkish sailing ships, he sank nine and captured a tenth in the Bay of Salona. Hastings had not yet learnt of the armistice agreement. The joint Turkish-Egyptian fleet at Navarino had, however, been chafing under the terms of the armistice, and was understandably infuriated to learn of his attack.

Ibrahim Pasha, their commander, demanded the right to chase Cochrane from Admiral Codrington, commander of the British fleet that had arrived to enforce the armistice. He refused. In October 1827 Codrington learnt that two ships had sailed out of Navarino Bay in pursuit of Cochrane in the Gulf of Corinth, and he in turn sent ships to give chase, catching them up and forcing them to return to their anchorage. Deeply angered, Ibrahim sent his shore troops to slaughter the inhabitants further inland in an orgy of brutality. Meanwhile Codrington had ordered Cochrane and General Church, commanding the Greek land forces, to suspend operations under the terms of the armistice.

Codrington was appalled to learn that the Turks were now violating the armistice on land. On 20 October he sailed into the Bay of Navarino at the head of ten British warships, eight Russian and seven French ships. The Duke of Clarence, later William IV, had declared before Codrington set sail, 'Go in, my dear Ned, and smash those bloody Turks.'

No one knows exactly how the fighting began, but musket shots turned to cannon, with the disciplined allied fleet firing broadside after broadside into the ill-organized joint Turkish-Egyptian fleet. As the Turkish army of 20,000 encamped above watched in horror, the whole bay was soon ablaze with ships and wreckage. In one of the greatest naval massacres of all time, fifty-three ships were sunk, the rest being appallingly damaged, and some 7000 sailors were killed. In Britain this savagery drew admiration and criticism in equal measure – the latter particularly from those who feared the power of Russia. Codrington wrote drily to the Greeks: 'The maritime armistice is, in fact, observed on the side of the Turks, since their fleet no longer exists. Take care of yours, for we will destroy it also, if the case requires it.'

Cochrane's work had been done for him. Nevertheless a second steamship, the *Epicheiresis*, had arrived in September 1827. He tried to find a crew to man her, without success. He travelled to Britain to lobby for the lifting of the Foreign Enlistment Act and recruit the men there, but failed. He was depressed and moody, and took it out on Kitty, who was living in Paris in his absence, who wrote back with some spirit:

I regret to see that you are still in the same uneasy state of mind. Do not, my dear Cochrane, fancy such nonsense. Why are we not to be happy, at least why not as much as we have ever been? I cannot understand your state of mind or feeling;

what can you dread? There is no fighting now in Greece. You surely cannot be well or such vile blue devils would not hold you so tight. I would strongly advise you to look on the bright side and leave that sad train of thoughts. Try reading, writing, walking, in fact try anything but thinking. Give your poor head a holiday. You will addle your brains and you will look so old. Do not, my Ever, fidget. Your life is made miserable by such melancholy thoughts.

All of this made eminent good sense. In the exchanges she comes out head-and-shoulders above Cochrane, who was now clearly in the depressive state of mania.

Cochrane returned to Greece, where he generously refused the further £20,000 he was owed, giving it to a fund for officers' wives and children, and handed over his two prizes. The Greeks received this with ill grace. Cochrane, however, had made a considerable sum through the rise in the value of Greek funds. He was much criticized in Britain for this as gambling on his own success, which seems a little unfair (in the event the success was not his own, but he had invested in a perfectly reasonable speculative venture).

It had been his most financially successful campaign but a military failure, although the Greeks had achieved their objective. The Turkish and Egyptian armies had to be evacuated from the Pelepponese in 1828, as the navy that supplied them had been destroyed. The Russian commander generously put a corvette at Cochrane's disposal to take him to Malta – the Greeks having denied him any such luxury – where Admiral Sir Pulteney Malcolm, his old colleague from Aix Roads, gave him a Royal Navy ship to convey him to England.

Cochrane had always been a perfectionist, a master of his art. While deprived of official recognition, he had the satisfaction of knowing that he had performed one job after another superbly, almost without fail and with a minimum of casualties. In Greece the wretched quality of his crews had deprived him of that satisfaction; and for the first time in his career that indomitable spirit appeared to be shattered, plunged into self-criticism, depression and disillusion, lashing out at those dearest to him.

He returned to Britain to be informed of another tempting offer by his old friend Captain Grenfell, still in Brazil:

> We have now a far finer squadron as to ships than when your lordship was here, and there are plenty of men to be had, but we have no commanders. I think if your lordship would, they would be glad to arrange with you, with a handsome income, to rehoist your flag. But the secret is this. The Emperor wants an independent force on whom he can depend, let whatever party be in power, and with the Emperor alone your lordship should treat.

This bore the stamp of Cochrane's old admirer, Pedro himself, and suggested the former had been forgiven for his hijack of the *Piranga*. Had Cochrane responded he might have commanded the British supporting fleet that was later to win back Portugal for the Emperor's daughter, Maria de Gloria (it was in the event gloriously led by Sir Charles Napier). But Cochrane wrote back glumly to Grenfell: 'The mental fever I contracted in Greece has not subsided, nor will it probably for some months to come.'

Two further blows were rained upon him in this grim mood. The first was the death of his younger brother Archibald, who had served so gallantly beside him in the *Généreux* and aboard the *Speedy*. The second was Kitty's delivery of a stillborn child at the end of her fifth pregnancy; even her strong nature appears to have been momentarily crushed by the blow, and although her devotion to Cochrane's reputation never wavered, the scales seemed to fall from her eyes as to his egocentric nature.

PART FOUR

Honour in His
Own Country

Of Lord Cochrane it can be said that he was the
victim of his generous enthusiasm for the oppressed.
During the greater portion of his life he rested under a
heavy cloud, and it was only in extreme old age that
he had the satisfaction of having his name rehabili-
tated, and of regaining the honours and rank of which
he had been so unjustly deprived.

G. A. Henty, *Cochrane the Dauntless* (1897)

CHAPTER 20

Rehabilitation

After the dreadful year of 1829 Cochrane's state of mind seemed to be picking up at last, and he even took Kitty on a visit to France. In June the unlamented George IV died, to be succeeded by his sailor brother William IV. At last the monarchy began to bask in the unfamiliar glow of popularity. Bluff, plain-spoken and an admirer of all things nautical, as well as of Cochrane himself, a wind of change was blowing under the new King.

It swept out the longstanding Tory administration now run by Cochrane's old enemy, the Duke of Wellington. At the end of 1830 Earl Grey came to office, along with Brougham as Lord Chancellor, in an administration committed to enacting the very parliamentary reforms so long advocated by Cochrane himself. Always in advance of his time, he saw the new age for British politics that he had worked for so long dawn at last.

The franchise was to be considerably extended, and the pocket and rotten boroughs abolished under the Reform Act which finally passed in 1832. People waited with bated breath to see if revolution would ensue, as the diehards had predicted. Along with Wellington, his protégé John Wilson Croker, the vengeful and entrenched secretary of the Admiralty, had fallen at last. Cochrane had lived to see his political dreams fulfilled.

He now devoted himself to three principal causes: vindication of his career and the establishment of his innocence in the Stock Exchange fraud; the development of ingenious new weaponry for the Royal Navy; and reinstatement to the navy so that he could return to active service. His political ambitions were forgotten with the triumph of the Radicals' position on universal suffrage and the introduction of a new reforming broom in the Admiralty. Besides, on 1 July 1831, his father died in Paris where he was ensconced, aged eighty-three, in cosy but limited circumstances with his mistress. Cochrane was now tenth Earl of Dundonald, a Scottish peerage with no automatic right to sit in the Lords – Scottish peers elected a small number from among their own ranks – but he was disqualified from standing for the Commons. In fighting for his personal honour, Cochrane wrote to the new Prime Minister, Grey. He received an encouraging reply:

> I need not say that it would give me great satisfaction if it should be found possible to comply with the prayer of your petition. This opinion I expressed some years ago in a letter which, I believe, was communicated to you. To the sentiments expressed in that letter I refer, which, if I remember aright, acquitted you of all blame, except such as might have been incurred by inadvertence and by having suffered yourself to be led by others into measures of the consequences of which you were not sufficiently aware.

But both Brougham and Grey, at a meeting with the spirited Kitty (Cochrane was absent perhaps because he was plunged into another of his post-Greece fits of melancholy) warned that there were obstacles to his rehabilitation – almost certainly the rearguard actions of conservatives in the Admiralty and the law officers who still held important baronial fiefdoms in the cabinet.

In November Cochrane took his case to the new King at the Royal Pavilion in Brighton, where he was listened to sympathetically and was promised that his case would be 'fairly looked into'. Privately Grey outlined the problem in a letter to Brougham:

> You may be assured that I have this matter at heart; but I am very unwilling to have it brought into public notice at a moment when the bitter and hostile spirit which prevails in the party most opposed to the Government would be likely to seize upon it as a good question for annoyance.

Kitty, now glorying in her position as the new Countess of Dundonald, a far cry from her impoverished and bastard childhood, had the temerity to ask her husband to seek a Royal pardon, which could be issued without formal Cabinet approval. Cochrane was convinced that this would imply he had committed an offence for which he needed to be pardoned, but she prevailed and herself courageously importuned the King again on the issue (this avoided Cochrane's having to beg for it). On 2 May the pardon was issued and Cochrane was appointed a rear-admiral of the fleet with immediate effect. He was received graciously by the King at the royal levee in St James's.

There was still, though, the matter of the Order of the Bath which had been ignobly stripped from him and had not been restored, which he regarded as a continuing sign of official belief in his guilt. He refused to take up any appointment in the Navy until he was restored to the order. The verdict of the stuffy and cautious Admiralty bureaucracy was implacable: too many service officers would be upset if this embodiment of naval insubordination was restored to so high an honour. Cochrane pressed on determinedly.

With the accession of a fervent young admirer of his exploits, Queen Victoria, in 1837, Cochrane had new cause for hope. But still the successive governments of Lord Melbourne and Sir Robert Peel refused to budge. Not until May 1846, when he was seventy years old, was Cochrane assigned the next vacancy to the Order. In July he was installed at Westminster Abbey. Here his enemies were forced to accept him at last as a senior member of the establishment he had fought for so long.

Lord Ellenborough, the son of the vindictive Chief Justice who had sentenced Cochrane, acted as one of his sponsors (although his own son was to write a vigorous defence of his grandfather and an indictment of Cochrane years later), and the Duke of Wellington, elderly and frail, came forward to congratulate him at last – the first friendly meeting between Britain's greatest living soldier and sailor, who had for so long been bitter enemies. Cochrane was not formally knighted at Buckingham Palace, which delighted him because it suggested that his old honour had been reinstated, not a new one conferred.

His cup of personal satisfaction overflowed when, to his astonishment, he received a letter from the First Lord of the Admiralty, Lord Auckland, in December 1847:

> I shall shortly have to name a Commander-in-Chief for the North American and West Indian Station. Will you accept the appointment? I shall feel it to be an honour and a pleasure to have named you to it, and I am satisfied that your nomination will be agreeable to her Majesty, as it will be to the country, and, particularly, to the Navy.

At the age of seventy-two, he was to feel a moving quarterdeck under his feet again – although there was, of course, no war in the Atlantic. He had achieved his second great objective – restoration of his command in the Navy as well as his reputation.

He had not been idle in the intervening eighteen years. They were marked by his dogged inventiveness. In what must surely have been the remark of the century even for an Admiralty mired in inertia and corruption, Lord Melville, First Lord, had declared in 1826:

> Their Lordships feel it their bounded duty to discourage to the utmost of their ability the employment of steam vessels, as they consider that the introduction of steam is calculated to strike a fatal blow to the naval supremacy of the Empire.

Thus Canute still ruled the waves.

Cochrane struck up a friendship with Marc Isambard Brunel, the inventor, whose ideas for developing steam tugs to tow warships had predictably been turned down by the Admiralty. Brunel had then tried to tunnel under the Thames near Blackwall, but the roof kept breaking through. In 1830 Cochrane produced a compressed air device which solved the problem. The same idea was used to develop the Hudson River

Tunnel in the United States by the great engineer, Mr Hoskin.

Cochrane and Brunel applied the lesson to developing an efficient steam engine to drive propellers in ships and locomotive engines. The challenge was to create a rotary engine in place of two twin engines with pistons going backwards and forwards propelling the paddles of steamers. The reaction of the new authorities in the Admiralty was cautiously favourable.

Meanwhile Marc Brunel in 1834 had persuaded senior officials of the Manchester & Liverpool Railway to look at his new rotary engine, which Cochrane argued would stop the terrible rocking motion of Stephenson's design. They were unimpressed by trials, however, when Cochrane sought to adapt the engine to Stephenson's *Rocket* itself.

But the London & Greenwich Railway was interested, and encouraged Cochrane to come up with several designs, which involved the spending of a further £4000 of his own money, before adopting it in a manner he disapproved of and without his permission. The whole concept failed on the size and weight of the boiler necessary to propel the engine safely. The project collapsed among legal wrangling and acrimony, which further added to his costs. With this failure and financial disaster behind him, Cochrane returned to his design for steamships, arguing passionately to the Admiralty:

A couple of heavy line-of-battle ships, suddenly fitted, on the outbreak of war, with adequate steam-power, would decide the successful result of a general action; and I am assured that I could show your lordship how to fit a steam-ship which, in scouring the Channel or ranging the coast, could take or destroy every steam-ship belonging to France that came within view.

Cochrane poured his Greek prize money into the project, spending no less than £16,000, and the Admiralty eventually agreed to build a frigate on his steam designs. By this time Cochrane had also developed his ship's propeller. By 1845 the new steamship, HMS *Janus*, had been built, but as with the

Karteria the boilers exploded, not being big enough to stand the pressure. Cochrane turned his attention to the problem. Once again, the old curmudgeons of Horse Guards Parade dragged their feet. However by 1847 Lord John Hope was writing to him:

> I am so thoroughly convinced of the numerous advantages of having one boat (at least) in all our large ships fitted with a high-pressure engine, that I had great satisfaction in recommending the plan you sent to the board for adoption – and I should like to have one or more ready for the ship that carries your flag.

His high expectations were dented when the *Janus*'s engine blew up through the lack of a proper oil supply pipe. But his admirer, the new First Lord, Lord Auckland, paid him a visit as he sought to remedy this with his own bare hands in the engine room. 'I was glad he found me down there, with a tallow candle in my hand, for it proved I was in earnest.'

Cochrane's design ideas for steamships were also visionary: his frigate would have 'the uniform delineation of parabolic curves, forming a series of lines presenting the least resistance in the submerged portion of ships and vessels'. The other inventions Cochrane continued to press on the Admiralty were his old secret designs for poison gas and mortar ships. He argued to the Admiralty in 1840, in rebuttal of a remark by Wellington:

> Your Lordship will perceive, that 'although two can play at the game', the one who first understands it can alone be successful. In the event of war, I beg to offer my endeavours to place the navy of France under your control, or at once effectually to annihilate it.

Six years later Auckland set up a select committee to look into three secret projects long suggested by Cochrane – camouflage, mortar vessels and gas attack. The first was adopted, the second and third rejected. The committee spelt out its reasoning:

We have resolved that it is not desirable that any experiments should be made. We assume it to be possible that the plan contains power for producing the sweeping destruction the inventor ascribes to it; but it is clear this power could not be retained exclusively by this country, because its first employment would develop its principle and application. We considered, in the next place, how far the adoption of the proposed secret plans would accord with the feelings and principles of civilised warfare. We are of unanimous opinion that Plans Nos. 2 and 3 (the sulphur attack) would not do so, and therefore recommend that, as hitherto, plans Nos. 2 and 3 should remain concealed. We feel that great credit is due to Lord Dundonald for the right feeling that prompted him to disclose his secret plans when serving in war as naval commander-in-chief of the forces of other nations under very trying circumstances, in the conviction that these plans might eventually be of the highest importance to his country.

Undaunted, Cochrane came up with another idea for a mosquito fleet:

Give me a fast small steamer with a heavy long-range gun in the bow, and another in the hold to fall back upon, and I would not hesitate to attack the largest ship afloat.

His view of stationary defence foreshadowed military thinking by nearly a century:

Immovable stations of defence, as a protection against invasion, are not only costly and of doubtful utility, but a reliance on them is, in my mind, an indication of a declining state. It is little short of imbecility to suppose that because we erect great imposing fortifications an enemy will come to them when he can operate elsewhere without the slightest regard to them; and the more so as the common experience of warfare will tell him, that numerous fortifications are in the highest degree national weakness, by splitting into detail the army which ought to be in the field against him, but who are compelled to remain and take care of their fortifications. Yet half the sum required for fortifications as defences in time of war would suffice to place the Navy in a condition of affording far more effectual protection. There is no security equal to that which may be obtained by putting it out of the power of the enemy to execute hostile intentions.

His work had been visionary. His frigate created a primary design later to be modified by the Admiralty. His tunnelling ideas had been revolutionary, as had his propeller design, and were recognized as such by the first Brunel. His ideas for total warfare were to be adopted early in the next century. To the modern person, they may seem to illustrate an unappealing side to his character: but he always believed that to win wars overwhelmingly was to shorten the suffering or prevent them altogether. He was the forerunner of the theory of deterrence.

What was perhaps less defensible at this period was his continuing to lavish large sums on these projects to the neglect of his family, with sad results. Cochrane, like the ninth Earl, had fathered a large family, to which his letters show he was deeply attached. He had installed Kitty and his five children in a house which at last did justice to her status as the new Countess of Dundonald – Hanover Lodge in Regent's Park. The running costs were a staggering £4000 a year, which he claimed he could barely afford. She and her children had been dragged around the world in his wake, and by now she was ready for her reward, holding a *fête champêtre* which, according to the newspapers, was

another proof how much this species of entertainment wins its way in the fashionable world. It [the house and grounds] united to a delightful situation, all the beauties of nature and art combined, surrounded by gardens, wherein are the most beautiful promenades. The interior of the villa is adorned with groups of the most classic busts and statues, both ancient and modern: added to which are paintings by the first masters of the gallant Admiral's achievements, by sea and land.

The visitants began to arrive at three o'clock; at the hour of six the dejeuner a la fourchette commenced in a noble temporary room, communicating with a beautiful corridor or gallery; at eight o'clock dancing commenced: at nine the grounds were really an illuminated garden; – the effect was magical, and produced by an infinity of variegated lamps. All were delighted with the graceful manners of the accomplished hostess and her amiable daughters. The party did not break up until midnight.

But Cochrane disapproved of this kind of ostentation and missed the occasion. The consequences for his family of a usually absent father were soon apparent. By 1836 Tom, trained at Sandhurst and now twenty-three, was in serious financial difficulties. Cochrane wrote to Tom's brother Horace (Horatio):

I am afraid that your brother has wholly ruined himself. He is yet here, without leave of absence; not daring to return to Plymouth where, under existing circumstances, not an officer would speak to him. He has been reported to the Horse Guards as having obtained money and drawn bills under false pretences; and I should not be surprised if he is compelled to quit the army – and God knows then what will become of him: I am now trying to get him off to India, where if he is not more prudent he will leave his bones.

But Horace was soon to follow in his elder brother's footsteps. Cochrane wrote to him three years later:

I shall endeavour to prevail on Dear Mam to permit two thousand of the French stock to be sold to prevent your ruin, and I shall give any security I have got to make up the difference of her little income, already too small to keep up a decent appearance; for where she is there is our home. As to myself I am accustomed to live in a very quiet and cheap way in every respect.

Kitty, in an increasingly hysterical state as her children went to ruin, and with good reason angry at Cochrane's obsessive expenditure of money on his inventions (although she was certainly extravagant herself) had effectively broken up the marriage and departed to Boulogne. Now it was her daughter Elizabeth's turn to suffer, in a marriage to John Fleming, heir to the stately home of Stoneham Park in Herefordshire. She spent her time racketing at Almanacks, the Caledonian meetings, operas, plays and other places and delivering a succession of small children before running off with a lover, citing Fleming's brutality.

Tom seemed to regain his equilibrium in Hong Kong and married an heiress to a Scottish fortune. Lizzie was later provided a reasonably generous settlement by Fleming. Cochrane's fourth, Arthur, was asked to behave with greater propriety than his brothers:

> You have been well and religiously reared by your dear Mamma, which gives me great confidence in you. I am indebted to the instruction of my most worthy grandmother for having avoided every kind of vice which surrounded me on entering the Navy. Never let a cigar or pipe get into your mouth; it is a practice that leads to drinking, and drinking leads to ruin. God bless you and make you that which dearest Mamma has endeavoured to effect, an open, true and honourable man, and being so success in life is sure.

Whether through inhibition, or being put off by this succession of domestic disasters, Arthur never married but enjoyed a distinguished naval career, becoming Admiral Sir Arthur Cochrane. His younger brother Eustace also went into the Navy and became a captain. Cochrane made clear his disappointment with Kitty in a letter to him about marriage:

> I hope your brother and yourself, if such an event shall be

contemplated, will secure enough, not for your living alone, but for the consequences of married life: for, believe me, that after the honeymoon is past there is the education of children to provide for, their advancement too in life – But above all, there is the necessity that the Hon. Mrs Horace shall not get out of humour, and make your life one continued scene of bickering and reproach, because the Hon. Mrs somebody else keeps a carriage; can give better or more numerous parties – or dress better! My dear boy, guard against this species of ever-preying misery above all else! For, like the perpetual drop of water, it will wear the heart, or harden it to stone.

She, with at least equal justice, remarked of him in another letter: 'I hate the inventive faculty.'

Cochrane must have been relieved to get away from his domestic difficulties and back on board ship again. He sailed across to Newfoundland, where his insatiable curiosity about both scientific and social conditions was soon in evidence. His men adored him. As one remarked:

I was never tired of hearing of the fine old fellow's exploits when, as young Lord Cochrane, he fought the French and Spaniards in Nelson's days. He was a fine old man with typical Scotch features. He was an ideal officer, and was so beloved by the men that his name on the lower deck was 'Dad'.

He travelled south to the Caribbean and the Radical in him was appalled by the conditions he found in Jamaica:

Is it reasonable to instruct the negroes in their rights as men, and open their minds to the humble ambition of acquiring spots of land, and then throw every impediment possible in the way of its gratification? I perceive by the imposts and expenses on the transfer of small properties, that a barrier almost insurmountable is raised to their acquisition by the coloured population . . . It is lamentable to see the negroes in rags, lying about the streets of Kingston; to learn that the gaols are full, whilst the port is destitute of shipping, the wharves abandoned, and the storehouses empty; while much, if not all of this might be remedied.

In Trinidad, his inventive instincts had been aroused by the pitch lake, which he hoped would produce bitumen to fuel his steamships. He also believed it could be used as manure, as asphalt for London's streets (it was judged too smooth for horses, wrongly), and as the material for building a Thames embankment, sewers and insulating wires. None of this came to anything.

In June 1851 he returned from his last tour of duty at the age of seventy-five, to find that Kitty's mental health had deteriorated and the children were quarrelling bitterly. While she remained in Boulogne, he took bachelor lodgings in Pimlico, a sign that the marriage was breaking down.

In March 1854, the Crimean War began and at the age of seventy-eight Cochrane volunteered for the role of commander-in-chief of the Baltic Fleet. Lord Aberdeen's ministry seriously considered sending him, but the First Lord of the Admiralty, Sir James Graham, wrote to the Queen that he was, in effect, too irresponsible for the post:

> Lord Dundonald is seventy-nine years of age; and though his energies and faculties are unbroken, and though, with his accustomed courage, he volunteers for the service, yet, on the whole, there is reason to apprehend that he might deeply commit the force under his command in some desperate enterprise, where the chance of success would not countervail the risk of failure and of the fatal consequences, which might ensue. Age has not abated the adventurous spirit of this gallant officer, which no authority could restrain; and being uncontrollable it might lead to most unfortunate results.

Undaunted, Cochrane urged the use of his secret weapons, in particular 'stink vessels'. Graham replied politely: 'On the whole

after careful consideration they have come to the unanimous
conclusion that it is inexpedient to try the experiment in present
circumstances.' Cochrane retorted:

> The unreasoning portion of the public have made an outcry
> against old admirals, as if it were essential that they should be
> able to clear their way with a broadsword. But, my dear Sir
> James, were it necessary – which it is not – that I should place
> myself in an armchair on the poop with each leg on a cushion,
> I will undertake to subdue every insular fortification at
> Kronstadt within four hours from the commencement of the
> attack.

The Baltic Fleet commander, Sir Charles Napier, failed to take
Kronstadt and retired. Cochrane pressed the new prime minister,
Lord Palmerston, to adopt his secret weapon: 500 tons of sulphur
and 2000 tons of coke in a lethal brew would be sufficient. In
addition, naphtha, he advocated, should be flushed into the sea
and ignited by a 'ball of potassium'. Palmerston seriously entertained the idea, writing cynically:

> I agree with you that if Dundonald will go out himself to
> superintend and direct the execution of his scheme, we ought
> to accept his offer and try his plan. If it succeeds, it will, as you
> say, save a great number of English and French lives; if it fails
> in his hands, we shall be exempt from blame, and if we come
> in for a small share of the ridicule, we can bear it, and the
> greater part will fall on him.

But with the fall of Sebastopol in the Crimea after terrible
suffering, it proved unnecessary.

Cochrane, in Kitty's absence in France, appeared to have
taken up female company: Kitty alleged so, and confided this in
a letter to Arthur – although the identity of the woman remains
shrouded in mystery: one prosaic possibility was his house-
keeper. At eighty-two years of age it was certainly merely a
desire for companionship by the old man. An increasingly critical

Kitty, enjoying the patronage of the anglophile Duc and Duchesse de Gramont, complained that Cochrane had wasted £70,000 of his money on politics and another £30,000– £40,000 on inventions and disastrous business ventures. She complained bitterly of the 'imprudent doings of a very weak headstrong old dotard wilfully independent, who is lowering his position to the level of idiotancy'.

The old man employed a ghost-writer to help him in his *Narrative of Services in the Liberation of Chile, Peru and Brazil,* published in 1859, and his *Autobiography of a Seaman,* published the following year. The *Illustrated Times* described him at about this time as:

> a broad-built Scotchman, rather seared than conquered by age, with hair of snowy white, and a face in which intellect still beams through traces of struggle and sorrow, and the marks of eighty years of active life. A slight stoop takes away from a height that is almost commanding. Add to these a vision of good old-fashioned courtesy colouring the whole man, his gestures and speech, and you have some idea of the Earl of Dundonald in this present June 1855.

He was certainly not the senile old man described by Kitty, but nor was she the demented shrew portrayed by his sympathisers. He was now living in his son Tom's house at Queen's Gate.

On 30 October 1860, following an operation on his kidney stones, Cochrane died at the ripe old age of eighty-four. The procession of his hearse and six black carriages travelled down Piccadilly and St James's Square, along Pall Mall and down to Westminster Abbey. His old friends Brougham, Grenfell and Seymour were all present. There was no official government representation, a throwback to ancient hatreds of him. *The Times* reported of him:

> One of the great characters of a past generation has just

departed. After attaining to an age beyond man's ordinary lot; after outliving envy, obloquy and malice; after suffering much, doing more, and triumphing at last, Lord Dundonald has closed in peace and honour the days of his eventful life.

History can produce few examples of such a man or of such achievements. There have been greater heroes, because there have been heroes with greater opportunities; but no soldier or sailor of modern times ever displayed a more extraordinary capacity than the man who now lies dead. He not only never knew fear, but he never knew perplexity, and was invariably found master of the circumstances in which he was placed . . .

He was a Radical, whereas those were the palmy days of Toryism. He was outspoken, whereas officials admire reticence and discretion. He was resolute in exposing abuses, and therefore constantly creating trouble. He was impracticable – a term still in favour for describing inconvenient excellence; and he had a strong spirit of independence – a quality which as very recent controversies have shown is singularly obnoxious to the official mind.

Kitty was at last reconciled to his memory when she appeared before the House of Lords to challenge Arthur's attempt to prove that his parents were not married in Scotland at all, but only after the birth of Tom and Horace, and thus that the third son was heir to the earldom. She spoke movingly:

I cannot bear to be sitting here to vindicate the honour of such a man. It is too much to speak and tell my feelings, it would be impossible. He was a glorious man. He was incapable of deception such as is imputed to him by the world, I know. Such a God of a man! A man who could have ruled the world upon the sea. That I, his wife, should sit here to vindicate the honour of such a man as that. Oh God have mercy upon me and upon us. It is too much, I cannot stand it.

That honoured name! That name for ages, for ages and for ages that has run the world with his deeds. The hero of a hundred fights. I have followed the fortunes of that great man.

I have stood upon the battle deck. I have seen the men fall. I have raised them. I have fired a gun to save the life of a man for the honour of my husband and would do it again. He was a glory to the nation in which he was born, and there is not a member of the family of Dundonald that need not be proud of belonging to such a noble man as he was.

Nor, finally, did he leave his family destitute. The British government in 1877 paid £5000 in respect of his successes, while the Brazilian government paid out £40,000 of the £100,000 he had claimed. The Chileans paid out £6000 of the £26,000 he had demanded. Kitty died in 1865 at the age of sixty-nine. His son Tom was the chief beneficiary of his will, while Horace, who he had supported, lived in straitened circumstances for most of his life, and Arthur and Eustace enjoyed distinguished naval careers. Douglas Cochrane, Tom's son, performed heroically in the Boer War and the First World War. Both the Chileans and the Brazilians now have annual ceremonies of tribute and commemoration at Cochrane's tomb in Westminster Abbey.

Thomas Cochrane had been a man of three careers: as an inventor, like his father, he was undoubtedly an imaginative genius and, equally, an impractical failure in putting his inventions into effect, nearly ruining his distraught family; as a parliamentarian he was a man ahead of his time, of great courage and a champion of the underdog, recklessly unconcerned about the consequences of his actions: the improvement in the life of the ordinary seaman during the nineteenth century can partially be set at his door. As a fighting captain he was among the best that Britain ever produced – one of the greatest seamen of all time. His reputation in the latter role has been clouded by his reputation in the first two, and deserves to be allowed to shine with all the brilliance it deserves.

Cochrane was an elusive, contradictory personality: the pleasant, gentle, kind, courteous man who was so protective of his crews and was a fierce and fearless fighter, also ranted and raved against the establishment, always apparently greedy for money, was said to lack judgment, and advanced weapons of mass destruction. It was suggested that unlike the greatest British seamen he was a deeply flawed personality. So much dirt still lingers from his conviction.

Yet what are the charges Cochrane is called to answer? His initial misjudgement was insubordination: he would not quietly accept orders from less gifted commanders than himself and spoke his own mind. Whether this is a failing or not depends on whether one has an iron belief in the need for service discipline, or believes that crass orders should be questioned. Certainly he never endangered lives by speaking out.

True, he was self-promoting, both in terms of his own causes and prize money. But he also assiduously promoted the interests of his own men and in the scramble for place in those days was hardly an exception in pusuing his own; unlike most of his competitors, he had displayed abilities that deserved promotion. His corrupt conduct during the Honiton by-election was deeply at fault and an affront to his later anti-corruption campaigns, but was no more than standard for the time and a product of youthful indiscretion. He deserves to be faulted for it, nevertheless.

His crusade against Admiralty abuses by contrast was bold and relentless – a defence of ordinary officers and seamen against the armchair profiteers enriched by the risks the former took and by the support they received from greedy shipyard owners and Admiralty courts. His attack on Gambier was justified by the various other accounts of the Battle of Aix Roads, even if his actual performance in court was poor. His alleged role in the Stock Exchange scandal was, as this book suggests, palpably trumped-up, one of the most disgraceful trials used to dispose of a political opponent in British legal history; his only fault on this occasion was excessive loyalty to his rogue uncle.

His attempt to defend Burdett's house in Piccadilly, and his escape from jail, as well as his earlier escapades in Malta, are often cited as proof of a fatal levity and lack of judgment. Yet each would today be classified as a publicity stunt designed to draw attention to an outrage by a member of what was, after all, a mass movement with a handful of seats in parliament.

His decision to fight under foreign flags was understandable – his naval and political career had come to a spectacular end in Britain. All three causes he espoused – Chile, Brazil and Greece – were struggles by an oppressed people against tyranny. True, he also sought to enrich himself – yet this was justifiable for a man stripped of his family fortune. His determination to marry Kitty in spite of losing his uncle's inheritance gives the lie to the idea that he was motivated more by money than idealism.

In South America, his bitter complaints that, in spite of a brilliant performance, he and his men were being denied their just reward, has a ring of truth, just as do his grumbles in Greece about the indiscipline of his crews. His relentless campaign for vindication, while certainly self-centred, is not an uncommon feature of old age. His inventiveness and deeply imaginative naval tactics displayed a remarkable mind, exposed the culpable laziness of the authorities, and hurt none but his own family finances.

On only two charges does Cochrane emerge deeply flawed: he was a rotten husband, incapable of realizing the damage that his single-minded pursuit of his career, and worse his huge expenditure on inventions, would inflict on his long-suffering wife and children – although in his absent-minded way he was a deeply affectionate husband and father. And, precisely because he was insubordinate, chronically restless, and fought the powers-that-be on behalf of himself and those below him, he goaded the Admiralty, at war, to deny him proper recognition of his astonishing naval feats. Cochrane took on the naval authorities frontally and fearlessly, and his relative obscurity to this day shows that he lost – except in the minds of the great writers of naval fiction. Cochrane's reputation for bloody-mindedness owes as much as anything to the grumpy, self-justifying nature of his memoirs: but these were dictated by an old man in a hurry at the end of his life.

So the pieces of the jigsaw that made up this most elusive of personalities at last fit together. He was a brilliant man, a far-seeing dreamer, military strategist and inventor of considerable talent; he was soft-spoken, well-mannered and extraordinarily protective towards those in his charge, as well as always affectionate, even when separated, towards pretty, strong-willed Kitty, doting on his children – but neglectful of their interests in his pursuit of greater things, a common trait in public figures. He was possibly the greatest individual sea-captain ever to have lived, and one who played a huge part in the creation of two new nations. He was a dogged fighter for the underdog, both in the Royal Navy and in society, with a streak of insubordination that caused the authorities to seek to expunge him from the official record – almost, but not quite, successfully.

SELECTED BIBLIOGRAPHY

As mentioned in the acknowledgments, the two best long academic biographies of Cochrane are *Cochrane* by Donald Thomas and *The Sea Wolf* by Ian Grimble. Christopher Lloyd's *Lord Cochrane* (Longmans, Green & Co., 1947) is a fine short study, and Cochrane's own autobiography, especially Volume One, makes gripping reading, while Maria Graham's *Journal* is fascinating and finely written. *Nelson's Navy* by Brian Lavery is a superbly researched treasure trove of useful information, as is *The Wooden World* by N. A. M. Rodger (Fontana, 1988) about a slightly earlier period. *The Frigates* by James Henderson (Wordsworth Military Library) is also a useful introduction to naval life in Cochrane's time. Other reading includes:

Allen, Joseph, *Life of the Earl of Dundonald* (1861)

Atlay, James B., *The Trial of Lord Cochrane before Lord Ellenborough* (1897)

Berenger, Charles Random de, *The Noble Stock-jobber* (1816)

Brenton, Edward, *Life and Correspondence of John, Earl of St Vincent* (2 vols, 1838)

Bunster, Enrique, *Lord Cochrane* (Santiago, 1966)

Cecil, Henry, *A Matter of Speculation: the Case of Lord Cochrane* (1965)

Chatterton, Georgiana, Lady, *Memorials Personal and Historical of Admiral Lord Gambier* (2 vols, 1861)

Cochrane, Archibald, *Account of the Qualities and Uses of Coal Tar* (1785)

Cochrane, Thomas, Lord, *The Trial of Lord Cochrane for Conspiracy* (1814)

— *A Letter to Lord Ellenborough* (1815)

— *Lord Cochrane's Reasons for Escaping* (1816)

— *Narrative of Services in the Liberation of Chile, Peru and Brazil* (2 vols, 1858)

— *The Autobiography of a Seaman* (2 vols, 1860)

Cochrane, Thomas, 11th Earl of Dundonald, *The Life of Thomas Cochrane, 10th Earl of Dundonald* (1869)

Cochrane-Johnstone, Andrew, *Defence of the Honourable Andrew Cochrane-Johnstone* (Edinburgh)

Cruz, Ernesto de la, *Epistolario de D. Bernardo O'Higgins* (2 vols, Santiago, 1916)

Ellenborough, Lord, *The Guilt of Lord Cochrane in 1814* (1914)

Finlay, George, *History of the Greek Revolution* (2 vols, 1861)

Gambier, Lord, *Minutes of a Court Martial* (1809)

Giffard, Edward, *Deeds of Naval Daring* (1852)

Grimble, Ian, *The Sea Wolf* (Blond and Briggs, London, 1978)

Gurney, W. B., *The Trial of Lord Gambier* (1809)

Hodgkin, Thomas, *An Essay on Naval Discipline* (1813)

Jervis, John, Earl of St Vincent, *Letters* (Naval Records Society, 1955)

Lavery, Brian, *Building the Wooden Walls* (Conway Maritime, 1991)

Lavery, Brian and O'Brian, Patrick, *Nelson's Navy* (Conway Maritime, 1989)

Lloyd, Christopher, *Lord Cochrane* (1947)

Mallalieu, J. P. W., *Extraordinary Seaman* (1957)

Marryat, Florence (ed.), *Life and Letters of Captain Marryat* (2 vols, 1872)

Martel, Alamiro de Avila, *Cochrane y la independencia del Pacifico* (Santiago, 1976)

McRae, Alexander, *A Disclosure of the Hoax Practised upon the Stock Exchange* (1815)

Pope, Dudley, *Life in Nelson's Navy* (Chatham, 1997)

Rodger, N. A. M., *The Wooden World* (Fontana/W. W. Norton, 1988)

Thomas, Donald, *Cochrane* (André Deutsch, London, 1978)

Tute, Warren, *Cochrane* (1965)

Twitchett, E. G., *Life of a Seaman* (1951)

Zenteno, J. L., *Documentos justificativos sobre la expedicion libertadora del Peru* (Santiago, 1861)

INDEX